The Years that are Past

The Face that We Lost

The author

The Years that are Past

FRANCES LLOYD GEORGE

HUTCHINSON OF LONDON

HUTCHINSON & CO (*Publishers*) LTD
178–202 Great Portland Street, London W1

London Melbourne Sydney
Auckland Bombay Toronto
Johannesburg New York

First published 1967

*This book has been set in Garamond, printed in Great Britain
on Antique Wove paper by Anchor Press, and
bound by Wm. Brendon, both of Tiptree, Essex*

Contents

Illustrations

Foreword

I should not like this book to appear without expressing my gratitude to all those who have helped me in making the sustained effort which has been necessary in its compilation.

I want to thank all those who have been so kind as to check my work: the Rev. Malcolm Thomson, my former colleague on L.G.'s staff, now working happily in the parish of East Coker; Sir Basil Liddell Hart, who has allowed me to quote from his works and has given me wise and understanding advice from his experience and knowledge and friendship; Miss Nancy Maurice, who did her best to keep me right in the chapter about her father; and many others who have given me permission to use material which concerned them or their relatives.

And chiefly I would like to pay an affectionate tribute to my sister, Muriel Stevenson, for looking after me like a mother in all the crises of authorship, for putting up with me when I got into a muddle with my papers and encouraging me when I became depressed or absent-minded, or unhappy (as one must often be in calling up the past).

F.L.G.

I

My Family and Childhood

I often think that I owe my perpetually optimistic view of life to the fact that my mother, Louise Augustine Armanino, married at the age of nineteen a man with whom she was romantically in love, and who loved her after the fashion of Scotsmen, well but wisely.

It was a curious attraction, my mother being of French and Italian descent. Her father, an Italian and an artist, had left his home in Genoa while still a youth. The family of Armanino had been for many generations merchants in Genoa, specialising, as they do even to this day, in the production of playing cards; but my grandfather had, much to the annoyance of his family, decided to develop the artistic side of his nature, and had gone to Paris to study painting in the Latin Quarter. There he met and married my grandmother, who with her sister had set up a school in Montmartre. (I realise that they must have been teaching there when Clemenceau was Mayor of Montmartre.) When the siege of Paris was imminent in 1870, my grandfather, being a foreigner and not allowed to carry arms, was advised to take his little family away so that there would be fewer mouths to feed, and they left Paris by the last train before the Germans tore up the rails. Having artist friends in London, my grandfather decided to make his home there, and never returned to Paris to live. They settled in Kennington, to be near the Kennington Art School, which was flourishing at that time, and at which many Frenchmen studied. My mother's brother, Paul, also studied there, and won a bronze medal in Rome for a charcoal drawing which I still have. He died, alas, when he was barely nineteen, after having shown great promise.

My grandfather was entirely dependent on what he earned as an artist; and the household was, I think, often short of cash. But although it was a Bohemian *ménage*, they seem to have been very happy. I remember my mother telling me of evenings when they rolled up the carpets and danced to the music of friends.

My father's forbears, by contrast, were Lowland Scottish farmers, and Sir Auckland Geddes, who had made a study of such things, told me that my type was 'pure Nordic,' so I suppose that my father's ancestors came from among the Norsemen who settled in the east of Scotland. Stevensons had farmed the same farm in Lanarkshire for hundreds of years. It was the farm of the 'Earl's Mill', the Earl being Lord Douglas, the head of the clan, and it was situated close to the Earl's residence. It was a typical dairy farm of those days, where the byre had direct access from the living rooms, so that it was not necessary for the farmer to go out into the weather to attend to his cattle, or to milk them. But my paternal grandfather, seeking other fields than farming, came south to London. This was ultimately to bring about the meeting of my father and my mother.

My father's parents were sternly religious. After my grandfather's early death, my grandmother brought up her large family in conventional strictness. When staying with her, as I often did, I was made to say my prayers every night and every morning, and I was first taken to church by her— much to my boredom, I remember. I was beginning to play the piano, taught by my other grandmother, but I was forbidden to touch the piano on a Sunday except to play hymns. To my delight, however, I found a Cake-walk called 'Stepping Heavenward', and this I was allowed to play.

A letter written in 1874 to my father by my grandfather, whose health at the time was already breaking down, sheds light on his character.

You must make up your mind to give your whole attention to business until you are completely master of all the details of it; and make up your mind to do your duty and to give satisfaction; you will never get on unless you do. Above all things, study your health; let your meals be plain and take them regularly, and be sure to be temperate and to keep good hours. Get up in the morning early and never be up late at night. And be sure to avoid bad company. . . .
Have you any Protestant place of worship in Saval? If so, I hope you will attend Church regularly.

My father was at the time in France. When he left school he took a 'situation' in France in order to learn French and to get acquainted with conditions there. He did, in time, become quite a French scholar and spoke the language well. A French relative told me that he spoke French better than my mother.

My father kept faith with his early training. Tall, fair and good looking, he had a simple code of behaviour, based upon the Ten Commandments, of which I do not think he can have broken one in the whole course of his life. It was unthinkable to him to tell a lie, whatever the consequences. He had the courage of a lion. I have seen him stop a runaway horse without hesitating a second—indeed, if he had hesitated he would not have stopped it. I have heard such courage attributed to a lack of imagination, and indeed that may have been true; but it was nevertheless courage. To us children he was perfection—the embodiment of truth, justice and kindness. There was no one like him. Our home was filled with the love which he generated.

My mother, olive-skinned and dark-haired, was, I think, more typically Italian than French. She had a force of character which in after years became dominating, but which was disguised by her intelligence and her sense of humour. She was sentimental, and had it not been that sex was a thing which she appeared to regard with horror, I should have said that she was passionate. She was certainly quick-tempered. She was prompt to resent a slight—even an imagined one. I suppose the modern word for this trait would be 'touchiness'. She too had courage of a kind that would dare anything and she would deny herself anything for those she loved. But where simplicity was the keynote of my father's character, my mother's Latin blood made her complex, mercurial, sometimes difficult.

It was no doubt partly the difference in temperament and outlook that attracted my father and mother to each other, for no two persons could have been more utterly unlike. But however unlike they were in character, they were completely agreed in mutual adoration. They were a shining example of loyalty and of the keeping of marriage vows in the spirit as well as in the letter; of tenderness and trust and tolerance.

The news of their engagement was received very differently by the families of the young people, for while my mother's parents took immediately to their prospective son-in-law, my father's family (his mother and his several sisters) viewed with alarm which amounted almost to horror the thought of having in the family a Frenchwoman who was probably a Papist. This disapproval, I may say, though modified later on the part of my grandmother, who was a Christian in the true sense of the word, remained in the case of my father's sisters, only slightly altered until the end of their lives. And I may add that this somewhat reluctant toleration was not helped forward by my mother, who was fully alive to their criticisms and strongly resented them, even on occasions anticipating them.

Among my most carefully guarded possessions are the love letters which my mother and father wrote to each other—letters from a very innocent girl to the man she adored; letters from a very unsophisticated young man to the woman of his choice—and I believe that this feeling which they had for each other remained unchanged until the young man, now old, whispered to his wife on her death-bed in 1945, '*Au revoir, Augustine!*'

And so love gave me a good start in life. I have never been able to remain downcast for very long at a time, always preferring hope as a companion rather than despair, and leaping from depression to buoyancy with a resilience which has never ceased to astonish me, and, I think, others also.

When my father and mother married they decided, not having much money, to live in rooms for a while. But it soon became clear that my mother's parents needed someone to look after them, and my parents took a house in South London which was able to contain us all. It had a pleasant garden in which we children could play, and where my grandmother could find an outlet for her gardening proclivities. My grandfather was able to have a studio at the top of the house. He had become very much interested in the development of colour lithography, and was doing coloured advertisements for the firms of Cadbury and Rowntree. But money was scarce, and there was not much for luxuries, though he did manage to keep a bottle of red wine on the table, and my mother would attempt to buy him figs and pears when they were in season. What he resented most, however, in this country was the lack of sunshine, and sunshine was a favourite topic with this rather sad exile—who always had enough money in his pocket to buy me a bar of chocolate when we went for a walk together!

I was born in 1888, before my mother had reached her twenty-first year. (It was the year that L.G. married, and his eldest son was born shortly after I was.) Soon—too soon, I think—other children were born to my father and mother, and before long they had four very young offspring on their hands. My father, who was secretary to a firm of French import agents, had only a very slender salary with which to provide for his growing family; but he was happy and contented in his work. He found his employers congenial people and they in turn liked and trusted him. My mother deplored his lack of ambition and his failure to take advantage of the opportunities for advancing himself which were presented from time to time, but as these usually involved risks he did not consider that his family responsibilities justified him in embarking upon schemes that would not in any case make him any happier than he was. And he was so devoid of guile that I very much doubt if he would have made any headway in a business of his own.

Though we naturally took everything for granted then, I realise now that my mother, in spite of her youth and inexperience, managed her little family extremely intelligently. We had the right amount of the right kind of food. I remember lovely teas with hot toast and dripping, as a change from bread-and-butter and jam. L.G. later told me that in his childhood *they* were never given *two* spreads — '*dau enllyn*'—on their bread. It was either butter *or* jam or an equivalent, but never both. But we, as children, were never stinted of butter, careful though my mother had to be. She preferred to sit up late at night, stitching our clothes and economising in that way.

The Sunday-morning breakfasts are vivid in my memory. It was the only morning when my father did not have to hurry from his breakfast, and my mother made it a kind of solemn feast. We sat around the table in our Sunday clothes —'Sunday best' really meant something in those days— with starched pinafores, to enjoy the ham and sardines and the milk loaf which were spread before us on that day. It was at one of those Sunday breakfasts that my younger sister solemnly asked my father: 'Dada, weren't you happy when you lived with Grandma?' My father, astonished, replied that indeed he was. 'Well, why did you come to live with us then?'

We invented a series of extremely boisterous games, aided and abetted by a neighbouring family of cousins, who were in complete sympathy with us. As the eldest, I was made responsible for what 'the others' did and what happened to them. I was inclined to resent the responsibility that fate had forced upon me, except when I realised that there were certain privileges attached to my office, such as being exempted from having to wear outgrown clothes, which my sisters bitterly resented. We thought our clothes were plain and dull, but my mother pointed to pictures of the royal children to show us how simply the best children were dressed. And so, like the little Princes and Princess Mary, we had clothes that were mainly navy blue or white, according to the season, with occasional variations when my mother happened to pick up a bargain or a remnant in the sales at the Army and Navy Stores. The little Princes and the Princess were held up to us as models in all things, and I feel sure we must have been told at one time or another that they were never naughty.

Although we were poor by many standards—by any standard—our home was not in our estimation a 'humble' one by any means. We seemed to have a strong sense of superiority, of sufficiency. No other home, no other parents, could possibly be quite like ours. It was our stronghold, inviolate, unique, complete, built on a foundation of loyalty and trust and love.

So we played, my sisters, my brother and I. We were happy, were naughty, quarrelsome and tiresome, repentant and self-righteous in turn.

And in my happier and more comforting dreams I visit again that unpretentious house, walk up the staircase and roam in the pleasant garden, somewhat distorted, as is the case with dreams; and feel again the security against the world which in my childhood I never supposed could be violated. But as is the case in dreams, I wake up strangely desolate to find that the guardians of my childhood are silent and gone. The centre of the universe has shifted for me many, many times since then, but at no time since has it seemed to me so much my own, so unshakable, so inviolate, so impregnable, as it did in those long, absorbing innocent days.

And yet the future could not rule itself out. In the half-real world which obtruded itself between waking and sleeping I would formulate wonderful schemes. And I remember one night when my mother looked into my bedroom, expecting to find me asleep, I pulled her down to me and whispered, in extreme confidence: 'Mama, I have decided that I want to do two things: to play with the little Princes and to write a book!' This astonishing piece of news my mother received with tolerant deprecation. It was one of those moments, however, that stay with ineffaceable permanence in the memory. Sometimes they are trivial, and one wonders why they have become indelible when so many more important moments escape. This one I had cause to remember long after, when both the wishes had come true—when I had danced and played tennis with the King's sons, and had also written a book. So does the tapestry of life weave backwards and forwards.

I must not give the impression that our house was a particularly peaceful one. The temperaments which composed it were too strong and too incompatible for harmony, and often there was the clash of political discord. The Boer War, for instance, aroused the most violent controversy—my mother being a passionate pro-Boer and my father supporting the British Government's attitude. My grandmother loved her son-in-law so dearly that she always hesitated to contradict his opinion, but my grandfather, who resented England not so much because of her policies as because he was an exile from his own beautiful land of sun and fruit and flowers, was always on his daughter's side. So from my very early days I became familiar with the arguments for and against the British Empire.

The Dreyfus case was another event which brought discord into our family and thus burned itself into my memory. The heated arguments were carried on in French and English, and this in itself was an education.

My French was taken in hand systematically by my grandmother, who always spoke to us in French, so that in spite of ourselves we grew up bilingual. I remember sitting on her bed and being introduced to the comedies of Molière and the fun of Lafontaine. I enjoyed our readings of *Le Bourgeois Gentilhomme* and *Les Précieuses Ridicules*. She could make the characters live. She would read us, too, articles from the French periodicals which she received regularly; but the *Journal des Débats* and the *Revue des Deux Mondes* were (fortunately, I thought) considered for some time to be beyond me. I realised long afterwards that the politics which emerged from these publications leaned decidedly towards the left, though at that time they seemed to me to be merely common sense!

She also taught us the piano, and while I enjoyed playing I resented the long hours of practice, which I could not avoid, since my teacher was living in the same house. We were given set times for practising, to which she listened in her bedroom, knocking on the floor with her stick whenever a mistake was detected. I fear that gratitude plays a small part in the mind of a child, but in later years I realised how much I owed to my grandmother for her refusal to accept a half-learned verse or a badly played scale; and for the fact that she enabled me to regard great music as a source of healing, so that on occasions when my heart has been very troubled I have received, as it were, a blessing from listening to it.

She was a grand needlewoman too, and helped my mother a great deal over many years, as we quickly grew out of our clothes. There were, too, in those days many

B

underclothes to make—and all underclothes were elabor-
ately trimmed with embroidery. Even our buttonholes
were stitched with the greatest care, for my grandmother
would never pass anything that was hastily or carelessly
made. (My mother was rather more slapdash in her needle-
work—a characteristic which I have inherited.)

My grandmother also supervised the garden, and gave
me my first lessons in gardening. She set me on my horti-
cultural way by showing me the glory that a packet of
nasturtium seeds can produce, or one of phlox drummondi;
and I was given a lily bulb and would watch with wonder
the multiplication of the lovely orange flowers year by year.
At that time little boys would bring in pails of horse manure
from the roads at a penny a time, and my grandmother had
a regular contract with them.

She would talk to me, from time to time, about her own
grandfather, an officer who had fought in fourteen campaigns under Napoleon, and had been decorated with the
Legion of Honour on the battlefield for conspicuous service.

She was, undoubtedly, a very intelligent woman and an
important part of the household. I feel sorry that in these
days young people do not realise the advantage of having
the old folks with them.

There is another moment of memory which has stayed
with me all my life. I must have been about twelve years old
when I remember my heart being suddenly uplifted one
evening in early spring. My mother had sent me on an
errand on coming home from school, and as I walked down
the road in the dusk I saw an almond tree in full blossom
against a lavender sky, with a silver crescent moon faintly
appearing. The beauty of it made me catch my breath. My
spirit seemed to soar, and I whispered to myself, 'I will
never grow old!'

This small experience is impressed upon my memory, as
evident as a 'still' from a strip of a movie film. What was
behind my sudden exaltation I do not know, except that the

loveliness of nature has always the power to move me in this way to thoughts of immortality. My grandfather, crushed by disappointment and failure, had lately died, and death, brought home to me in this way, had become repugnant, and on this lovely evening unreal. But I think it was rather the sudden quickening of my senses, the sharpening of perceptions, which seemed to make that moment a milestone in my life.

We were encouraged to say our prayers—my paternal grandmother saw to that. I prayed in faith but also in fear—lest God should remember the one thing I forgot, and get back on me, so to speak. I wonder if many children pray in that way? But in spite of my frequent asking that my grandfather should not die, one night when my mother told me that he was very ill, he was indeed dead by the following morning. After that my prayers followed a different, more fatalistic pattern.

Many years later L.G. told me that he himself experienced quite suddenly the same fear that, as he put it, 'there was no one at the other end of the telephone'. He was walking to chapel from Llanystumdwy to Criccieth, and he showed me the exact spot on the road where, at the age of eleven, his beliefs suddenly fell away, and he was left to wrestle with doubt. He recovered them on a broader basis, so he told me, when as a young man he read for the first time *Sartor Resartus*. I am not sure that Carlyle was not responsible for clarifying L.G.'s political as well as his religious creeds. 'Let us take these outworn vestments to bind the sore and bleeding wounds of humanity' became L.G.'s watchword henceforth. He turned away from Doubting Castle towards the Delectable Mountains and the Vision Splendid.

As a child I read greedily. Books then were not so easily come by as they are now, and were much more precious. In those days we read our books over and over again, and loved them none the less for doing so. As children we had to be content with those already on our bookshelves and

any that were given us. I formed an early acquaintance with
Dickens, weeping copiously over Little Dorrit and Little
Nell; and I knew by heart many of the passages in the
Ingoldsby Legends, a volume that had been given me as a
Christmas present when I was ten years old! The poems
fascinated and horrified me, as did also the Cruickshank
illustrations to the book. I wept over the 'Wide, Wide
World' and 'Home Influence', but I lost myself in a magical
world while reading the poems of Scott. I think I read them
all during one summer holiday, in a special spot in our
garden; my mother reproving me for being a 'bookworm',
and unwilling to give her help when needed.

Even before my teens my reading entered upon the
romantic stage. I read *Quo Vadis* and longed to be a Christian martyr: I read Rider Haggard's *She* and wished for
nothing so much as to be 'the World's Desire'; then *Robert
Ellesmere* and I knew that the most wonderful thing in the
world would be to marry a *good* man—preferably a clergy-
man—and to devote my life to good works.

2

Growing Up: School and College

As soon as we were old enough we were sent, my sisters and my little brother and I, to a school nearby which provided excellent educational facilities, being attached to a training college for teachers. The head mistress, strangely enough, was an American, with a forbidding exterior but with great capacity and a keen sense of humour. Though I did not realise it at the time, she was a wonderful administrator, with advanced ideas. It was only later that I realised how well I had been grounded. I knew that I liked my teachers and I enjoyed my lessons, but I think my high spirits must sometimes have made me rather troublesome. I remember one occasion when I was about twelve years old I was subjected to considerable humiliation as the result of being the ringleader in an episode which appeared to exasperate one of the mistresses, for I was reported to the head mistress, a grave occurrence. The following morning I was called up at prayer time in the presence of the whole school, my crime, to which I admitted, was explained in detail, and I was condemned to sit for the rest of the day on a chair by the head mistress's desk. As the school was built with glass partitions to the schoolrooms, which radiated from Miss Birkin's room, I was the cynosure of the whole school. My humiliation was I think rendered more complete by the fact that my sisters were amongst the witnesses of my degradation. I bore my discomfiture as well as I could until

I went home for lunch, but then I burst into tears in my mother's arms sobbing, 'I *won't* go back! I *won't* go back!' Her reply was: 'You must go back, darling. You must take your punishment. It will soon be over.'

Such wise words! Many years later L.G. would tell me that if ever he had to be punished he would want it to be over quickly. 'Delayed punishment in any form,' he declared, 'is much worse.'

On this particular occasion I was rewarded, for on going back to the afternoon classes, I was told that my punishment was over and I could go back to my class. A wise head mistress indeed! My resentment was changed to gratitude and my humiliation was soon forgotten.

Fortunately, I have always been able to forget my grievances very quickly, which has made it easier to forgive my enemies. My memory for these things has always been so short that I have sometimes caught myself wondering *why* I quarrelled with so-and-so. My mother, her Latin blood strong in her veins, used in later years to say to me, 'You forget and forgive too easily'. But then I could never bear a quarrel, or to have unpleasantness about me; life was too full of so many wonderful things for it to be spoilt by bad temper, so that it was a good thing to be possessed of a short memory in such matters.

We remained at this school—or college, as it was known— until, when I was thirteen, a fifth child was born to my mother. She then decided, with great courage I think in those days, to send us all to a council school, from which she knew that some of us at any rate might obtain scholarships. My father's family were indignant with her for thus lowering the family respectability, but our finances were particularly strained at that moment, and my mother adhered to her decision. She proved to be quite right. My brother and I quickly obtained scholarships, I to Clapham High School, he to Christ's Hospital; and the intermediate members of our family, who did not appear likely to shine in this way, were subsequently sent to a more select school to finish their education. But in some ways my mother was excessively Victorian. 'No daughter of mine,' she pronounced in our early days, 'shall ever ride a bicycle,' quite unconscious of the fact that her three daughters were already riding their friends' bicycles whenever they had the opportunity. However, later, after Queen Victoria was dead and under Edward VII things were looking up a bit for women, and when my cousins acquired bicycles of their own, my mother relented, and finally decided to ride one herself.

Just before going to Clapham High School, and before my grandmother died, I learned that I had won a travelling scholarship in France from the Institut Français. I remember running straight to my grandmother's room to show her the letter. I was old enough to remember that it was largely to her that I owed my success, and to be glad that she should be thus rewarded. She was already very ill, and she died alas! soon after, before my visit to France took place.

The scholarship was only for ten pounds, but as I was able to stay with my French relatives, this sum would go a long way. And since my relatives spoke no English, this would be very good for my French. They were living at that time in a little village on the Marne—a village which in the 1914—18 war was to be twice occupied by the Germans— and it was decided that I should spend the whole of my summer holidays in France.

There was great preparation for my first journey abroad: a few new clothes—very few, I fear—but messages and presents to my great-aunt (my grandmother's sister) and her daughter, with whom I was going to stay. The Continent in those days seemed to be so much farther away than it is now, and in any case a journey of this kind was something which had not occurred in our family for years.

I was placed at Victoria Station in the charge of two schoolmistresses who were travelling in the same carriage. It was a comfort to have companions on the journey, and experienced travellers at that. My cousin met me in Paris, and took me straight to the little village of Lizy-sur-Ourcq. It was the heart of the French countryside. This was my first opportunity of seeing at close quarters not only the French countryside but any countryside, and it can be imagined with what wonder I surveyed the golden corn-fields, the still rivers, the spacious farmhouses of that fair land.

Looking back, I can see that that year, my sixteenth, marked a very definite stage in my development. The death of my grandmother, whom I dearly loved, had stirred me emotionally; the new scenes and people now presenting themselves, and with which I had to cope unhelped, were forcing upon me a new intellectual phase. The little English girl now staying with her French relatives in this quiet village was the point of curiosity—and she instinctively felt that she had a dignity to uphold. I remember becoming involved in an argument on the Boer War in which the French members of the circle denounced Britain for her action in it. Whatever had been the pros and cons as presented in the discussion between the members of our family at home, there was only one course to adopt abroad. Crossing my fingers, I put, as well as I could in French, the case for my country, and was rewarded by hearing an elderly French solicitor say: '*Mais elle a raison, la petite.*'

My second cousin, Suzanne, a highly intelligent and cultured woman of about thirty, took me under her wing and devoted herself to me during my stay. I could have had no better guide or more congenial companion. I was taken to Meaux to see the wonderful old Cathedral, and the pulpit of Bossuet, whose sermons I was given to read. (I found them excessively dull.) I was taken to Soissons. . . . And, glory of glories, I was taken to Paris.

My mother's godmother, Madame Debray, who had retired for the summer to a villa at Meudon, lent us her flat in Paris; and from here, every morning after our bowl of chocolate and our croissants (unaccustomed but delicious meal!), we would sally forth to see the sights of Paris—to Notre Dame, the Palais de Justice, the Luxembourg, the Louvre, the Panthéon, the Museum at Cluny, and to many of the lesser treasures to which tourists are never introduced. I not only saw these places, but I learnt the history of them from a Frenchwoman, and it is strange how the memories of this visit to Paris transcend all later ones. We went up to Montmartre to see the new church that was being built, the Sacré Cœur, but after the beautiful old churches I had seen in Paris, I found this one unimpressive, as indeed, but for its situation, I still do.

My cousin insisted that my first sight of the Arc de Triomphe should be in the very early morning, when the streets were clean and the air quite pure, and that is how I shall always think of that great monument, shining in the sun of a summer morning, with the stillness of the magic city around it. I saw the sculptures of Rodin, including his famous statue of Balzac, which, after having been rejected by the French Society which commissioned it, was now restored to a place of honour at the intersection between the Boulevard Raspail and the Boulevard Montparnasse.

We would have our goûter at a patisserie, and pursue our sightseeing until lunch time; and often after lunch we would emerge again, to sit perhaps in the Luxembourg Gardens, or the Parc Monceau, or the Jardin des Plantes, or perhaps go on a visit to one of my cousin's friends. These visits I did not much care for. Although I was anxious to do my cousin credit, I knew that I was under close scrutiny on these occasions and I found it somewhat of a strain. Of the Opéra and the theatres we only saw the outside. I think most of them were closed in any case at that time of the year, but I am not sure that our finances would have run to the extravagance of a performance.

I may add that I saw nothing, absolutely nothing, of the more sophisticated side of Paris of which I had heard and read vague accounts: '*Les français n'y vont pas*' was my cousin's terse reply when I asked about them. '*Ce sont seulement pour les étrangers.*' I evidently did not come into the category of '*étrangers*', which I think I regarded as a compliment.

It was the era of the horse-bus, and no one who has not experienced this mode of travel can imagine how terrifying was the lurching and the clatter as these enormous vehicles rushed along the boulevards, and the narrower streets of Paris, supplemented, when the journey neared an incline, by a third excitable horse produced with even more noise and clatter. The addition of another animal enabled the journey to be continued at an even greater rate, and I was always thankful when our ordeal was at an end and we found ourselves once more on *terra firma*. Indeed, I would infinitely have preferred to make the whole of the journey on foot rather than entrust myself to one of these heaving, swaying and frightening vehicles.

We went, of course, one day to Versailles, which I found almost too vast, and so thorough was my guide that on subsequent visits in later years there seemed to be nothing that I had missed, either inside the great Palace itself, or in the Trianons, or in the surrounding Park, even to the carp in the little stream and the wooden bridge across it.

When it got too hot in Paris we retired for a time to the villa at Meudon, where I remember collecting French curses from the old man who used to swear in the garden next to ours, and retailing them in apparent innocence to my cousin and Madame Debray.

Thence back to the Marne, to the pear trees and plum trees laden with fruit, the ancient dovecotes with their flurrying hordes, the white, hot country roads, the shade of the river—to my aunt, gaunt and unforgetful of the siege of Paris, during which her baby son, who died later as a result of undernourishment, was born; to the kind and hardworking country folk.

And in September back to London—an anticlimax in some ways, although I was glad to get back to my home. I had at times felt very homesick on this my first separation from my family.

Moreover, there was the experience of my new school in prospect. My nervousness at entering a totally different kind of scholastic centre from that to which I had been accustomed was mitigated by the fresh vistas of possible achievement which were open to me. Having progressed so far, so many things appeared to be possible. Would I, perhaps, be able to obtain a scholarship to a university? It was no longer only the privileged who were admitted to the desirable precincts of Oxford and Cambridge. But I had a long way to go yet. And I do not think that I was ever consciously ambitious. I was content to take each step as I reached it, sustained by the happiness and fullness of the present rather than by the promises of the future. I think it has always been so.

And at Clapham High School I tasted real happiness and a release from inhibitions. I thought it the most beautiful building I had ever been in, with its polished floors and staircases, its lovely central hall in which stood a statue of the Venus de Milo; the reproductions of Old Masters on the walls, and, above all, its opportunities for friendships with both girls and mistresses. There was an atmosphere of culture which my previous school had not possessed, and a regard for the individual which, to a certain extent, had been lacking there. One of my colleagues in the fifth form was Mair Lloyd George, the eldest daughter of the Liberal statesman. The family lived nearby. Mair was a gentle and charming personality and I had particular reason to like her and be grateful to her, as she would often come to my help in my mathematical difficulties. She was good at mathematics: I was not, and she was always ready to explain away my problems. I liked her very much.

I achieved the unusual by passing my matriculation

examination in the first class when I was still in the fifth
form, a distinction reserved for the members of the sixth—
and one which the members of the sixth seemed inclined
to regard as an impertinence.

My head mistress, Mrs. Woodhouse, a most remarkable
woman, whom I regarded with infinite respect and admiration, was also deeply religious. My love, however, was reserved for my classics mistress, Miss Trenerry, who, I
thought, not without reason, was the most beautiful and
most gifted woman I had ever seen. I sat in the front of my
class and absorbed her lessons with delight, trembling with
adoration when she entered the room. She was kind, but
she sternly discouraged my undisguised admiration. Even
to this day the memory of her and the mention of her name
stirs my heart.

As a result of this passion, I was filled with a desire to
become myself a classics scholar, and to go to Cambridge.
This project was increased as a result of a visit to Girton
and Newnham organised by Miss Trenerry. I more than
ever felt that I must somehow or other obtain a scholarship
to one of these desirable colleges.

But it was not to be. When I was eighteen, my head
mistress in her wisdom thought that I should try for a
scholarship to the London University. I thought it un-
reasonable in any case to be made to sit for the scholarship
in the same year that I was taking my intermediate examination, but to please her I did so, not caring whether I won
it, for I had no intention of taking it up. I still had one more
year to spend at Clapham High School, in which I planned
to study hard for a Cambridge exhibition. There were not,
I think, many competitors for the London scholarship in
question, and I won it—a very handsome one—and to my dismay Mrs. Woodhouse argued that it was my duty to take it.

Supposing, she said, I refused this opportunity, and failed
in my efforts to get to Cambridge? In any case, even if I
were to win a Cambridge exhibition, it would not be nearly

enough to pay all my expenses, and where was the rest of the money to come from? I did not know the answer to the second argument, though I would have been perfectly willing to take a chance on the first. I knew that the Cambridge exhibition was very small in comparison with the scholarship I had won. And so, almost broken-heartedly, I gave up my precious year which I still had in hand and brought my school career to an end a year earlier than I had hoped. It was arranged that I should go to the Royal Holloway College as a classical student.

If my years at Clapham High School had effected a transformation in my life the following years at the Royal Holloway College were something of a revolution. I had never been away at boarding school, and consequently this was my first experience of living away from home. The emancipation—the complete freedom of movement and thought and decision—were like wine to me, and my spirits soared. At home I had been subjected to the alternating domination of my mother's very forceful personality, and the pretty vigorous school discipline which my studies and the necessity of passing examinations imposed upon me. Now the matter was reversed—it was for me to take decisions as to what my curriculum should consist of—subject, of course, to consultation with my lecturers and tutors. My spare time was my own, and I could do what I liked and go where I liked—subject, of course, to college rules. It took me some time to think of myself as an adult—I was, I think, very young for my age—and the shadow of regimentation was long in disappearing. My mother had the power of keeping her dominion over her family even when removed from her: she was, as I see it now, jealous of influences in our lives which weakened the bonds at home. She was the traditional French mother whose daughters remained in her orbit and subject to her influence as long as she lived.

When I was sixteen I had been confirmed, with my sister,

in the Church of England, and I think that my parents
considered that, as far as they were concerned, my religious
education was at an end. But my mother never ceased to
be concerned about our *moral* education. With a Puritanism
strange in a Frenchwoman, she strongly discouraged any
ideas we might have on making ourselves attractive to the
other sex. We were told that 'a good man' would love us
for ourselves alone, and that if we were to dress ourselves
in the plainest and most unattractive way, indulge in no
feminine wiles whatever, but preserve a prim and even forbidding countenance, the right sort of man (how dull he
would have been, I fear!) would somehow discern beneath
this very unprepossessing appearance qualities of sterling
worth which would place us on a pedestal above all other
women. But for myself I did not *want* to be put on a pedestal:
what I was beginning to want was a little male company,
and of this, owing to the fact that my brother was very
young, I was fated to get very little. My mother was suspicious of all young men, and did not encourage them to
come to our home.

And such is feminine instinct that I was unimpressed by
my mother's outlook and counsel—I took great trouble in
making myself what I thought very attractive clothes. Looking back on the fashions of that day and my very dubious
and immature taste, I think they must have been not so
much pretty, as pretty awful.

In addition to the fact of becoming a member of a more
or less free community, I found myself at Holloway College
in lovely surroundings. The English countryside was a
thing which was almost foreign to me—our holidays had
always been taken once a year, at the seaside, and the
woods and the fields and lovely river nearby were a revelation to me, a constant cause of astonishment and pleasure.

It has always been the custom to sneer at the mass of red-
brick buildings with the crenellated and turreted roofs
which constitute the Royal Holloway College, and the fact

that it was built and endowed by the maker of Holloway's pills and ointment. But to me the quadrangles and cloisters and corridors of the College did not appear to be undignified in their spaciousness, and the gardens in which they were set were undoubtedly lovely in their semi-wildness. It is true that in the centre of one of the quadrangles there was a statue of Queen Victoria, but that did not necessarily make it ridiculous.

The fact that I had *two* rooms of my very own added to the congeniality of the College, and completed my sum of happiness. Here I could entertain my friends, or putting up 'Engaged' on my door could work uninterruptedly. I was a free woman. It was liberation on a grand scale.

The first term at college was marred by the news which reached us of the death of Mair Lloyd George.[1] I think it was the first time I had experienced the death of someone of my own age. I was shocked and shattered and found it difficult to realise that one with whom I had sat in class such a short time ago had been cut down in the flower of her youth. Her father, David Lloyd George, had lately obtained Cabinet rank when the Liberals came into office. I thought of him, and the cruel destiny that had given him high office, the realisation of his ambition, with one hand, and taken away his beloved child with the other.

The heady wine of freedom, congenial friends, and lovely surroundings so bewildered me during my first year that my work became a secondary preoccupation. Unfortunately —in a sense—I had passed my intermediate examination in my last year at school, and while most of the students were studying to take this at the end of their first year, I had no aim to strive for, and took life very easily—too easily, for at the end of the year my classics lecturer wrote me a stern letter advising me, unless there was to be some improvement, to give up the idea of sitting for a classics honours degree, and take a pass instead. Stung by the humiliation, I decided

1. November 30th, 1907.

to mend my ways, and indeed I was obliged to do. The following years were no less enchanted, but more disciplined, less dissipated, and in the vacations I spent many hours in the British Museum supplementing my classical knowledge. I decided to take Greek sculpture as one of my secondary subjects.

But I was not an ideal student—I think I was too full of the joy of life for that. I was reproved on more than one occasion by another classical lecturer (female) for flippancy in my comments on the great Greek tragedians; and my efforts to render Euripides into corresponding Shakespearian lines were not encouraged. I was also mildly reproached by the same lecturer for finding my friends outside the classical school. This I could not help, but I was too polite to give her the obvious answer.

Professor T. Allen used to come over from Oxford once a week to lecture us on Homer. He was a handsome figure, who lectured without once looking at his class; we felt that he was not even aware of our existence, and somewhat resented the fact. On doing a translation for him from the *Odyssey* I ventured to put several exclamation marks in the margin of my translation of Ulysses' remark to Alcinous when he finds Nausicaa and her maidens playing on the beach: 'For the young are ever foolish.'[1] He retorted by writing underneath: 'N.B. masculine gender.'

One great attraction of Englefield Green was its proximity to Windsor Park and the town of Windsor. The distance on a bicycle through the Park to Windsor was a trifling one, and the students made regular excursions in that direction. We must have looked very prim with our long skirts, our stiff collars and our boaters, but there was no primness in our hearts. Innocence there was, for our college life was a conventional one, and most of us were content to have it so. One afternoon as we were bicycling through the Park we came suddenly upon King Edward VII

1. *Odyssey*, VII, 294.

and the Kaiser in a clearing. They were resting during a shoot, and dismounting from our bicycles we looked on at the little party only a few yards away—a stout gentleman who was the King of England, and the German Emperor, an arrogant handsome figure in flowing green cape and Tyrolean hat. We saw him again during my last year at college (1910) when he came to Windsor for the funeral of King Edward, and we went over to Windsor to see the procession. He looked even more majestic in his white cape and gilded helmet, and even a shade more arrogant, I thought.

On vacation I went to stay with a friend at the rectory at Worplesdon, where, being an orphan, she lived with her uncle, the rector, Mr. Duncan Tovey, and her cousin Donald. The delight of that visit remains permanently in my memory. The old rector, who was a considerable scholar, discussed Virgil with me, and we agreed upon the enchanting qualities of the Georgics, a translation of which, by Mackail, he presented to me. In the evenings Donald Tovey played Beethoven and Bach to us. And there were tennis parties in the long sunny afternoons, when god-like young men from nearby Aldershot met the lovely maidens of the neighbourhood. It was a glorious, golden, top-heavy world, soon to be destroyed for ever.

One of the neighbouring families was that of Colonel Frederick Selous, of German East Africa fame. He had a museum of his trophies in his garden at Worplesdon, and he showed it to me with great pride. He himself was killed in Africa in World War I, and his elder son was also killed, in the Flanders campaign.

There was a flourishing Choral Society in Windsor under the direction of Sir Walter Parratt, and this some of us joined. We thoroughly enjoyed the weekly rehearsals, and the concerts were a real event in our musical lives. There was plenty of music at Holloway—to belong to the chapel choir was an education as well as a privilege—and almost

C

every Sunday evening there was music after dinner in the hall, sometimes by visiting performers and sometimes by the students or the more musically minded lecturers, of which there were not a few.

The principal, Miss Higgins, was herself a keen musician. She was an austere person, handsome though mannish in her appearance, caustic in comment. At that time women wore long skirts, and I seem to remember that hers even had a train. The swish of her skirts and her long mannish strides through the corridors remain a vivid memory with me, as does the wise advice she handed out to me on more than one occasion when I stood in need of it.

But although my three years at college are a blissful memory of happy friendships which have continued, many of them into after life, and of broadening interests, my recurring and chief nightmare is of an examination—my finals—for which I am utterly unprepared, and which is inexorably and remorselessly imminent. I have not rubbed up my Greek grammar, and I have not even glanced at my set books. It is impossible to do anything in the short time in front of me to remedy the state of my ignorance. I wake in a sweat of apprehension, for it is a real nightmare, which even when it has passed I am unable to believe is not true. The responsibility and care which I so gaily put aside then has had its revenge upon me in all these after years. I can never get away from the awful spectre which, kept at bay, fortunately, at the actual time of crisis, has lain in wait for me ever since. And my heart goes out to young students faced with this ultimate test of their knowledge, and I hope that they will not be haunted by this grim reminder. I was 'capped' in 1910 by Lord Rosebery, a dignified, handsome figure, who resented the ragging indulged in by attendant students, and at one point sat down and refused to proceed with the ceremony until the noise ceased.

To politics I did not give much thought in those days, except in so far as they concerned women's franchise, which

I supported very enthusiastically, believing, I seem to remember, everything that was said by the suffragists about the Government that refused to give them the vote. But the social reforms which were being initiated under the direction of the Chancellor of the Exchequer do not appear to have made any great impression on my mind at that time. The study of classics took me into the realms of ancient, not modern, history.

3

First Meetings with L.G.

While I was at college my mother, who was always, I think, without being told, aware of what was going on in my mind (she had throughout her life an uncanny instinct of what was happening to her children) became rather fearful of the influences which were beginning to impinge upon my development. I was reading avidly all the books of H. G. Wells as they were published, and although my mother did not make the mistake of forbidding me to read them, she strongly disapproved of this author, regarding such novels as *Ann Veronica* and *The New Machievelli* as unsuitable for the education of a young woman. And when a young man of our acquaintance—the son of an artist friend of the family and a Fabian—sent me a copy of *Tono Bungay*, he was never invited to our house again, and my mother made it quite clear that she thought our acquaintance ought to cease— I think she told him so.

It was perfectly true that H. G. Wells' ideas had a tremendous influence upon me. I was exceedingly interested at that time in the emancipation of women, and Wells' contribution towards the breaking of the barriers which hitherto had hemmed us in and discriminated between the sexes appealed to me inevitably. I was standing on the threshold of my life, and I knew instinctively that it would not be a sheltered one. I took pleasure in the thought that my name 'Frances' meant 'free'. I was, moreover, keenly interested

36

in the Fabian Movement. I joined the Fabian Society, went to hear Shaw lecture at the meetings whenever I could, and to see his plays when I could afford it. My father and mother were both strongly suspicious of Shaw and his influence upon the young mind. The former never altered his opinion, but would say, disapprovingly, 'He destroys; but he sets nothing in the place of what he has destroyed.'

It was inevitable also that the women's suffrage movement should claim me as a member. On leaving college my interest in the 'Votes for Women' movement took a more active form and I became an ardent suffragist, and here my mother was torn two ways, for though she herself was in favour of women's suffrage, she was alarmed at the idea that I might throw in my lot with the women who were chaining themselves to the railings of the House of Commons and Downing Street and being put into prison and forcibly fed. My father, too, besought me not to become involved in any of these shameful things. And although I attended the meetings at the Queen's Hall and the Albert Hall at which Mrs. Pankhurst and her daughter Christabel spoke most eloquently and inspired women to deeds of law-breaking, I did not join the W.S.P.U., but remained contented—or was it discontented?—with being a member of a non-militant organisation. I think this was due partly to my dislike of hurting my parents, partly because I had my own living to earn, and partly no doubt to physical cowardice and natural shyness. But my sympathies were strongly with the militants and I would defend them against all criticism. I did on one occasion join two friends of mine, both members of the W.S.P.U., on a walking tour in Perthshire in the summer of 1912. One of them, a good speaker, addressed meetings in the small villages we passed through, and we came in for a good deal of banter and heckling. On one occasion the local miller poured a bag of flour over us. But it was all very harmless and completely lawful, though I should doubt very much if we made any converts. One of my friends was shortly afterwards engaged in much more serious activities, and went to prison as a result.

I did not know then that a few years later I would be able to help the Suffrage movement in another way and would have made their acquaintance in an official capacity. In 1915 Mrs. Pankhurst and her followers offered to recruit women for the munitions factories, and I, as secretary to the Minister of Munitions, was very closely concerned with the scheme. But of this more later.

After obtaining my degree I cast about for a teaching post, much as I loathed the idea of teaching. But at that time, without further training, there was little open to a young woman in the way of a job; and further training my parents could not afford. A teaching agency sent me particulars of a post in a large council school in Hull, and, being placed on the short list, I travelled north for an interview. I looked younger than my age (twenty-two) and in spite of the fact that in those days a distinction was drawn between youth and maturity by putting up one's hair and letting down one's skirts, I am afraid that I still looked rather immature and most unlike a schoolmistress. The head mistress who interviewed me turned me down on the grounds of youth and inexperience, and, terrified by the vast size of the school and the smell of fish which I encountered everywhere in the town, I was not sorry. I returned home infinitely relieved but still in search of a job, and when a resident one was offered to me in a girls' boarding school at Wimbledon, within easy, though not daily, reach of my home, I accepted it.

The school was an expensive one—not a finishing school in the accepted sense of the word, as there were a good many young children there. But the school had been founded with the idea of putting a polish, so to speak, on young girls of good families, and the teaching of French and music was an important part of the curriculum; as was the improving of accents whether foreign or provincial.

I remember feeling angry with the parents who sent their daughters to have their Scottish accents obliterated. Other subjects came after. The girls were for the most part intelligent and interested in their work, many of them gay and amusing. Some of them were only a little younger than I was; many of them were more sophisticated. When they left they would enter the social life which was the normal occupation in those days for young women of means. I grew to like the school, though I remember that on my first visit home, so strange was this new experience of earning my living, I wept and said that I could not go back. But my mother comforted me and told me, as she had done on a previous occasion, that I ought to go back, and that all would be well. She was again right.

The younger children were my especial charge, I suppose on the analogy that the youngest mistress looked after the youngest children. At first I thought, with my academic distinction, that this was somewhat of an indignity. But I soon came to enjoy my association with the young ones, especially as I was given older classes to teach as well. I am sure, however, that teaching was not my *métier*. I was not nearly strict enough: I saw the children's point of view too well and too easily. To the young ones I was a good storyteller, preferring to teach them their history and literature in this way. To the older ones I was a confidante. They called me affectionately 'Pussy'—a nickname which stuck to me afterwards.

I came in for some rather spiteful banter from some members of the staff who were opposed to Women's Suffrage, and in that very respectable establishment found myself sometimes hard put to it to keep my end up. Surprisingly enough, I found that I was supported by some of the older girls, but here I had to be very careful of the extent to which I encouraged emancipating tendencies! I might have had irate parents on my track, as did once actually happen when, in a lesson on the Reformation, I

rather rashly remarked: 'No one really believes in the
Thirty-nine Articles nowadays!' One of my pupils had a
canon for a father, and shortly afterwards I was reprimanded
by the head mistress for my indiscretion.

The music teacher was a Welsh woman, and we became
good friends. She had a lovely voice, and through her I
became acquainted for the first time with the enchanting
songs of Wales.

It was about this time that I had my first glimpse of L.G.
The housekeeper at the school, who was exceedingly kind
to me, and with whom I became great friends, was also a
Welshwoman and I began to go with her on Sunday afternoons to her Welsh chapel (Baptist) in Castle Street, near
Oxford Circus. It seems a coincidence—or was it fate?—
that this was also the chapel attended by L.G. and his family
when in London, and it was the custom on the last Sunday
in June—the Flower Sunday—for L.G. to attend and
address the members of the congregation. My Welsh friend
offered me a special treat and took me with her to the June
service in 1911, and there for the first time I came into contact with the Welsh Chancellor of the Exchequer and in-
stantly fell under the sway of his electric personality. I
listened to his silver voice, observed his mastery over his
audience. He seemed to establish a personal relationship
immediately with every member of it, and although he spoke
almost entirely in Welsh, I felt myself in some mysterious
way drawn into the orbit of his influence. At that time I was
scarcely interested in politics at all, but I had heard such
divers accounts of this now famous politician that I was
naturally delighted to see him for myself and form my own
estimate of this much-discussed character. And on this June
afternoon my feelings were aroused to something beyond
satisfied curiosity at seeing this Welshman amongst his own
people, without pomposity and without condescension. He
was at home and at ease, receiving a welcome in which
affection was more evident than homage. He was amongst

The author's grandmother (by her grandfather)

The author's mother and father at the time of their marriage

Frances Stevenson, aged 19

Lloyd George in 1913

Richard Lloyd

his own people—in a Welsh oasis in London, as the Welsh chapels are indeed.

I began to go often to these Sunday gatherings, which are different from the English church services, in that the afternoon service was followed by tea and a sort of social ceremony in the big room underneath the chapel itself—an interlude before the evening service. And so started my aquaintance with the Welsh colony in London, and my understanding of the Welsh people. I was completely won over by their sympathetic nature, their gaiety, their easy friendship.

But destiny very soon forged another link between the Welshman and myself—and I have never ceased to wonder at the strange way in which my next meeting with him was brought about. It appeared that the Chancellor of the Exchequer was disturbed at the lack of education that his youngest daughter Megan was receiving; she was living at No. 11 Downing Street with parents whose time was very much taken up with public affairs, and while she was being given a great deal of attention in some respects, she was being completely neglected in others. Her father decided to send her to boarding school, but discovering that she was backward in elementary subjects, he thought it would be a good plan for her to be coached during the summer holidays, and he applied to his elder daughter's head mistress for a suitable person for this purpose. (It so happened as I have said that his two elder daughters and I had gone to the same school, Clapham High School.) Mrs. Woodhouse, a woman, incidentally, of the most outstanding gifts, and a distinguished head mistress in her day, first asked my great friend, who was also teaching, if she would like the job. But my friend had already arranged her summer holiday, whereas she knew that I had not, and so it came about, through a series of chance events, that I was eventually asked to go to an interview with the Chancellor of the Exchequer at 11 Downing Street one day at the end of July 1911. Nervous and pale, and looking, I think, much younger than I was, I was shown into the large drawing room upstairs. Soon the door opened and I found myself confronting, but this time at nearer quarters, the man whom I had seen in the Welsh chapel a few weeks before. My nervousness was dispersed in a few moments by the warmth of his voice and the kindliness of manner which put me entirely at my ease. His image as I saw him then is graven on my mind: the sensitive face, with deep furrows between the eyes: the eyes themselves, in which were all knowledge of human nature, grave and gay almost simultaneously—which, when they scrutinised yours, convinced you that they understood all the workings of your heart and mind, sympathised with all your difficulties, set you in a place apart. The broad brow; the beautiful profile—straight nose, neat insolent chin, and a complexion as young and fresh as a child's. (He was very proud of his skin.) Later in life, when his chest and shoulders became broader and he wore his hair longer, his head became more leonine in aspect.

But there was something more even than this which distinguished him from all other men I had ever met—from all whom I ever did meet thereafter—a magnetism which made my heart leap and swept aside my judgment, producing an excitement which seemed to permeate my entire being. I was strung to the utmost point of awareness by this strange encounter, which meant so much for me, then and for ever after.

We discussed the job and my qualifications for it, and he must have seen how eager I was to be given it. It was quickly arranged that I should go down to Criccieth almost immediately and spend the summer there, teaching Megan the elementaries of elementary things, and in addition a little French and music!

He would send his car for me on the appointed day (it was my first drive in a private car) and I was to come first of all to Downing Street for lunch, and then be taken to Paddington and put on the train for Wales. He himself was coming down to Wales a little later.

I left Downing Street under the impression that I was a free and independent person: in truth, I was enslaved for the rest of my life.

The next few days were spent in a whirl of excitement; the horizon of my life was suddenly extended and I walked with wings.

The lunch at Downing Street the following week petrified and exhilarated me. The Attorney General, Sir Rufus Isaacs (later Lord Reading), was there, full of raillery and charm, handsome and debonair, and high spirits were the order of the day. I had never before listened to such witty and stimulating conversation. I realised the quality of L.G.'s voice, but Sir Rufus had a beautiful voice too. L.G. and Rufus at that time were the greatest friends, seeing each other every day, cracking jokes and talking serious politics alternately. The fortunes of the Liberal Party were still very high, the two elections of 1910 had been fought and won, and L.G. was an outstanding personality in the Government. His chief companions were at that time, in addition to Rufus Isaacs, Charles Masterman and George Riddell, and these he saw and talked with practically every day. The Insurance Bill was on its way to becoming an Act, and L.G. was immersed in all the intricacies and controversies connected with its passage through Parliament.

The journey to Wales was, as it even now is, a long and tiring one, but the end of it was for me full of wonder and delight, as I passed through the Welsh landscape for the first time, and along the lovely stretch of Cardigan Bay leading to Criccieth. It was dark and late when I arrived, but, late as it was, Megan had insisted upon waiting up to see her new instructress, and during supper I felt the scrutiny of these young eyes upon me, weighing me up and assessing the possibilities. Dame Margaret (then Mrs. L.G.) was kind and homely. It would not have been extraordinary had she resented the presence of a strange young woman in her household during the summer holidays, when her family would be around her.

Part of the day was given over to lessons, and at other times we bathed, walked, or talked. When Gwilym and Richard, the two boys, came home the household was an extremely lively one.

During that time at Criccieth I made the acquaintance of 'Uncle Lloyd'[1]—a courteous old gentleman with a penetrating eye—rather uncertain of his English. He would come up to Brynawelon soon after breakfast every day to find out what the latest news was of 'his boy', and Megan and I would often walk back with him into the town. He himself wrote to L.G. almost every day. These letters, written half in Welsh and half in English, form a study in themselves, and are a running commentary on L.G.'s progress. Of quiet and dignified bearing, and gentle manner, he would yet sway his congregation when preaching in the Baptist chapel, as I could see for myself. I was touched by his utter devotion to the man whom he had watched over from childhood, for whom he had made such sacrifices, and whose success was rewarding him now so handsomely.

After the House of Commons had risen for the summer recess L.G. arrived with C. F. G. Masterman and Mrs. Masterman. Thereafter the tempo of the household was considerably enlivened. The atmosphere was electric. Masterman and L.G. together at mealtimes provided a conversational feast of the first order. The former, soon to become Financial Secretary to the Treasury, i.e. to L.G.'s department, was a very lovable person, of extremely untidy habits, and with a long nose, down which he would look while making his most cynical or insolent remarks. He and

1. Richard Lloyd, brother of L.G.'s mother, who took her and her children to his home at Llanystumdwy on her husband's early death in 1864.

L.G., while belonging to completely different orders, were entirely in sympathy on the subject of social reform, and Masterman was a tower of strength to L.G. during the framing and passage of the Insurance Act. The present generation, to whom a country without N.H.I. would seem an impossibility, would find it difficult to believe the attacks to which L.G. and Masterman were subjected during its passage through Parliament. No stratagem was left untried by the Conservative Party to block its progress; and a powerful and relentless 'stunt' campaign was organised by the Northcliffe Press, *The Times* and the *Daily Mail*. *The Times*, to quote only one extract from its pages at that time, announced: 'Work of 100 years undone by the Insurance Act.' 'No State Medical Service', bawled the *Daily Mail*. In fact Northcliffe and the Conservative Party had sworn an oath to break the Act before it came into operation.

It was a thousand pities that Masterman and L.G. were to fall out eventually over a stupid disagreement on a constituency. Masterman, not a very good political candidate in spite of his intellect and ability, had lost two by-elections and finally L.G. got him the offer of what was practically a safe seat in Swansea. There were some technical difficulties, but L.G. advised Masterman to go ahead. Masterman preferred, however (or so L.G. thought), to take Asquith's advice on the matter, and Asquith advised against Swansea. Masterman could not have dreamed that L.G. would regard this incident as a slight both to himself and to Wales, but the fact was that he did take great offence, and the two friends drifted apart. Much later they were reunited on L.G.'s plans for land reforms in 1926, but by that time Masterman was failing in health, and died soon afterwards.

Now, however, he was in his heyday, revelling in the carrying out of a great scheme of reform. The atmosphere at Brynawelon glowed. In the mornings L.G. sat for his portrait to Mr. Christopher Williams, a Welsh artist, in his Chancellor's robes; L.G. was always a bad sitter for a portrait, and Megan and I would often sit and talk to him to while away the time. In the afternoons there were picnics on the banks of the Dwyfor, sheepdog trials above Beddge-lert, or drives in the wonderful surrounding country. On Sunday evenings there was the singing of glorious Welsh hymns after chapel on the seashore.

At other times there were walks up on the golf links, with the most wonderful view in the world; a midnight walk up Snowdon to see the sun rise, a sunrise which was not visible owing to the morning mist! There would be excursions every day to some place of interest, or a picnic by the river at Llanystumdwy, where we all took off our shoes and stockings, the men rolling up their trousers (I noted that L.G. had a shapely calf), to cross the stream by the large stones in the river bed, careful, on L.G.'s instruc-tions, to avoid the slippery ones—otherwise a wetting ensued. We made a fire to boil the kettle for tea. L.G. was always a good improviser and he then conceived the idea of making mushrooms on toast on a tin lid over the fire. I may add that they were uneatable, tasting of nothing but smoke. On another occasion he insisted on climbing a tree which overhung the river. He dared us to do likewise but I do not recollect that anyone accepted the challenge.

One day Megan and I had gone down alone and crossed the river and were trespassing on the opposite bank when we were startled by shouts on the other side. We jumped up and were about to run, thinking that the noise proceeded from an irate keeper, but on further investigation realised it was L.G. and Masterman, who were having their fun by alarming us in this fashion.

In the evenings we would often have music and songs and hymns. Megan was not allowed to stay up to dinner and strongly resented this. One night the door of the drawing room opened and a small white-robed figure en-tered on her own initiative to join the party. I cannot remember whether her mother's annoyance or her father's indulgence triumphed on that occasion. I think there was a compromise, and that he took her back to her room and remained with her till she slept.

Visiting Brynawelon at this time also was a lady who was helping L.G. to produce his voice without undue strain upon his throat. He had from boyhood had a delicate throat, and after the elections of 1910–11 a serious condition supervened. Miss Hicks was recommended to him as an expert on voice production and so successful was her treatment that L.G. had no serious trouble with his throat thereafter. One piece of advice which she gave him, and which he took, was never to wear a scarf around his neck. This, she said, weakened the throat and its powers of resistance.

Mr. Kennedy Jones, the editor of the *Daily Mail*, also came on a short visit. This somewhat bewildered L.G.'s local supporters, who rather naturally regarded anyone connected with that paper as an enemy and beyond the bounds of hospitality. They were unfamiliar with the policy of encouraging an enemy if he showed signs of wanting to be a friend.

That summer did so much to me and for me. It was 1911, the summer of perpetual sunshine: sea, sun and mountains —such a combination of beauty I had never before experienced. To teach an enchanting child in the mornings, even if sometimes her attention did wander—so much was going on, and we often had to have our lessons in a room where other people were talking—was no hardship. Around me were the warmth and kindness of the Welsh people: and inside me a sense of gratitude for this new and wonderful experience.

4

Appointment as L.G.'s Personal Secretary

It was decided that Megan should come to school at Allens-wood—the school where I was teaching—as a weekly boarder. The other members of the staff were prepared to be contemptuous of a child who was bound, so they thought, to be insufferable, after having received so much publicity and being so widely photographed: but she won their hearts completely with her charming ways and outwardly docile temperament. She was wiser than her years and able even then, to sum up her surroundings and assess her gaolers. And she went home every week-end to resume her sway of the Downing Street household.

I paid several visits to Downing Street in the autumn that followed. The invitations usually originated from the Chancellor of the Exchequer himself, who would often come to the school to pick up Megan. My visits were always on Sundays. I was subsequently to realise that Mrs. Lloyd George never took the initiative in matters either great or small: her life was made for her, and she accepted it all. The visitors to the house in Downing Street were her husband's visitors, sometimes her children's, scarcely ever her own. She was, in effect, a visitor in her husband's house —except at Criccieth, where he was a visitor in hers. L.G. had in fact had the house built in her name—not that she did not enjoy full sway as hostess in both houses, for L.G. was anxious for her to hold with dignity her official position;

and this she did. But it was L.G. who gave the real welcome, as it was inevitably he who was the centre of the company.

Mrs. L.G. was passionately Welsh, and grudged every moment that she was obliged to spend outside the Principality. L.G. used to say that she would have been happier if he had remained a successful Welsh solicitor, living in Wales. As it was, she was a tremendous help to him with the Welsh nonconformists, and indeed with all nonconformists. When he became Prime Minister she filled her place as the hostess of No. 10 with natural dignity, and I know of many who went there expecting to see a simple peasant woman being surprised to meet a personality of common sense and humour who, although she would have preferred to greet them in Wales, was perfectly able to make them feel at home in an official residence. From what L.G. told me, after Mair's death they had drifted apart. They each had their poignant grief but could not go to each other for sympathy and understanding—there was no sharing of the trouble, both blaming the other, perhaps, for what went wrong, the delay in calling the doctor, the carrying out of an emergency operation without a highly skilled staff and hospital amenities. The gap of incompatibility which had always been there became emphasised and more difficult to bridge.

All this I did not realise at the time. I only knew that I looked forward avidly to the Sunday afternoons when I was invited to tea at No. 11. I remember one occasion when we went after tea to the evening service at the Castle Street chapel and since we were returning to a house empty of servants, for they were away in their own chapel, we bought delicatessen at Appenrodt's (whose existence ceased with the outbreak of war in 1914) and waited on ourselves for supper. Later, L.G. made me play some of the glorious Welsh hymns, and everyone sang lustily, none more lustily than L.G. himself. After which I took the Tube back to school at Wimbledon.

D

On another occasion I remember a friend of Richard's was there, a young man named Clement Davies; and he and Richard greatly entertained us all by their witty chaff, and their teasing of Megan, the spoiled baby of the family. I do not think L.G. was there that afternoon—the family were always less restrained in his absence, having things, as it were, to themselves. When L.G. was present anywhere all attention was necessarily focussed on him. He would always hold the initiative, whether in great things, or small —a political campaign or a picnic party. The tempo of a household would change when he entered it from one of quiet and order to something exciting and almost feverish. Everything naturally, it seemed, revolved around him, and nobody else.

L.G. knew at that time that I was resolved to give up teaching at the earliest possible moment. About Easter he asked me if I would like to summarise for him a French book on the land system, and this I gladly did in my holidays. Although I was not unhappy in my job—I was determined not to fail in it—I was finding myself increasingly 'cribbed, cabin'ed and confined' in the boarding school at Wimbledon, and was casting about for more emancipated occupation. From time to time I visited the offices of the more highbrow newspapers to enquire if my services would be acceptable to them, but I had no experience of journalism and my offers were politely declined. I did discover, however, that shorthand might be a useful asset, and set about learning it. I remember that after reading the French edition of *Woman: A Vindication*, by Ludovici, I wrote in an endeavour to widen my horizon, and asked if I might be allowed to translate it into English (an ambitious project!), but received a courteous reply to the effect that this had already been arranged for.

Later, however, in the summer holidays, I did some more work for L.G. in connection with the land campaign which he was contemplating as soon as the Insurance Act was out of the way. The Act was still giving him a lot of trouble. The duchesses and domestic servants held a combined meeting at the Albert Hall to protest against 'stamplicking'. The Northcliffe Press was on the watch for any advantage that might be snatched to damage the Act.

In addition, the Welsh Disestablishment Bill had been introduced, in which L.G. was naturally intimately concerned. And he had already started organising his campaign for land reform.

I remember going to the House of Commons to see him for some instructions on the work I was doing for him one summer's evening before the House rose for the recess. He was very tired and his eyes were red-rimmed with late-night sittings. 'I have to flog myself, otherwise I could not go on,' he said to me. My heart went out to him, and I wanted more than anything to help him.

In the autumn I went several times to the House of Commons in the evenings at his invitation to listen to debates, and a note would be handed to me in the Gallery to come to his room for a chat, or on one or two occasions we dined at a nearby restaurant—often Gatti's, which he liked very much. We wrote to each other almost daily. I burnt his letters after reading them, as I imagine he did mine. We were handed our letters by the head mistress after prayers, and I remember the look of strong disapproval on her face as she handed me the letters addressed in L.G.'s distinctive handwriting. I began to realise that he looked forward to seeing me, as I did to seeing him. I felt I ought to give up my visits, but I could not bring myself to do this, and so the link inevitably tightened, and when the possibility of working for him altogether was put forward it did not take me long to make up my mind. The point of no return had been reached—and passed.

My head mistress, with whom L.G. was already not too popular owing to the continual whisking off of Megan at irregular times and her late returns to school, was angry

beyond words when I announced my intention of leaving
the school. 'The man has upset me enough with his Insurance stamps,' she raged, 'and now he takes away one of
my staff.' She tried to persuade me to stay, saying that if
I liked I could 'reach the top of the tree'. 'But I don't want
to reach the top of *this* tree,' I replied.

I had arranged to stay with some friends in Scotland at
the end of the term. L.G. had already made it clear to me
that he would like to have me as a secretary at the Treasury
—but I realised that this would be on his own terms, which
were in direct conflict with my essentially Victorian upbringing. In my heart I wanted to marry and have a home
and children. L.G. gave me at that time a copy of the book
on Parnell by Katherine O'Shea. He always contended that
by marrying Kitty O'Shea, Parnell had destroyed his own
career and destroyed the Irish Party; and he held that no
man has a right to imperil his political party and its objective for the sake of a woman—which meant that no divorce
was possible, and that I must not hope for marriage unless
and until he could make me his legal wife; with a corollary
that if he ever could he would do so.

L.G. described to me, in telling, me of Parnell's fall, how
Parnell came into the House of Commons after the divorce
and took his seat on a solitary bench; how no one came near
him until an old Quaker left his seat and sat down next to
Parnell and talked to him.

I was very innocent and inexperienced for my age and
by the time I went to Scotland I had heard too much of
L.G.'s caressing voice and become too fond of him to
doubt that true happiness could be found without marriage.
I decided, however, to think the matter over very carefully
while in Scotland. Then in Scotland I met a young man who
had fallen in love with me during my visit the previous
summer and wanted to marry me. He was in every way a
desirable '*parti*', highly intelligent, musical, a civil servant

with a future. His approach, however, was academic rather than romantic. I wrote and told L.G. about him and his offer of marriage, and L.G. replied at once that I must do what I thought right and that he would not stand in my way. He did not try to persuade me against it; the decision was with *me*.

Almost immediately I received another urgent letter; it simply said that something terrible had happened and that he needed me. I was unable to imagine what the misfortune could be. I returned to London at once. It was the Marconi scandal[1] which was about to break, with all its threat of ruin and disaster to L.G.'s career and to all the reforms which he had made his own. There had been rumours and rumblings of the affair for some time, but L.G., knowing his complete innocence, did not think that they could affect him personally and had felt justified in treating the matter lightly. Now, however, it was assuming more serious proportions. He was going through an agonising time, and I knew he needed me. His suffering was all the greater because he knew he was innocent of the accusation which was being brought against him in connection with Marconi shares which Rufus Isaacs had persuaded him to buy. The accusation was that L.G. had used his position as Chancellor of the Exchequer to buy shares, which he thought would eventually sell at a profit, in the American Marconi Company when the British P.O. was discussing a contract with the British Marconi Company. Although a Select Committee of the House of Commons ultimately acquitted him handsomely and a Vote of Confidence was passed on L.G., the mud—and a good deal of it—stuck for all time. Not knowing how the scandal would end he was tormenting himself, not so much for what would happen if he had to resign his office, but how he had let down his nonconformist supporters by his transactions (even though in the event he was hundreds of pounds the poorer as a result). He was

1. 1912.

suffering, too, because of what old Uncle Lloyd would think of 'his boy' for being so foolish when he had attained such high office and responsibility.

L.G. had good friends who rallied to him and did their best to comfort him. C. P. Scott used his paper to the utmost to defend L.G. and Churchill's loyalty and affection were as a strong rock. C. F. G. Masterman was also a loyal friend, and I think it was on his suggestion that I visited newspaper offices in an endeavour to find out whether there had been any public mention of the American Marconi shares which would have made them available to the general public. This would have exonerated L.G. and Rufus Isaacs. However, after many weary but hopeful days I could find nothing to help him. I could only comfort him, talk to him, try to cheer him and help him to cross the raging torrent of political hatred which would gladly have compassed his downfall.

Asquith refused L.G.'s and Rufus Isaacs' offers to resign, and throughout this lamentable period acted with the utmost loyalty to his Ministers. And in the House of Commons later, he said:

Their honour, both their private and their public honour, is at this moment absolutely unstained. They have, as this Committee has shown by its unanimous verdict, abused no public trust. They retain, I can say with full assurance, the complete confidence of their colleagues and of their political associates.

In fact, Isaacs was made Lord Chief Justice very soon afterwards. L.G. recommended him to the King as Viceroy of India when he was Prime Minister. But the personal relations of L.G. and Reading were never quite the same after the Marconi affair.

L.G. was devoted to Reading in the early days of office and preferred his company to that of all other men. He was a fascinating man, with his good looks and brilliant brain.

His gaiety almost equalled L.G.'s and he had the legal mind which L.G. greatly admired. L.G. was always attracted by the Jewish characteristics, and Jews were attracted by him. He would not listen to the denunciation of Jews which some people indulge in, and he would often go through a list of the great Jews and what they had done for mankind. When he visited Hitler in 1936 he remonstrated with him about the persecution that Jews were undergoing in Nazi Germany. Hitler defended himself by giving a catalogue of what the Jews were supposed to be doing in Germany—corrupting the young people by low forms of entertainment in theatre, music-hall and newspapers: the only thing was to exterminate them. It has often seemed to me since that Germany was not the only country whose young people were thus corrupted, and *not* by Jews.

But when it came to outlook, L.G. and Rufus Isaacs parted, for the latter had what might be called the 'cafeteria' mind—self-service only. Ambition was his ruling quality, quietly he sought and obtained advancement until he became Viceroy of India—he, a Jew!

Mr. Roy Jenkins is probably right when he says in his biography of Asquith: 'Lloyd George and Isaacs were both lucky in the Prime Minister under whom they made their errors of judgment.' Had Asquith so willed, he could have ruined L.G., and the fact that this course of behaviour was alien to him might have made L.G. his grateful servant for ever.

When I returned to London from Scotland soon after Christmas (1912) in response to L.G.'s letter I returned to place myself in his hands unconditionally, that is to say, on *his* conditions. So great was the power and mastery that he had already exercised over me that I did not doubt for one moment that *he* was in command of the situation. He had made me realise that I was necessary to him. I knew instinctively that in the relationship I was contemplating there would be hurts and humiliations, but it seemed to me that nothing I could ever do would be so worth while as to help this man with whom I wished to join my life. L.G. himself, with his knowledge of the world, must have visualised the possible danger to his own career from our re-relationship, but I, in my inexperience, felt complete confidence in his power to shield us both.

The decision was a heart-shocking one for me, due to my upbringing and the opinions I held regarding any woman who *lived* with a man to whom she was not married. I held myself up to the light, so to speak, and passed judgment on myself, longing for some comfort but realising the awful things which the future might hold.

I decided to make a confession to my mother, to seek from her some form of forgiveness or reassurance that redemption was possible, or might be. But with her strong and definite moral outlook she turned on me the whole of her anger at the thought that her daughter could be capable of such an action, however extenuating the circumstances. It was useless for me to try to defend myself. The excoriating contempt which met my apologia made me deeply conscious of the barrier which had come between us. She actually quoted the classical words: 'I would rather see you dead at my feet.' My father and mother, to my horror, asked to see L.G. He invited them to Downing Street to dine, but it was not a success and the attempt was not repeated. I was sorry for L.G. but angry with my parents. For them such a situation would admit of no compromise. It was a world in which my parents had never walked and could only lead to unhappiness (oh! but so much happiness, and fulfilment as well!). My mother never forgave L.G., and I think that to the end of her life she was hoping that I would leave him.

It was a good thing that during these months he had the work of his land enquiry to occupy him, in addition to his routine Treasury work. L.G. had decided that his next

task, after the completion of the Insurance Act, would be
to attempt to improve the lot of the agricultural labourer.
This meant an attack upon the landlords and the whole
agricultural system. A committee had been set up—what
we would now call a 'fact-finding committee'—to produce
a report which would form a basis of the new campaign.
The moving spirit of the new committee was Seebohm
Rowntree. This remarkable man was a Quaker possessed
of a wonderful business sense. A pattern of rectitude and
self-discipline, with a twinkling eye and a teasing manner,
he had already become well known for the inquiries he had
conducted into the conditions under which certain sections
of the working classes lived. His book *How the Labourer
Lives*, with its facts on wages, housing, and unemployment,
had just been published and had created something of a
sensation. He and L.G. found an affinity with each other,
and L.G. could think of no person better suited than
Seebohm Rowntree to prepare the facts and figures which
he would require for his land campaign and at the same time
'obtain an accurate and impartial account of the social and
economic conditions in the rural parts of Great Britain'.

The Land Enquiry Committee had their premises in
Palace Chambers, very near the Treasury, and it was part
of my work to go backwards and forwards when L.G. was
preparing his speeches, collecting the necessary material
and giving messages on his behalf. By now I had completely
identified myself with L.G.'s interests. But I was received
rather coldly by the Treasury staff. They definitely resented
this intrusion by a young female into their domain. L.G. had
already put the cat amongst the pigeons by introducing a
female shorthand typist: on going to the Treasury he had
found a male shorthand writer who transcribed his notes
in longhand! And now another innovation. I shared a
room, however, with L.G.'s other personal secretary (who
had also been recruited outside the bounds of the Civil
Service)—J. T. Davies, who took me under his wing from

the first moment and was for ever afterwards my friend. He himself had only lately come there, and had just had a rather terrifying experience of his chief's idiosyncrasies. L.G. had been away on the Continent for a fortnight, during which time correspondence had greatly accumulated. On his return L.G. asked to see anything of importance, and J.T. went to him with a pile of papers reaching up to his chin, on the top of which lay an invitation to dinner from a well-known London hostess. 'This is the most urgent, sir,' he said, handing the letter to L.G. This so angered the Chancellor of the Exchequer that he seized the whole pile out of J.T.'s hands and hurled it across the room. Thereafter it can be imagined with what care, and trepidation, and with what economy J.T. selected the letters which he brought to his chief's attention.

I became immersed in my new work. My shorthand and typing were now proficient, so that I was able to help in the preparation of the speeches for the new campaign. I was more than excited—I was thrilled to find myself thus in the centre of the political scene and identified, in a very humble way, with momentous events. I did not spare myself. I worked early and late, as indeed L.G. expected everyone employed by him to do. I had no leisure: from now on I was dedicated to L.G. and his works. I saw less and less of my friends.

I began at this time to become acquainted with some of L.G.'s more personal friends. In addition to Masterman, one of the men who was constantly in L.G.'s company was Sir George Riddell (later Lord Riddell). I found him at first rather forbidding, with his piercing blue eyes, gaunt figure, and his habit of cross-examining everyone with whom he came into contact. He had an insatiable curiosity, and he simply had, if possible, to get at one's private life, more, I think, because he liked to be able to form a complete picture of the person in question than from any morbid motive. Nevertheless, it was a habit

which those who did not know him well found rather embarrassing. But he would take the same keen interest in
those in humble stations of life—a servant, a clerk or a
tradesman—as in very important people—such as Cabinet
Ministers! It was human nature that interested him. At
the time of which I am speaking he had attached himself
to L.G. and the latter found his company congenial and
convenient. Riddell as a newspaper proprietor had all the
political gossip of the day, and since politics dominated
L.G.'s every working hour, he naturally found Riddell a
good companion. Moreover Riddell gradually made himself indispensable to L.G. He arranged games of golf
whenever L.G. could spare the time, and saw that L.G.
had a house on the edge of the Walton Heath golf course,
which was an immeasurable boon to a man who needed
fresh air and exercise to keep him fit for his work.

Riddell was a strangely paradoxical creature. He could
be mean and generous, hard and kind. While keenly interested in the making of money, he was not interested in
spending it upon himself. His clothes were shabby, his
hat battered and old, and he was indifferent to food and
drink. He preferred an austere room in the Dormy House
at Walton Heath to his mansion in London overlooking
St. James's Park.

I came to like Riddell very much, and to count him as a
real friend. I never quite trusted him, but when one is
forewarned one is forearmed. Nevertheless I am grateful
to this day to him for many kindnesses.

The man, however, who was closest to L.G. politically
and mentally was Winston Churchill. These two men had
already been fast friends for years, and were destined to
be very near to each other for many years to come—indeed
until death parted them. They dined together, so L.G. told
me, for several nights running, at the Café Royal when
Campbell Bannerman was forming his new Government
in December 1905. Masterman, Elibank, Reading and Jack

Seely were also of the company. One by one they were sent for, L.G. first of all, the others waiting their turn in hope and trepidation.

The friendship between the two men was a curious one. It was not identity of interest, for Churchill had no interest in social reform, which L.G. had in his bones. Both were born politicians, and interested in politics on the grand scale. Both had the same daring outlook and the same love of the political arena in all its fascination and peril. And, of course, both had genius. But whereas, generally speaking, one genius tends to become segregated from another, these two, although revolving in their own orbits, worshipped the same sun and thus were drawn to each other in a common understanding. They were both cast on a great scale: their ideas were uninhibited by convention or creed: their minds towered over others like the tall towers of San Gimignano. When L.G. became Chancellor of the Exchequer he almost inevitably came into conflict with Churchill over the Navy Estimates. Churchill, quite naturally, wished for a powerful Navy: L.G., on the contrary, wanted to spend money on the social services. There was a distinct clash. L.G. had recourse to his friend C. P. Scott, whose advice he sought now as always in his life during crises.

The conflict of interests between L.G. and Churchill, which continued almost up to the outbreak of war in 1914, and broke out from time to time throughout their lives, did not at all interfere with their friendship. They met constantly at each other's houses, in the House of Commons, or around a friendly table elsewhere, to discuss politics at large, in their ebullient fashion. Both men were in the prime of life, but Churchill was eleven years younger than L.G.

5

War Comes to interrupt Reform

The land campaign was launched in a speech at Bedford on October 10th, 1913, and this was followed by speeches at Swindon on October 22nd and in November at the Oxford Union. At the beginning of 1914 the attacks were widened to include the abuses of urban land, and some terrific evidence was produced against the titled landowners of urban properties. L.G. ran true to form and derived great satisfaction from focussing his attacks upon the dukes, who, so it happened, were amongst the largest landowners and provided, so he thought, the most flagrant cases. They were, in fact, fair game.

But even a duke will turn if you prod him and goad him too mercilessly. The Tories decided to fight the cause of the dukes in the Commons, to throw them, as it were, in L.G.'s face. The Dukes of Bedford, Westminster, Montrose and Sutherland had been successively attacked by L.G. He had a magnificent case, and he used it to advantage. It was now obvious that having succeeded in establishing his National Health Insurance Schemes, he intended to introduce legislation to improve the agricultural conditions. But the Tories were infuriated by this new onslaught upon their ancient privileges. The National Unionist Association of Conservative Organisations sent out an instruction to their agents asking for reports from the villages about the new campaign.

61

One that they received read as follows:

The Radicals started their land campaign here about a fortnight ago with an open air meeting promising the labourers
£1 *a week* [my italics], better houses, etc. The meeting I am informed was well attended, and the proposals are much talked
about in the village publics afterwards. I would suggest that
meetings like this should be followed by one on our own side,
and these plausible statements contradicted before they have
time to sink in.

Another ran like this:

The villagers and the agricultural labourers are talking about
nothing but Lloyd George and the Minimum Wage. . . .

It was not only country conditions which L.G. attacked.
Urban landlords were pilloried, and the injustice of leaseholds laid bare. He spoke at Middlesbrough and Holloway
on this subject during the following months, and it was
obvious that the campaign was gathering momentum. At
Holloway he announced: 'The new dispensation is on the
way, when the resources of the country will be well ordered,
well husbanded, fairly distributed.' He told Charles Masterman before the meeting that he was 'going to let himself go
and brighten things up a bit'. This indeed he accomplished.

At last the Tories could stand it no longer. They determined to attack him on a grand scale in the House of
Commons. The Tory press were full of it. The debate was
fixed for March 10th, 1914, and L.G. according to the newspapers, was to have 'the time of his life.' The dukes were
about to be vindicated by the Tories in formal debate. Sir
John Randles put down a motion:

That this House contemplates with regret the repeated
inaccuracies of the Chancellor of the Exchequer and his gross
and unfounded personal attacks upon individuals.

I shall never forget the scene which presented itself in the House of Commons that evening. The debate was opened at 8.15 p.m. and the House itself was packed, members sitting in the gangway, and elbowing each other for seats. I had been fortunate enough to secure a seat in the Ladies' Gallery, which was also packed. Mrs. Asquith was not present, but Violet Asquith (Lady Violet Bonham-Carter) was in the seat of honour at one end of the front row, while Lady Londonderry, the great hostess of the Conservative Party, in all her splendid aggressiveness was at the other end. The atmosphere, in the Ladies' Gallery as well as in the House itself, was tense.

I was on tenterhooks, for I knew that, in fact, L.G. had committed one or two inaccuracies in his speech at Holloway regarding leaseholds in St. Pancras, due to faulty information which had not been properly sifted, and I could not see how he was going to ward off his enemies. They in turn, were aware of the weak points in L.G.'s defence, and they thought they had him at bay.

The indictment by Sir John Randles was not a particularly formidable one. It attacked L.G.'s Glasgow speech where he had accused the Duke of Sutherland amongst other things of falsifying the value of his land, and for saying:

In the old days the Chieftains had the right of hanging their subjects. In 1748 the Government thought, on the whole, they had better take that away from them, and the Duke of Sutherland claimed £10,000 compensation. He got £1,000.

Randles defended the Duke of Montrose against L.G.'s suggestion that he had sold land to the Stirlingshire County Council at 2,000 years' purchase. He had recourse to a quotation that L.G. 'keeps one eye on the crowd, the other is blinded by limelight'.

Mr. Felix Cassel (he was made a baronet during L.G.'s

Premiership in 1920), an able and eminent lawyer who followed, was much more formidable. His first mistake, however, was to refer to L.G.'s attack on the Duke of Westminster which had been made five years earlier in L.G.'s Limehouse speech.[1] It was not really relevant to the debate, but it enabled L.G. to make great play on this point and to devote (legitimately) a valuable part of his time in replying to dealing with Cassel's questions. The case against L.G., however, was now being built up.

The Chancellor of the Exchequer has such an animus against landowners that he is ready to take any material to his hand without investigation and without enquiry if only it will have the effect of damaging landowners.

Cassel accused L.G. of desiring to 'arouse feelings of cupidity and envy in the audiences he was addressing'.

Then he went on to defend the landlords of St. Pancras (his own constituency) against the charges which L.G. had brought against them in his speech at Holloway, in connection with leaseholds; he ended by accusing L.G. of 'imperilling the credit and the dignity which attaches to the high office which the Rt. Hon. Gentleman holds'.

Both L.G.'s attackers had insisted that they were making their speeches brief in order to give L.G. plenty of time for reply. L.G., however, in the opening sentences of his reply took the precaution (for what reason it was soon obvious) of complaining that his accusers had not left *him* time to deal with all the matters they had raised. However, he made full use of his time. To see him on his mettle in the House of Commons, with head tilted back and insolence in his whole bearing, was a sight worth remembering. I have in my possession a bronze bust made by Mr. Felix Weiss, in which this insolent attitude has been captured, and I am glad to have this permanent witness of what I call 'the gladiator look'.

1. July 30th, 1909.

L.G. dealt with his accusers and their accusations in turn, but in the process he artfully drew red herrings across the trail for the benefit of F. E. Smith (later Lord Birkenhead) who was to follow and wind up. The House warmed up, and interruptions were frequent. The Deputy Speaker had constantly to call members to order. L.G. tackled Cassel, cornered him, and then accused him of running away. There was never a more perfect example of L.G.'s technique of choosing his own strategic position, changing it at the psychological moment, knowing when it was strong, and avoiding the weak places. Nor had I ever seen him better at throwing his enemies into confusion with his adroit handling of their accusations and his skilful defences. Here was the happy warrior indeed. The Tories became angry. They had thought they had got the little devil at last, and here he was eluding them in triumph. Lady Londonderry, in her place in the Ladies' Gallery, an almost terrifying figure, and strengthened by her admiration of F.E., became angriest of all, and the attendant had to request her to keep silence.

L.G. continued to put confusion into the Tory camp by quoting Mr. Joseph Chamberlain, who had said:

I cannot recall to mind one single great or beneficent reform which has been promoted at the instigation of the landed gentry, or which has not received their personal hostility. It was two inveterate cockneys, Mr. Bright and Mr. Cobden, that aroused the nation to a sense of the iniquities of the system which taxed the bread of the people in order to raise the rents of the landlord..

L.G. added:

. . . The Right Hon. and learned Gentleman the Member for Walton [F. E. Smith] the other day delivered a glowing eulogism upon that very statesman. He said: 'He was one of the three great Englishmen of the last century—Chatham, Beaconsfield—and *Chamberlain.*'

E

L.G.'s eloquence mounted, and he returned to his attack on the Duke of Sutherland and the derelict Scottish acres upon which the Duke put such a high price. But he insisted that he must keep to his time and that he must allow his opponent, F. E. Smith, adequate time for winding up. He had dealt with the Gorringe case (Duke of Westminster), with the Cathcart case (Duke of Montrose), with the Sutherland case (the Duke of Sutherland), and—much to his chagrin!—he found it necessary to sit down without having time to deal with the St. Pancras case—the one on which his enemies really thought they had him! 'I promised the Rt. Hon. and learned Gentleman I would sit down to time' . . . 'I cannot deal with the other cases—I had all the cases here—therefore I should like to sum up, and this is what I have to say.' Then followed a terrible attack on the Tories, finishing on a note of challenge and triumph. When L.G. sat down the scene was indescribable. The Tories were howling for his blood. They saw red. Lady Londonderry in the Ladies' Gallery cried out in her wrath, and was again called to order by the attendant. But L.G.'s speech had taken all the sparkle out of F.E., who, instead of demolishing the Chancellor of the Exchequer with wit and satire as he had been expected to do, stumbled over his points and became involved in his arguments. He was reduced to resurrecting the gibe about pheasants and mangold wurzels.

The Chancellor of the Exchequer . . . had made a discovery, novel, valuable, possibly true, but one which—I say this confidently—had escaped the observation of every previous authority alike upon horticulture and ornithology. . . .

He was pathetically below form, and made a mess of his peroration. L.G. was left in victorious possession at 11 p.m. and the motion was lost by 240 votes to 304.

The excitement on this occasion was high, the tension

terrific. There seemed to be much *weightier*, and much *deeper* issues at stake between the two parties then—possibly because there were only two parties, and they faced each other in full battle array. It was the last ditch of the land-lords, and they knew L.G. as their bitter foe, which he had indeed been since his boyhood in a little Welsh village, when the local landlord had turned the parents of his friends out of their homes for voting Liberal at the election. (The war and the Coalition put an end to all this.)

I used to send him a little note into the House after any speech he had made, and now I hurried into the ante-room behind the Gallery to scribble him a message of excited congratulation and hand it to a messenger to be taken into him. He loved to receive such messages after a speech, to reassure him. With the true temperament of the artist he was glad to receive praise for his work. This one said:

First class. It was everything I could have wished. Every point, however quietly made, went home, and you had the rapt attention of the House. It was a complete success. P.

What with the land campaign and Ireland, that spring was a full one. L.G. was still defending the Insurance Act against Tory onslaught in the House of Commons. On March 5th Worthington-Evans moved 'That the vote on the National Insurance Act be reduced by £100' and a lively debate followed. There were, of course, still many leakages and weak points in the Act, and the Tories made the most of them. L.G. on this occasion criticised the attacks that were being circulated on the Act in the poor London districts and quoted one particularly offensive quatrain. 'Where is your sense of humour?' asked a Tory member, and L.G. retorted: 'What does the Hon. Gentle-man mean by "sense of humour"? A sense of humour means that you go down to constituencies and tell the poor people that officials who are working hard are simply sitting around smoking and lolling about upon the money which the poor people are compelled to pay. That is very funny—extraordinarily funny! It is one of the most amusing things I have ever heard.'

Those who did not actually hear L.G. when making a retort of this kind would find it difficult to conjure up the ring of scorn in his voice and the flashing eye, the accusing finger pointed at the delinquent on the bench opposite and under which he wilted.

Looking back, it is interesting—even amusing—to read the violent attacks on him by Tories who, before very long, were to look to him as a possible saviour of the country.

The Budget and the work which it entailed in the House of Commons necessarily occupied much of his time, but the real hard work was over the Irish question in which he took a prominent part. The Ulster Plot in April caused matters in Ireland, always on the boiling point, to boil over, and the British Government had to act firmly. With his gift for negotiation, and his passionate determination to 'find a way', L.G. was inevitably in the forefront in the talks with the Irish leaders on both sides. There were constant talks and correspondence between John Redmond, Joe Devlin, John Dillon, Sir Edward Carson, and other distinguished Irishmen on both sides. L.G. was busy and happy, happy because he was busy.

On Saturdays there would be golf at Walton Heath, usually with George Riddell.

Thanks to Riddell, L.G. now had a house within a stone's throw of the golf club—a house furnished from left-overs from L.G.'s former houses—lacking comfort and adequate heating. I remember that there was no heating at all in the spare bedroom, which used to get horribly damp when unoccupied. It was not until Philip Kerr, some years after, caught a bad chill when sleeping there that it was decided to put in a gas fire. The house was looked after by an old Welshwoman who would cook L.G. simple meals but did not believe in luxuries! When I suggested that L.G. might sometimes be given cream with his food as it would be good for him, she replied that she could not include that extravagance in her account to Dame Margaret. Nevertheless L.G. loved to get away down there, and would sometimes drive down in the week, when the day's work was done, 'to sleep and wake up in the fresh air', as he put it. And when he was preparing a speech he would often stay and work there, in preference to town, where there would be more interruption.

One night after a dinner in London he was driving down alone, when on Banstead Downs, some miles from home, something went wrong with the car, and the driver stopped and opened the bonnet to examine the works. It was a fine night, and L.G. also got out of the car. The driver, having put right what was wrong, got into his seat and drove away, and arriving at Walton Heath, opened the door of the car for L.G. to alight. To the astonishment and bewilderment of the housekeeper, the chauffeur without a word hurriedly shut the car door again, jumped into his seat and drove off, realising his error too late, and full of shame at leaving his master on the lonely heath at that late hour. L.G. had had no other alternative but to start to walk, and he used to say that he wondered what would have happened if the police had encountered him—a strange figure in an evening cape and opera hat. He would have explained that he was the Chancellor of the Exchequer, but they would probably have pointed to the Banstead Lunatic Asylum close by, and said, 'Come inside'.

On another occasion when L.G. was driving up from Walton Heath with Sir George Riddell one morning the car broke down at Streatham. There was an important Cabinet Meeting at eleven o'clock and L.G. decided that if he wanted to arrive in time the best plan was to take a tram to Westminster (there seemed to be no taxis about). He and Riddell accordingly did so, but when the conductor came for their fares it was found that neither L.G. nor Riddell had any money in their pockets! However, some of the passengers came to their rescue, although the spectacle of the Chancellor of the Exchequer without a penny in his pocket may have seemed rather paradoxical to them.

The achievement of Home Rule for Ireland, which had been one of L.G.'s heart's desires from his earliest days, was now once more postponed. As a result of untiring negotiation he succeeded in persuading Redmond and his Nationalist followers to accept an Amending Bill giving the right for six years to any of the Ulster counties to vote themselves out of the Home Rule Bill. The Lords, however, destroyed the hopes which this agreement had raised, and civil war in Ireland seemed almost certain, when the outbreak of the European war called a halt to this particular plan as it did to so many others. It was left to L.G. as Prime Minister, five years later, to tackle and solve the problem.

On Sunday, June 29th, 1914, I was at 11 Downing Street in the afternoon working on a speech which L.G. was shortly to make to the bankers in the City. I remember the day well, because it was my mother's birthday, and she was cross that I should have another engagement on that day. (Birthdays were important dates in our family, as were all anniversaries.) I was upset at annoying my mother, and L.G. was annoyed with me for being upset. My mother and L.G. were never good friends and I was constantly being pulled both ways because of this.

During the afternoon the red despatch box came in from the Foreign Office, while L.G. was resting, and at tea time I took it into him. He unlocked it and drew out the telegram announcing the assassination of the Austrian Archduke and his wife at Sarajevo. 'This means war,' he said, as he handed it to me to read. But I am sure that 'war' meant to him only another upheaval in the Balkans, with Austria in the background. It never entered his mind that a flame had been lighted which would spread wave upon wave until it affected most of the world.

I went towards the end of July with members of my family to the speech day at Christ's Hospital, where my brother was now a joint Head Grecian, with John Woods, later head of the Civil Service. My brother had gained an exhibition to St. John's College, Oxford. We little knew that he would never take it up, and that before the next speech day he would lie buried in France.

We were very proud of our brother. It was his last speech day at school, and he intended later to try for the Higher Division of the Civil Service. He was tall and good-looking and nineteen. In addition to his scholarship he was leaving school with one gold medal for Greek and Latin composition, and another for Latin hexameter verses, the Charles Lamb silver medal for English prose, two silver medals and two bronze ones for athletics. Small wonder, then, that in the eyes of his family he was '*primus inter pares*'.

Of his companions and rivals, one, John Woods, and another, Eric Speed, achieved distinction in the Civil Service after the war. It is difficult not to speculate sometimes as to 'what might have been' had my brother lived; he was only one of the multitude of whom it was written 'age shall not weary them, nor the years condemn'; who 'by being faithful unto death, have won a crown of everlasting life'; but whose brilliant qualities were lost to their generation.

Edmund Blunden, himself a Christ's Hospital scholar, wrote:

What war was, all who were present in Chapel felt with intense shock in May, 1915, when Dr. Upcott [the head master], announced the death of P. W. J. Stevenson, a most popular, promising and modest Grecian who had left the school only a few months. It became also a common enough occurrence as the War dragged on for a boy fresh in the minds of all to be struck down; but that was the first universally comprehended tragedy, I believe, given out in Chapel.

When war broke out my brother, having been a member
of the O.T.C. at school, obtained a commission. He was
full of high enthusiasm for the conflict, which to these
young idealists took the nature of a crusade. When he went
out to France in the following March he refused to take his
greatcoat with him. 'We shall soon be on the move,' he
said, 'and I don't want to have a lot of heavy things to
carry.' He sent for it very soon, however, and what he must
have suffered from the cold in the intervening period I do
not care to imagine. What he must have suffered, too, when
he discovered the conditions under which our men were
fighting, with little ammunition and no explosives, he was
never able to tell us, for he was killed in May, before having
time to come home on leave.

Somehow my mother knew that he was dead before
the news reached her. She was very quiet, and when my
sister asked her if she did not intend to make the usual
weekly cake to send to Paul, she shook her head. The only
time I ever saw my father weep was after the telegram
arrived telling that my brother had 'died of wounds'.

Towards the end of July L.G.'s family packed up, when
the children's holidays started, and went to Criccieth for
the summer. When this happened the custom was for all
the rooms to be shrouded in dust sheets, and a minimum
of staff left at No. 11 until such time as L.G. should be
able himself to travel to Wales. The fact that he might in
the interval want to entertain did not enter into the scheme
of things at all. His minimum wants were provided for and
that had to be sufficient. Perhaps the theory was that he
would not dally in London under those conditions.

So that during that fateful week-end when war broke
out L.G., as far as his family were concerned, was alone in
Downing Street, except for a minimum staff which included
Sarah Jones, a great character by whom L.G. was often
kept in order. Sarah was a friend of mine from the first,
and my position in Downing Street was greatly eased and

abetted by her. I was not averse to taking advice from this wise old Welshwoman. L.G. was her 'child' over whom she watched, unselfishly, devoted to his welfare, and often incurring the displeasure of his family by her fearless words. L.G. could depend upon her help for looking after me when he wanted me in Downing Street. She had not been too pleased when the family moved from a pleasant house in Chelsea to which they had gone after the death of Mair, and L.G. thought she would be influenced by the lovely (extremely old-fashioned) kitchen at No. 11 with its walls lined with shelves of copper kitchen utensils, relics of the Victorian era. Instead, she flung up her hands and cried: '*Duw Anwyl* (Dear God) *what* am I to do with all these pots and pans?' But she had a devoted staff from her home town (Criccieth) and I do not remember there ever being a domestic shortage in 11 or 10 Downing Street as long as L.G. was there.

So much has been written—he has written his own account of it—of his attitude at that time that it would be superfluous for me to detail it here.

The week-end that war was declared I was in No. 11 the whole of the week-end, desperately unhappy at first at L.G.'s attitude *against* supporting the French and declaring war ourselves. He was certainly no pro-German, but he felt in the first place that we were not prepared for war, and secondly his instinct was against war. He was pressed all the time by his colleagues who *wanted* war with Germany (e.g. Churchill, who was for any war at any time, and Asquith, who realised probably that war was inevitable). And the anti-war people were certainly not amongst his friends—Simon, for instance, and John Burns, and John Morley. (Simon, L.G. said, will sit on the fence until the iron enters his soul.)

My own opinion is that L.G.'s mind was really made up from the first, that he knew we would have to go in, and that the invasion of Belgium was, to be cynical, a heaven-sent excuse for supporting a declaration of war. He was fully aware that in taking the side of the pro-war party in the Government he would offend a large section of his supporters, but his first few speeches did a good deal to reassure a great number of them. His first great speech—in the Queen's Hall[1]—after the outbreak of war has become a famous one, with its magnificent peroration on sacrifice, using his beloved mountains for a simile. Now he stood aloof, however, and at one point on that eventful Sunday, with the crowds in Whitehall demanding war, he told me that his decision depended on whether the Germans invaded Belgium or not. In that event we were governed by a treaty. In those days I was not addicted to prayer, but I think as far as I could I prayed that the Germans would invade Belgium. L.G. came backwards and forwards from No. 10 to No. 11, telling me of the controversy that was taking place. At one time I knew that the Cabinet were hopelessly divided, and I knew that L.G. was hoping that the integrity of Belgium would be respected. If, however, the Germans did not honour their bond to protect Belgium I realised that L.G. would throw in his weight *for* war. This was what I hoped for, and by the time L.G. wrote his memoirs he said: 'We could have done no other.'

L.G. liked to deliver his important speeches on a Saturday afternoon, for thus they received the maximum amount of publicity—in the Saturday evening press, the Sunday papers, and again perforce in the Monday papers. It must be remembered that in those days there was no such thing as broadcasting. The Press was the only medium of publicity. Nor, I may mention here, were there any loudspeakers or microphones. L.G. had to rely solely on his own voice to reach the farthest corner of his audience. That was why he did not care to speak in the Albert Hall—it was too great a strain upon his voice. It is difficult for those who have grown up since the first war to realise what a

1. September 19th, 1914.

small proportion of the nation ever heard L.G.'s voice—
or, indeed, the voice of any Minister: whereas now there is
probably no one who has not heard the voice, at some
time or other, of every prominent statesman or politician.

How we worked at that Queen's Hall speech! And how
apprehensive he was before it was delivered! With his
Boer War record he realised how important it was—a
landmark in his career. People would have to be convinced
of his sincerity. Strangely enough, when the speech was
over, he was intensely depressed. We drove down to Walton
Heath and on the way he expressed the opinion that the
speech had been a complete failure. This may have been
partly due to the audience—composed very largely of smart
London people who had come not to receive guidance or
inspiration on the war but to quiz and possibly admire the
limehouse orator turned patriot!—the sort of audience
that L.G. described as 'a stodgy, fashionable crowd that
would chill any enthusiasm in my own or anyone else's
breast!' It is true that he had many friends in the audience,
but the atmosphere was stuffy and unresponsive. It was
not until the next day—a Sunday—when the papers, to
his great surprise, were lyrical in his praise, that he was
convinced of the success of his speech.

All through the months that followed he threw himself
into the tasks which confronted him as Chancellor of the
Exchequer, winning golden opinions from the City for the
measures he took to safeguard our finances. He dealt with
ease and understanding with the financial crisis which
necessarily arose on the outbreak of the war. Swift, satisfactory measures ensued. Paper money replaced gold in
this country for good and all. The City, to which he
had hitherto been anathema, now took him to their bosom.
The Governor of the Bank of England, Lord Cunliffe,
was a frequent visitor to the Treasury. Jovial and Conservative, and typically British, like a giant cherub with
a moustache and a sense of humour, he and L.G. became

firm friends. Later, when L.G. became immersed in the munitions problem, and was stressing the shortage, Lord Cunliffe sent him a wonderful old crossbow inlaid with ivory, almost too heavy for a man to lift. It is now to be seen in the Lloyd George Museum at Llanystumdwy.

But soon the sphere of L.G.'s activities inevitably widened beyond the Treasury precincts. He was one of the first of Asquith's Government to realise the true proportions of the struggle on which we had embarked, and by October 1914 he had written his first memorandum voicing his misgivings. By the end of the year he had paid a visit to the Front in company with Lord Reading, etc., and had seen for himself the shortcomings of the Allies. He had written a long letter of misgiving to the Prime Minister on the gravity of the outlook. He realised that we should need every ounce of our strength, and he took advantage of his position as Chancellor of the Exchequer to deal with the sale of intoxicating liquors, which were sapping the energy of the munition workers and the men in the dockyards. 'We are steeped in drink' I wrote to my brother just before the April Budget.

At the same time L.G. turned his attention to munitions, and the story of that heroic effort has been told by many, so that there is no need for me to relate it again. On May 19th, when Asquith formed his Coalition Government, L.G. was given charge of the Ministry of Munitions, a new department. Uncle Lloyd wrote begging his 'boy' not to leave the Treasury, that coveted jumping-off board for the Premiership. He realised that L.G. jeopardised the whole of his political career in giving up the Treasury for the Ministry of Munitions, for had he failed in the latter job—and at one time it seemed to be touch and go—he would have been cast on the political scrap-heap. As it was, his exit from the Treasury was the sign for all his enemies in the Liberal Party to endeavour to compass his downfall.

6

Ministry of Munitions: War Office

On the day that the Ministry of Munitions was born at 6 Whitehall Gardens, in May 1915, J. T. Davies and I walked into a room adjoining the one L.G. was to use. It possessed two chairs and a table, and as we were contemplating our new province two men arrived to take away the furniture. J.T. asked them where was the stuff to replace it? 'Dunno,' was the reply. 'That's not our job.' J.T.'s language does not bear repetition in print, but like L.G. we realised that our fight was on the home front and we fought it tooth and nail. We were an orphan department—no one wanted us—everyone resented us.

How the department took gradual shape, and began to function, I do not clearly remember: we were plunged too deeply into instantaneous work. While L.G. chose his heads of department and instructed them, J. T. Davies and I wrestled with mountains of correspondence, often sitting there till midnight in our endeavours to keep pace. We soon realised that we would have to have a registry and a secretariat, and competent people were engaged and accommodated.

Sir Hubert Llewellyn Smith was lent by the Board of Trade to organise the new Ministry on Civil Service lines: with him came a young man named William Beveridge. Humbert Wolfe was lent as a secretary. I thought his poetry beautiful (I still do), and he was handsome to look at, but

L.G. had no time for his looks or his poetry, and Wolfe was soon returned to the Board of Trade. Another young man, Stephen Tallents, joined us when he was invalided home from France. L.G. himself chose business men for the heads of his departments—Eric Geddes, Ernest Moir Percival Perry, Alexander Rogers, Alfred Herbert and others.

He needed them. One of the first things he discovered was that although there were hundreds of thousands of shell cases at Woolwich Arsenal they were actually being filled by hand with a ladle! Eric Geddes was put in charge of shells—and their filling.

One of the biggest problems which confronted L.G. was the fact that there was a complete shortage of machine tools; so that before making the actual munitions the tools themselves had to be made, and before the tools could be made, large factories had to be built to make them in. Small wonder that L.G. could not even find time to attend Cabinet meetings!

But L.G. was *par excellence* an innovator and these emergencies appealed to him, for they allowed him to introduce many reforms which otherwise would have taken years to pass. In addition to the measures he took against excessive drinking, he introduced a Welfare Department under Mr. Seebohm Rowntree into the Ministry of Munitions, and it was the function of this department to see that the conditions for the workers in all the factories were such as no one need be ashamed of. Not till then was it discovered in their entirety the appalling conditions under which some of the workers were expected to function. And never again have they been allowed to return to those conditions.

As I have already mentioned, the Pankhursts, who were moulded on a big scale, and other prominent Suffragettes such as Flora Drummond and Annie Kenny, offered their services for the recruiting of women for the munition factories. These women who had once been out for the Minister's blood, and who had set fire to his house at Walton Heath, became his warm allies. L.G. himself was a strong advocate of women's franchise—he used to say that he had been converted to it in his early Parliamentary days, after seeing a performance of Ibsen's *Doll's House*— and he was angry that the very people whom he was doing his best to help should try to upset his meetings. (He had actually been struck down by a man suffragist when about to enter a meeting on the Insurance Act.)

But now all this was changed, and the result was such a seizing of this tremendous opportunity for women to serve their country as to make the enfranchisement of women a certainty. The response to the call was magnificent: it helped substantially to solve the munitions problem.

How we got that lumbering, improvised machine of the Ministry of Munitions to move I cannot think. But with L.G. as driver it did move in spite of the fact that he had to keep getting down from the footplate to remove obstacles from his course. It was added to and altered as it went along, until it became immense and parts of it at first were very ramshackle; but it moved, and with increasing momentum. One thing never happened: it was never shunted into a siding! And it reached its destination well ahead of time. In a little over a year no one could stop the outflow of munitions; the troops had all they needed, and grateful messages were reaching L.G. from the Front for the transformation he had effected in the situation.

My brother's regiment had been one of the earliest to go to the Front. One day in May 1915, when L.G. was feeling tired out by the demands of the Ministry of Munitions, some friends, who thought he needed a break, took us out to dinner and on to see Barrie's new play *Rosy Rapture of the Beauty Chorus*. During the last act J. T. Davies came into the box and sat and talked to L.G. After the play L.G. took me back to Downing Street and there broke the news to me that my brother had been killed—he had died of wounds. Later L.G. took me home, where I found my father and mother in desperate need of comfort.

When the second war broke out, and Mr. Morrison became Minister of Munitions, he came down to Churt to get particulars from L.G. as to his methods and his organisation in the first war. L.G. placed at his disposal all the records he had, which, at any rate, enabled Mr. Morrison to start a stage further on than had been possible for L.G. in 1915 and to avoid some of the mistakes and pitfalls that the first Ministry of Munitions had inevitably encountered. But I doubt if he had better—if as good—lieutenants as L.G.'s key men at the Ministry of Munitions.

L.G.'s attendances at Cabinet meetings became more and more rare. 'What has become of the little man?' asked Balfour at one of them. 'We hardly ever see him these days.' But although he cut many Cabinet meetings, he found time to travel the whole length and breadth of the country, making speeches to hearten the munition workers, and to cheer the people. On these journeys he visited the factories, sometimes having to settle disputes, which were frequent owing to the new conditions of the war. He spent Christmas Day of 1915 in the train returning from Glasgow where he had been to settle a serious dispute. At a meeting there of factory foremen one man, a great bully of a fellow, advanced threateningly on him, but L.G., knowing his audience, remarked that he had been confident that in coming to Scotland he was meeting gentlemen. They responded immediately and there was no further trouble. His companions in the train on the return journey, besides his own staff, were journalists who had gone up to report the meeting, and who naturally resented being deprived of their Christmas Day at home. But the journey back I believe was such a merry one, L.G. being at the top of his form, and his spirits reacting on the company, that I do not think in the end anyone had any regrets. I believe that many stories of an amusing character were exchanged, and towards the end of the Christmas meal some songs were given by the more musical members of the party. I often heard the most heart-warming accounts of the Christmas Day in the train from Glasgow.

One of our frequent visitors to the Ministry of Munitions was Albert Thomas, the French Minister of Munitions. L.G. had met him early in the war at a conference in France, and they had quickly recognised each other as kindred spirits. Thomas was a typical Frenchman, ruddy of countenance, inclining to corpulence, with a quick sense of humour and a broad mind, his blue eyes twinkling behind his spectacles. He spoke no English, and had to have an interpreter—sometimes myself, but more often M. Paul Mantoux, almost as hirsute as Thomas, but with red hair and beard. Brilliantly bilingual, Mantoux acted as interpreter at most of the inter-Allied conferences, including the Peace Conference later on. Both were advanced Liberals; Thomas was in fact a Socialist, and in political matters, as well as in the prosecution of the war, he saw eye to eye with L.G. The munitions Ministries of France and England worked in complete harmony and unity, sharing ideas and helping each other where necessary. The same remarks did not apply to the Russian representatives. There was pandemonium in that quarter; it was quite impossible to get any decisions even as to what was required by Russia. We received appalling stories of the graft and corruption in high quarters, and quantities of stuff despatched by us to the Russian front never reached their destination. I remember that L.G. had a violent scene at a meeting in London with a Russian archduke who was the representative of his Government on the munitions question.

There was much manœuvring, if not actual graft, on this side too. When the shortage of rifles was acute we had mysterious visitors to the Ministry of Munitions who said

F

they could put us in touch with a source—I think it was in South America—where a million rifles could be obtained. Soon afterwards another customer turned up with the offer of, as we thought, another million rifles. Then a third offer appeared, and I think there was even a fourth. After probing thoroughly into the matter, however, it was discovered that all the offers related to the same million rifles, which in any case turned out to be obsolete. But each of the persons dealing with them expected obviously to get a rake-off on the transaction, and one can imagine the vast sum that it would have cost the country had the deal materialised.

In 1915 Mr. C. P. Scott brought Dr. Weizmann to see L.G. with a plan for converting wood alcohol into acetone, in order to increase the supply of high explosives. The story of Weizmann's visit to the Ministry of Munitions is a well-known one, with its bearing on L.G.'s promise of a National Home for the Jews as a reward. It is told in full by L.G. in his own memoirs.

C. P. Scott was L.G.'s mentor. When in political difficulty L.G. would write to C.P. and say in effect, 'Advise me', and Scott always gave his honest opinion. For him, Scott was his touchstone not only for what was Liberal and what was not but for right and wrong. Scott backed L.G. through thick and thin, even in the quarrels between Liberals. Later, in 1919, the *Manchester Guardian* was one of the papers that considered the terms of the Versailles Peace Treaty too harsh, but though Scott was critical, he did not break off relations. But for one period during the Irish trouble in 1920–1 he was to withdraw his approbation and his friendship altogether. He was angry with L.G. for permitting the 'Black-and-Tans' to have their way in Ireland, and albeit that his anger was mingled with sorrow for the outbreak, the *Manchester Guardian* weighed in with whole-hearted condemnation.

I truly believe that if L.G. had been questioned about Scott's attitude over the 'Black-and-Tans' L.G. would have admitted that in his heart of hearts he believed Scott was right. But then, he would have argued, Scott was not responsible for ruling Ireland, for dealing with an almost impossible situation—one which General Macready advised him could only be coped with by sending an army of 700,000 to Ireland—and for taking measures which led eventually to negotiations for a treaty on Home Rule. Scott would not have understood that more Machiavellian side of L.G. which said, as he said actually now in 1915, in a reckless mood it is true: 'I would make terms with Beelzebub if I thought he would help me to win the war.'

Scott would from time to time counsel restraint on L.G.'s part from retaliating when attacked. Sometimes out of affection for the counsellor and faith in his wisdom L.G. appeared to respond, but it did not last for long. He could not easily ignore an insult, nor submit to contradiction, and it was his nature to attack when provoked—sometimes before!

While L.G. was struggling with the munitions problem he was also studying the military aspect of events. The Allies had been unable to save Serbia. The little country was being overrun by the enemy, and we who had guaranteed her safety were unable to raise a hand to help her, so short were we of men and munitions. I remember L.G. dictating a memorandum after reading the latest war telegrams, with Mr. Churchill pacing up and down the room. They were both shattered, but impotent.

Cabinet meetings at this time were, according to L.G. almost a waste of time. Asquith, he would tell me after leaving one, had not got his mind on the demands of the war. L.G., and other Ministers, thought that the death of his son Raymond had destroyed his capacity as Prime Minister, but L.G. described on several occasions how Asquith was occupied with his correspondence with Lady Venetia Stanley, with whom he was no doubt in love at that time and who was proposing to marry Edwin Montagu. A messenger would come into the Cabinet Room with a letter for Asquith, and after having read it Asquith would settle himself down to reply to it at length, then ring for the messenger who would take the reply for despatch. Those letters have now become available and they are much quoted and to great advantage in Mr. Jenkins' biography of Asquith. Some of them gave details of the Cabinet discussions, and were, it is said, much more detailed than the Prime Minister's daily letters to the Sovereign giving accounts of the Cabinet meetings, which apparently Asquith judged to be of less importance than his correspondence. Be that as it may, there was a general feeling that Asquith was not giving the necessary attention to Cabinet decisions. For instance, after the last Cabinet before Asquith's resignation, there were three different versions, so Ministers said, of what had been the decision upon a debate (in the Cabinet) on the Air Ministry. And nothing was definitely decided. At that time no Minutes were taken of the discussions at Cabinet meetings. It was not until L.G. came into office that this was altered.

It was at this time that L.G. agreed to have his portrait painted by Augustus John. The canvas had been bought from John by Sir James Murray, an old friend of L.G., in aid of Red Cross funds, and the arrangement was that John should paint whomever Sir James designated. It can well be understood that the sittings were not very gay ones, for L.G. was in a grim mood; in addition to the news from Serbia, he was suffering from violent toothache.

The result was a most formidable portrait of L.G., much criticised by his family (to John's intense annoyance). It now hangs in the Aberdeen Art Gallery, a somewhat savage record of L.G.'s feelings of impotent despair at the way things were going at that time.

In 1916 L.G. paid a visit to the Front in company with M. Albert Thomas, to find out for himself what was the

effect of the increase on the supply of munitions. He was
well rewarded, the men in the trenches greeting him as a
hero. They realised that they now had a backing and were
grateful for the change in the quality and quantity of the
munitions supply. Sir Douglas Haig himself was confident
that the military outlook would soon improve, but there
is a telling photograph of him explaining to L.G. that the
cavalry were about to make a break-through, L.G. listening with
scepticism in every line of his face and bearing. M. Thomas
is standing by, his countenance registering utter incredulity.

   L.G. indeed was very apprehensive about the whole
military position. He feared that unless there was a change
in the conduct of the war all the munitions he was supplying
would be completely thrown away. During that spring he
seriously thought of resigning. He was not happy—indeed,
in spite of the now assured success of the Ministry of Munitions, he was desperately anxious as to the ultimate success
of the Allied effort. His mind was further occupied with
the introduction of conscription, for which he put up a
gallant fight. The Bill became law in May, and it is on
record that Sir William Robertson, who was never one of
L.G.'s particular friends, attributed the passing of the Act
to *L.G. alone*. There is a note in Robertson's handwriting
to this effect. But L.G. was bitterly attacked by some
Liberals in the process, and he parted company with Sir
John Simon, who opposed the measure and resigned from
the Government. His opinion of Sir John (later Lord
Simon) as a person to go tiger-hunting with had never
been very great, and L.G. was not surprised at his defection.
Many years later Sir John was instrumental in organising
a revolt in the Parliamentary Liberal Party against L.G.
during the 1929–31 Labour administration. He had previously in 1926 taken a very unfriendly attitude towards
L.G. in the general strike.

   Then came the dramatic news of Kitchener's death.[1] I had

   1 June 5th, 1916.

gone down to Falmouth to snatch a few days' holiday in June when the stunning message came. Although by this time some of the glitter of his name and personality had worn off, the tidings assumed the importance of a major disaster, for as Minister of War he was a great and impressive figurehead. I received the news before it was made public, for L.G. rang me up and urged my immediate return. (There was no B.B.C. in those days and news took longer to reach the public.) There would, he said, inevitably be changes in the Cabinet which might concern him.

He was right: they did concern him, but so reluctant was he to take Kitchener's mantle upon his shoulders that he wrote a letter to Asquith refusing the offer of Secretary of State for War. But second thoughts prevailed. The Ministry of Munitions was fully established, and a more than adequate supply of arms and ammunition guaranteed for our armies for an indefinite length of time. L.G. had built solidly: not even his most indefatigable enemies could undo his work. If he went on to the War Office he would get the chance of dealing with certain people who had been obstructive and also with one or two matters which had come outside the range of the Ministry of Munitions but which were intimately concerned with munition supplies. And so, rather doubtingly, but urged by Mr. Asquith, he accepted, suggesting Mr. Churchill as his successor to the Ministry of Munitions. But Asquith refused, Churchill remained in the wilderness, and Mr. Edwin Montagu became Minister of Munitions.

It was a very brief sojourn at the Ministry of War, and an unsatisfactory one. One thing, however, L.G. did achieve, and that was to get the railways *behind* the lines in France in working order so that the supply of ammunition to the front trenches should not be impeded. This was a matter which had been greatly worrying L.G. and which the military did not seem to understand at all. He got Haig's consent to putting Eric Geddes in charge of the

reorganisation, and because the C.-in-C. was very loath to
have a civilian in charge of the work, a way out was found
by making Geddes a major-general! The work, I need
hardly say, under the auspices of this skilled engineer of
forceful personality, went ahead with enormous rapidity,
and there was soon a network of light railways behind the
lines in France. Transport in Mesopotamia, which was in
a disgraceful state, was also reorganised.

Other reforms which L.G. attempted at the War Office
were not so successful. The brass hats were too powerfully
entrenched for a passing Secretary of State to make any
impression upon the labyrinthine system of procedure
which had prevailed and become engrafted over so many
years. Instructions given by L.G. were passed from one
department to another until it became almost impossible
to trace their progress. Correspondence became lost in the
recesses of the vast registry. I remember trying to check
up on the case of a soldier who I thought had an undeniable
grievance. Not being satisfied with the progress of the
investigation and being unable even to trace the original
documents themselves, I bearded the major-general who
was in charge of the department concerned, and urged an
answer. After some beating about the bush, he suddenly
said to me: 'Miss Stevenson, when we get a case like this we
lose the correspondence.' 'Not when Mr. Lloyd George is
Secretary of State,' I retorted angrily. My recollection is
that the Tommy got fair treatment in the end.

There were other weaknesses in connection with the
supplies to our armies that L.G. sought to deal with. There
were, for instance, abuses in the Army Clothing Department and inefficiency in some of the medical branches.
L.G. was, as usual, ruthless in his purges, but he was not
there long enough to effect any permanent improvement,
and when he left the denizens of the War Office—or a good
many of them—heaved a sigh of relief and returned very
quickly to the *status quo ante L.G.*

I should not like to give the impression that our fleeting
stay at the War Office was entirely unpleasant, or that everyone there was obstructive. Herbert Creedy, the Assistant
Principal Secretary, who became one of L.G.'s secretaries
for the brief period that he was there, was a delightful
person, with a sly sense of humour, and as helpful as, in
the circumstances, he could be. Sir John Cowans, the
Quartermaster General, was as charming a person as could
be met, a most efficient official, and L.G. had no quarrel
with his department. Indeed Cowans was only anxious to
help L.G. in any difficulty that arose. The Adjutant General,
Sir Neville Macready, was a tower of strength to L.G. then,
and afterwards. These men were outstanding personalities.
In general L.G. received the same hindrances and rebuffs
from 'the clique within a caste' that the young Wellington
had encountered a century before. One hundred years in
the sight of the War Office or the Horse Guards were but
as yesterday.

L.G. was at the War Office barely six months, and during
the latter part of that time he was occupied with his controversy with the Prime Minister over the direction of the
war which led to Asquith's resignation. 'It is hard for me,'
says L.G. in his memoirs, 'to convey an adequate picture
of the sense of frustration and tangled impotence which
oppressed me during those closing months of 1916.'
Corroborative testimony was given to this in a trenchant
criticism by L. S. Amery of the Prime Minister's handling
of the situation.

The supreme power of the State has fallen into the hands of
a man who combines unrivalled gifts of parliamentary leadership
with a complete incapacity to face facts or to come to any
decision on them. Again and again in the last few months Mr.
Asquith has averted a breakdown by the exercise of his amazing
skill in debate, but he has never shown the slightest trace of
understanding of the forces at work outside. . . . It would be
futile to attempt to strip off the outer integument of debating

points in order to get at the real Asquith underneath. There is no such person. For twenty years he has held a season ticket on the line of least resistance, and gone wherever the train of events has carried him, lucidly justifying his position at whatever point he has happened to find himself.

Victories are not won by this kind of generalship; and when a desperate situation has to be faced, forcing the issue between a man of action and one of inaction, it is the man of action who finds himself in control.

The story of L.G.'s accession to the Premiership has been told so often that it is not necessary for me to go over it again. The many accounts of it vary according to the political views of the narrators, their personal attitude towards L.G. himself, their real knowledge of the full facts, or their desire to paint L.G. as the villain of the piece. But out of the debris of conflicting stories it has gradually become clearly established that L.G. himself made no personal move to seize the Premiership; though it is equally an historical fact that he was utterly condemnatory of Asquith's leadership in the conduct of the war. His own memoranda, written at the time, show this, and his 'Too Late' speech on December 20th, 1915, prove that he was already critical of Asquith's Government:

Too late in moving here, too late in coming to this decision, too late in starting with enterprises, too late in preparing! In this war the footsteps of the Allied forces have been dogged by the mocking spectre of 'too late' and unless we quicken our movements, damnation will fall on the sacred cause for which so much gallant blood has flowed.

Yet throughout 1916 nothing seemed to be done to cure this situation. Members of the Cabinet complained that no decisions were taken at Cabinet meetings. The situation in Mesopotamia became disastrous. The Germans overran Roumania and wiped her out. L.G. badly missed Churchill, who was politically in the wilderness. Asquith had reduced him from the Admiralty to the Duchy of Lancaster when forming his first Coalition Cabinet, and Winston, throwing up this sinecure, had spent some six months fighting on the French front. The Tories, who hated him, had made him the scapegoat for the failure of the Dardanelles and Gallipoli campaigns, and L.G. vainly urged Asquith to appoint Churchill to the Ministry of Munitions when he himself moved over to the War Office.

In December 1916 L.G. 'blew up' again, and demanded an Inner War Council, a small body to take over full responsibility for the conduct of the war effort, subject to the approval of the Prime Minister. Asquith refused. He was persuaded by his close friends that if he resigned he would be asked to form another Ministry from which he would be able to exclude the tiresome Welshman. But it was Asquith himself who was excluded from the next Ministry by the consent of all the Conservative leaders, and the tiresome little Welshman who replaced him as Prime Minister. On Asquith's resignation, Bonar Law refused the Premiership, and so did Balfour. It was in fact owing to the action of the Conservatives that L.G. was made Prime Minister. History will confirm that he did not desire this office. He had not, indeed, that confidence which Mr. Churchill had when he accepted the Premiership in 1940, of his power to do all that was needed of him. 'I wonder if I can do it?' he said, half to himself, as we sat in a gloomy War Office after his return from Buckingham Palace from the ceremony of 'kissing hands'.

7

L.G. at No. 10

It was not surprising that L.G. viewed with apprehension the size of the problem confronting him when he accepted the Premiership; but had he known what was awaiting him and his Government in 1917 he might well have been more than doubtful of accepting. He was right in feeling some diffidence as to the future of the war. He had no confidence in the British direction of it in the field and he knew how many hurdles there were to be dealt with.

In the opening months of L.G.'s Premiership the war situation was becoming more and more critical, the only bright spot being the entry of America into the war on the Allied side; and this, unhappily, was counter-balanced by the collapse and withdrawal of Russia.

I can see L.G. standing in the large drawing room at No. 10 on an afternoon in March 1917, reading a telegram which I had handed to him announcing the Russian Revolution. I can, without effort, recapture the silence after he had read the despatch. Then he said: 'They will be no more use to us in this war.'

In August L.G. attended the Eisteddfod, an engagement he never missed in peace or war, and which that year was held at Birkenhead. It was a dramatic gathering, the winner of the Crown having been killed in France, and the Bardic Chair was draped in black. L.G. made a magnificent speech in spite of the fact that he was desperately tired and overworked. I will quote one passage from it—the kind of thing that heartened and sustained the nation through the grim months that followed:

. . . I have been in the habit once or twice of telling my Welsh fellow-countrymen, when there was anything that made them feel in the least depressed, to look upon the phenomena of their hills. On a clear day they look as if they were near. You could reach them in an easy march—you could climb the highest of them in an hour. That is wrong—you could not. Then comes a cloudy day, and the mists fall upon them and you say: 'There are no hills. They have vanished.' Again you are wrong. The optimist is wrong; the hills are not as near as he thought. The pessimist is still more wrong, because they are there. All you have to do is to keep on. Keep on. Falter not. We have many dangerous marshes to cross; we will cross them. We have steep and stony paths to climb; we will climb them. Our footprints may be stained with blood, but we will reach the heights; and beyond them we shall see the rich valleys and plains of the new world which we have sacrified so much to attain.

We stayed during the Eisteddfod with Lord Leverhulme at his house outside Port Sunlight. Lord Leverhulme showed us the model village which he had built for his workers—a most impressive achievement. Planning on any large scale was rare in those days. Building was haphazard, and anyone could build any atrocity anywhere. We were therefore full of admiration for this attractive village, with its pretty little houses. We found, however, that the complaint—a justifiable one, to my mind—of the tenants was that by living in Port Sunlight they were bound to their work—it was virtually a town of tied houses.

Amongst the guests at Thornton Hough was a grand old Welshman—Sir Henry Jones. It was my privilege to meet him here for the first time, and to meet him many times afterwards. I did not know then that the beard which he grew was to conceal a malignant disease for which he had already had an operation, and which in a few years was to kill him. He was a professor of moral philosophy, not, strangely enough, in Wales, but in Glasgow. No one could know him without loving him for his integrity, his sense of fun, and, above all, for his heroic bearing in the face of his grim disease. He continued his work almost to the last, and finished a remarkable series of Gifford lectures only a few weeks before his death. When articulation had become difficult, he said to a friend: 'The ultimate meaning of Reality is Love. If that is true, there must be a soul, a personal God, to do the loving. The task of philosophy is to justify that view.' Such was his faith that on his death-bed, though in a torment of pain, he could still declare: 'The Lord reigneth: let the earth rejoice.'

L.G. was devoted to him. Henry Jones was staying at Downing Street in December, 1916, during the struggle which resulted in Asquith's resignation and L.G.'s accession to the Premiership; and he wrote to a friend:

I want to exonerate Lloyd George in one respect. He had no more idea of supplanting Asquith than I had. Lloyd George's team . . . will get something done. Something will have to smash, and I guess it will be Germany. For the little country man is a very big man in a way; and there is no fatal interval between desire and deed in his case.

And again:

This is a momentous change. I wish in some ways it could have been avoided, and I am certain that it was not what Lloyd George wanted. I wish the two men could have worked together. The country needs them both. But it won't be a draw now.[1]

History will confirm that the changing of Prime Ministers was due entirely to the action of others who saw, first, that Asquith could not be left in charge if we were to win the

1. *The Life and Letters of Sir Henry Jones*, by H. J. W. Hetherington.

war, and, secondly, that L.G. was the person who could
win the war if anyone could. Carson, Balfour, Bonar Law,
Beaverbrook—all Conservatives—were from patriotic mo-
tives willing to put the reins of leadership into the hands
of a Liberal, who had proved that he could 'get things
done' and whose power of oratory could inspire the nation.
It was, I believe, Asquith's own family who persuaded him
that L.G. was plotting against him. In the Beaverbrook
papers are letters that Margot Asquith used to send L.G.,
pencilling them from her room next door in the early hours
of the morning.

There was a curious affinity between L.G. and Balfour
(now Foreign Minister), a mutual admiration, a respect for
each other's qualities. L.G. seemed to fascinate Balfour,
who even during the days of L.G.'s fiercest attacks upon
the Tories was drawn to the fiery little Welshman, probably
realising his sincerity. L.G. on the other hand was aware of
the outstanding *quality* of Balfour, of his utter detachment,
his integrity. It was not a close friendship, but it was a very
long and sincere one. As far back as 1911, L.G. and Balfour
had come together over the possibility of an agreed programme between the two parties—an amazing happening,
which unfortunately never achieved the planned conference
at Buckingham Palace.

Now in 1916 Balfour had refused the Premiership but
offered—nay, been anxious—to serve under L.G. He served
L.G. faithfully and enthusiastically until L.G. was turned
out by other and less loyal Tories in 1922. And he said, after
Baldwin's manœuvre at the Carlton Club meeting which
brought the Coalition to an end: 'There are some things that
gentlemen do not do.' Although L.G. discounted his ad-
ministrative abilities, he set high store by Balfour's intellectual equipment, and would seek his judgment upon all
important matters. Balfour could give the *arguments* for and
against, but he found it more difficult to give a *decision*. After
one most erudite dissertation at the Peace Conference, for

instance, in which Balfour closely examined every aspect of
a problem, and then concluded, Clemenceau turned a
puzzled face to L.G. and asked, 'But is he *for* or is he
against?' But Balfour's private letters to L.G. during the
Washington Conference of 1921 are masterly accounts of
the events there and monuments of sagacity.

One of C. P. Scott's journalists wrote to him in May 1917:

Balfour is an unmistakable success. They all found him not only
courteous, friendly and unaffected, but always to the point in
consultation and never ruffled.

And in the same month Theo Russell at the Foreign
Office received a letter from Cecil Dormer, on the occasion
of the visit of the French and British delegates to Washington's tomb:

Viviani is a fine orator and perspired freely, but Mr. Balfour
was splendid too and was a remarkable contrast by his quietness
and distinction.

Later, in July, Drummond heard from Geoffrey Butler
in Washington:

The President [Wilson] said that Balfour was one of the few
public men he had ever met who showed no trace of cynicism.
He said that the hardest thing that he himself had to face was
the tendency to grow cynical. He spoke of the great qualities
of this wonderful man.

When Balfour became ill in the twenties L.G. visited him
in his Surrey home. Balfour asked him, rather pathetically,
'There is one thing I would like to know: why did you want
me to leave the Admiralty in 1916?'

In the last days of the Asquith administration, when
L.G. was fighting for more energetic control, he had demanded Balfour's removal from the Admiralty. L.G. could
not tell him that what was necessary at the Admiralty at

that moment was a man of energy and of quick decisions. Instead, he said, 'I thought you would be better at the Foreign Office.'

I always think that it is one of the marks of L.G.'s greatness that he was able to attract a personality such as Balfour's, and to keep his allegiance, through thick and thin, until the end.

He pays Balfour a fine tribute in his own memoirs:

In personal charm he was easily first among all the Statesmen with whom I came into contact. As to his intellectual gifts, I doubt whether I ever met so illuminating an intelligence outside the Council Chamber.

I have recollections during those first few days of December of constant and prolonged meetings between L.G. and Bonar Law, Carson, Beaverbrook and others from which it emerged that none of them was willing to go on working with Asquith, that neither Bonar Law nor Balfour would accept the Premiership, but that both would work under L.G. I have recollections, too, after L.G. had agreed to try to form a Cabinet, of comings and goings at the War Office and 11 Downing Street from which a complete Cabinet finally emerged and L.G. was able to inform the King, much to the surprise and disgust of the Asquithians, that he had been successful in forming a new Government with which he hoped to win the war. L.G.'s new Government included three future Prime Ministers—Bonar Law himself, Stanley Baldwin and a Junior Lord of the Treasury, Neville Chamberlain, who became Minister of National Service. (L.G. in his memoirs said: 'He was not one of my successful selections.') L.G. would have liked to include a fourth, Mr. Winston Churchill, but Mr. Bonar Law, backed by other Tory Ministers, vetoed this. It was not until the following year, when L.G. had become securely established, that he was able to insist upon Churchill's inclusion in the Govern-

ment as Minister of Munitions. Even then he received
several threats of resignation from Conservative colleagues.
He ignored them and thought the risk was worth taking.

There was another outstanding member of L.G'.s Coalition Government who might, had he lived, have become
Prime Minister of a Conservative Government—F. E.
Smith, Lord Birkenhead. He was a tower of strength to
L.G., for he had a remarkable mind and great force of
character, and I know that L.G. had envisaged the possibility of entrusting to F.E. the formation of a code of law
in this country comparable to the *Code Napoléon* in France—
a reformation of our outdated legal system which would
sweep aside legal weaknesses and anomalies.

It is well known, I think, that F.E. had a personal failing,
but this did not affect the deliverance of his brilliant speeches
and judgments. I remember that during the Versailles
Conference L.G. and Clemenceau met at breakfast to discuss the much debated question of the Trial of the Kaiser.
Both wanted to get the line settled, and Clemenceau suggested to L.G. that he should send for his Lord Chancellor,
F.E., to give a legal opinion on the matter which would
guide them in their decisions. L.G. telephoned to Newnham
(his personal attendant) to get F.E. to where he and Clemenceau were breakfasting, and not to take 'No' for an answer.
Newnham presently telephoned to say that F.E. was fast
asleep, not having returned to his lodgings until 5 a.m.,
when he seemed to be in a parlous condition. Nevertheless,
L.G. insisted that he should be awakened and brought
along, and this was done. The question was put to him, and
he gave judgment on the matter, a judgment which was
accepted and carried through by the Big Four and the conference. Clemenceau afterwards said that it was the most
brilliant legal pronouncement he had ever heard.

It was a misfortune to this country that F.E. died a comparatively young man. His ability might have carried this
country through many of her trials and difficulties.

G

He was not a good patient. He came into my office in Downing Street after an illness which had pulled him down. I asked him how he was feeling and his reply was: 'You see, Miss Stevenson, I have never been ill in my life before.' No one could fail to be charmed by his gaiety and good humour, and very soon after first knowing him I realised what a gallant friend he was to L.G. and how much L.G. valued and admired his wise outlook. His good looks were combined with perfect manners, and when you add to that a striking wit and an aptness of phrase, there is the picture of 'a very parfit gentle knight' such as is not often found even amongst friends, and certainly not amongst politicians. His downfall while yet a young man was a disaster for politics and for the Conservative Party.

F.E. had a charming family who descended with him on Bron-y-de from time to time, and every summer a week-end was dedicated to a visit from them to eat cherries off a special tree which was kept for them. These cherries were grown on bush trees covered with netting to keep the birds away, and were of a flavour which deteriorated the moment they were picked, so that they had to be eaten immediately. L.G. himself greatly enjoyed these orgies and looked forward to them.

It is a curious thought that of all these great crises I have but a hazy recollection of the details. I suppose that there was so much to do, so many *particulars* to see to, that one missed inevitably the broad effect, the drama, the exhilaration, in the physical demands upon one's time and strength. The trivial, the irrelevant things, the crowds, for instance, outside No. 10 in the hope of catching a glimpse of the new Prime Minister—one's own self-consciousness at entering the front door for the first time on the way to one's new office—these, and not the first Cabinet meeting, the majestic entry of the Lord President of the Council and Leader of the House of Lords—Lord Curzon—seem to be those which survive in the memory.

As L.G. had remained at 11 Downing Street while at the
Ministry of Munitions and the War Office, the move to No.
10 was a simple one, especially as the greater part of the
furniture of both houses was official. Dame Margaret wrote
a note to Mrs. Asquith to tell her to take her time in moving
out, and I think the line that Mrs. Asquith took was that in
any case they would soon be moving in again. The opinion
in the entourage of the Asquith family was that even if L.G.
had been able to form a Government, certainly he would
not succeed in holding it together for long. They over-esti-
mated their own strength. The prospect of office is too
tantalising for there not to be *some* defections from one side
to the other. And Asquith had forgotten, or perhaps had
never heard of, the advice once given to L.G. by a veteran
politician: 'My boy, *never* resign.' Certainly in Asquith's case
it was fatal to resign with the idea that he would speedily
come back.

My urgent job was to arrange for an adequate number of
typists to deal with the ever-increasing correspondence—
and the additional work which would obviously be entailed
in the Prime Minister's office. My recollection is that Mr.
Asquith had only employed one typist. We certainly needed
more. Even the *opening* of L.G.'s mail was a lengthy process.
Mrs. Hoster's school came to our rescue and things went
smoothly ever after. We had a most capable secretariat.

I should like at this point to pay a tribute to the Church
Army, the organisation of that splendid philanthropist,
Prebendary Carlile. A very large proportion of L.G.'s
correspondence when he became Prime Minister was from
individuals who had suffered hardships as a result of the
war and who needed help or advice. It was almost an impossibility for me to make the necessary enquiries into each
case—a thing which troubled me, as so many of them came
from people who were homeless, hungry and ill, and I cast
about for a solution to this difficulty. A generous Indian
prince—the Maharajah of Gwalior—had given L.G. a sum

of money (about £6,000 is my recollection) for dealing with cases of hardship arising out of the war, and it occured to me that we might hand over part of this money to the Church Army if they would investigate cases for us and report on their merits, and, if possible, deal with them through the organisation. L.G. agreed to the plan, and in a long interview with the Prebendary it was agreed to by him. The results were most satisfactory, and my gratitude for this help has always been very lively.

Once again L.G. showed his skill as an innovator; but in the course of his innovating he was intolerant, almost oblivious, of obstacles. He blithely cut through red tape in his tilting at outworn methods. Difficulties were things to be surmounted, not shied at. He welcomed them, and they stimulated him. No spring-cleaning was ever so thorough as this complete mid-winter overhauling by L.G. of the obsolete and inefficient machinery which prevailed.

But perhaps the most important of all L.G.'s innovations on becoming Prime Minister was the creation of the Cabinet secretariat under Sir Maurice Hankey. This organisation made a note of all decisions taken at a Cabinet meeting and circulated the minutes to all members of the Cabinet concerned, as well as to the Sovereign, so that each had an opportunity of querying any of the statements attributed to him, and of knowing exactly what had been decided—an invaluable improvement on the state of affairs under Asquith. From then onwards Hankey or any one of his subordinates attended every conference, either at home or abroad. Sir Maurice Hankey was an exceptional personality and the ideal man for his job. The serenity—the gaiety almost—of his character was phenomenal. I do not ever remember him angry or put out. Clemenceau became very much attached to Hankey, and when a point was in question would say affectionately: 'I am sure Hankey can find the answer in that little bag of his!'

One of L.G.'s decisions was to establish in the *garden*(!)

of 10 Downing Street what became known as the 'garden
suburb'. In these hutments were housed persons of distinction and accomplishments whose duty it was to keep
an eye on the Government departments, to maintain a
liaison with the heads of these departments and keep the
Prime Minister informed of important items. There was
loud complaint that traditional customs were being violated,
but L.G. had no time in these grim days for ceremonial and
for long consultations. It was not that he was inaccessible to
his Ministers, but that a great deal of preliminary work in
arriving at decisions was done beforehand by his Secretariat, who sifted the facts and prepared memoranda and
often conveyed messages from him to his Ministers. Such
proceedure was most distasteful to some Ministers who
preferred the old-fashioned etiquette.

It was inevitable that this new arrangement should tread
on the corns and even wound the feelings of the more conventional members of L.G.'s Government. Long wails came
in particular from Lord Curzon, who in spite of his pomposity was a kind and genial soul, and on occasions a most
entertaining companion. But this tendency of his chief to
ride roughshod over precedent and procedure wounded and
shocked him, and he was at times goaded into protest. L.G.
had strengthened his own secretariat (as he himself put it in
his memoirs) by appointing Philip Kerr (later the Marquis of
Lothian) to his personal staff. So Philip was acting as a go-
between for L.G. with various Ministers, but chiefly with
the Foreign Secretary, whom L.G. was at times anxious to
keep at bay.

Lord Curzon disapproved, I think, of 10 Downing Street
as a whole at that time. He and L.G. were by temperament
and upbringing opposed to each other. Neither did Curzon
approve of L.G.'s chief secretary, J. T. Davies, a Welshman
who was not a civil servant—he had, in fact, been a school-
teacher. L.G. had flouted precedent in giving him such a
post. Later, when J.T. was given a knighthood, Curzon's

indignation broke bounds, and he exclaimed: 'Surely, nothing so absurd has happened since Caligula made his horse a pro-consul!' No one was more amused than J.T. at the outburst, which he himself would relate with relish.

I had a glimpse of two Curzons—one pompous and over-bearing, with a permanent hangover of vice-royalty, the Curzon who on his first day at the Foreign Office, rang his bell for his secretary, and pointing to the rather ordinary 'stock' inkstand on his desk, said: 'Remove this. The Secretary of State must have a crystal and silver, *not* gläss and bräss.' His speeches at Cabinet meetings were masterpieces of rotundity, of laboured lucidity which often degenerated into banality. L.G. would give a wonderful imitation of Curzon's statement on the problem of Azerbaijan—rolling out the last syllable to an incredible length. Thus Curzon was constantly rubbing L.G. the wrong way, provoking him to sharp retorts which Curzon bitterly and pathetically resented.

There was a painful incident at a Cabinet meeting in 1917. The Government proposed to requisition the British Museum for the Air Board. There was violent resistance by its Trustees and all the learned men. Sir Arthur Evans, the archaeologist, said it was 'the breaking in of the jungles'. He lashed out at the Philistines and there was a great outcry. The matter came before the Cabinet. At the meeting Curzon stated that he had asked the Archbishop of Canterbury, one of the Trustees of the B.M., to come and take part in the discussion. L.G., furious, attacked him in front of his colleagues. 'Why should you bring the Archbishop here?' he asked Curzon angrily. 'I didn't invite the manager of the Hotel Cecil to come to the Cabinet when we debated taking over his hotel.'

The result was a pained and pathetic letter from Curzon complaining of his treatment. Even Balfour said to L.G. 'I think, Prime Minister, you were a little hard on George this morning.'

He never sent a typed letter. All his letters to L.G.—

myriads of them—many of them mild protests on what L.G. had done or had not done—are in his own curious but distinctive handwriting, in accordance, I imagine, with old-established ideas of what correspondence between a Secretary of State and a Prime Minister should be.

But then there was the human Curzon—the one who took infinite trouble to make more humble people feel at their ease: I remember his telling me to come early before a party at Carlton House Terrace, to which I had been invited, in order that he might show me over the house with its treasures and points of interest; the Curzon who would sit up into the small hours of the morning doing the household accounts (or was this human in a Foreign Secretary?) and who would insist upon interviewing a prospective lady's maid for his wife. 'I always ask them to take their bonnets off,' he said to me.

Curzon was immensely proud of his wife, a very beautiful woman of great dignity. On the occasion I have mentioned he showed me her picture by de Laszlo with obvious satisfaction. I have always been particularly sensitive to beauty in a person—man or woman—not mere good looks or prettiness, but the perfection of face or form that makes your heart beat a fraction more quickly, that makes you want to look again and again, and to be grateful to the possessor for sharing his or her gift with you. It may be a pagan instinct, but I have never doubted the power of a single beautiful face to launch a thousand ships. On the other hand, had Helen been an ugly woman there might have been one war the less!

Curzon could never forgive L.G. for appointing Philip Kerr (who was an expert on foreign affairs) as liaison officer with the Foreign Office, which often meant that Philip would present to Curzon L.G.'s own ruling on a point of foreign policy without L.G. discussing it with him. This to Curzon was *lèse-majesté*. Alternatively if Curzon wanted to discuss a matter with L.G. he had often to do it through

Philip Kerr, a most humiliating procedure for a Foreign
Secretary who had vice-regal ideas of his position.

Philip Kerr was, in the circumstances, the best possible
person to deal with Curzon. He was, I think, of all people
the one on whom L.G. relied most during the time—five
years, 1916–21—that he was a member of L.G.'s staff.

A good many of the State documents which were drawn
up in connection with inter-Allied conferences, and especially at the Peace Conference in 1919, were drafted by Philip.
The 'Fontainebleau Document' which was presented to the
Allied heads of Government in May, 1919, and represented
the essential views of the British Government on the terms
of peace (in an effort actually to bring the French back to
sanity) was broadly speaking Philip's own work.

At that time Philip had no politics, though he supported
L.G.'s left-Liberal national outlook. He was a little suspect
by the more right-wing and intransigent European Prime
Ministers of that time, and I remember the Italian Prime
Minister's secretary confiding to me during an inter-Allied
conference that it was well known that Philip Kerr was 'the
head-centre of Bolshevism in Europe' and had far too much
influence over the British Prime Minister.

After the Peace Conference was over, Philip made an
effort to get some leisure. He had been L.G.'s constant companion seven days a week during his war Premiership and
during the exacting Peace Conference which followed, and
he really needed some rest. (He actually had a minor breakdown during the Paris Conference, but refused to give in.)
He therefore asked his chief for time off during the week-
ends in which to play golf. (His handicap was scratch; his
golf, like his work, was perfection.) Actually what Philip
wanted was a little more time for his own personal thinking.
L.G., quite surprised that anyone should ask such a favour,
said: 'Why, of course! Take your week-ends, my dear
Philip'—or words to that effect. Nevertheless Philip found
that he was *not* getting his week-ends. There was always an

Lloyd George by Augustus John

Frances Stevenson at Downing Street, 1916

At the front, 1917: Lloyd George on left and Albert Thomas in centre

Picnic near Beauvais, 1918: Sir William Robertson, far left; Lloyd George, seated on far right

V. S. Orlando

D Lloyd George

G Clemenceau

Woodrow Wilson

The Big Four at Versailles

urgent job in hand, or he would be wanted to play golf with L.G.!

And so, reluctantly, in 1921—almost, I thought, to save his freedom of soul—he parted company with his master, and Ned Grigg, afterwards Lord Altrincham, took his place.

Philip Kerr possessed that interior harmony for which we all strive but which is so difficult of achievement. He told me that he always tried to get away for a month every year, entirely alone, so that he could think and read—and possibly pray—at his leisure. His sincerity expressed itself in his benign and handsome countenance. He judged no one harshly, and I never saw him ruffled. He responded to L.G.'s tantrums with an amused smile, realising that they were often the result of some trouble or annoyance which L.G. had to distribute on someone who happened to be around—not necessarily the person who caused it. He knew, too, that sometimes they were deliberate, in order to gain a point. In fact he knew his chief through and through and he loved and admired him. But his veneration was reserved for God. He was a deeply religious man, and a great part of his time was devoted to his religion. He told me once that he only needed five hour's sleep, and that he studied and read into the small hours of the morning. He was born a Roman Catholic, but while at Oxford he became doubtful of his faith, and later, having returned from South Africa, he became, under the aegis of Nancy Astor, a Christian Scientist. It was a terrible experience for him when at his mother's funeral the priest denounced him as a renegade Roman Catholic.

He was the most unworldly person I have ever known. Although he was the heir to the Marquess of Lothian (which he subsequently became) and all the properties that went with the title, before inheriting he told me that his independent income consisted of thirty pounds a year. His clothes were always shabby and not too well fitting and his hats were a disgrace.

When L.G. went to stay in Lord Leverhulme's house in Lancashire in 1917 during the Birkenhead Eisteddfod at which L.G. was speaking, Philip went also, but travelled there independently. To his great amusement when he turned up in a shabby suit and hat and carrying an old suit-case, as a member of the P.M.'s party, the butler mistook him for L.G.'s valet and told him to go to the back entrance. It was typical of Philip that far from being outraged he was only amused.

But I believe that his chief reason for leaving L.G. after five years was because he found that his work at Downing Street encroached too much upon the time that he needed for his religion. We were sad at heart when he went, but in later years he was always ready to help L.G. in any particular scheme or plan if required, and we were always in touch with him. He came down to Churt to see L.G. after he returned in 1932 from India, where he had been leader of the Indian Franchise Committee. 'The man I was most impressed with,' he said 'was Jawaharlal Nehru.' He valued L.G.'s opinion on all matters. His death in Washington when he was still a comparatively young man filled all who knew him with grief.

L.G. appointed as his Parliamentary Private Secretary Major David Davies (Lord Davies of Llandinam)—a lovable personality with a strong sense of duty. He went with Lord Milner on the mission to Russia which L.G. appointed soon after becoming Prime Minister, in order to ascertain exactly what was happening there. L.G. suspected that something odd was going on, but Milner and the other members of the mission, who only saw officials, British and French and Russian, while reporting on the confusion, incompetence and discontent there, had obviously no inkling of the terrible upheaval that was about to take place. They returned from Russia extremely dejected, but gave no hint of revolution in their report. David Davies, however, with a smattering of Russian, went into the people's homes and into inns and

talked with the people themselves, and on his return reported that the country was on the brink of a revolution.

David Davies had an uncanny way of probing into a situation—of worrying at it and trying to unearth it, like one of
his own hounds. But unfortunately he introduced his
probing methods into his relations with L.G.

He had an unhappy habit of telling L.G., as a result of his
researches, all the unpleasant things that people were saying
of him—and it was not difficult in those days, or indeed at
any time, to collect all kinds of criticisms against L.G. As a
fellow-Welshman David Davies should have understood his
L.G. better, but for a Welshman he was singularly unimagin-
ative and blunt. To take a simple view, it was not kind to add
to the worries of a harassed and overworked Prime Minister by relaying unpleasant truths to him when nothing could
be gained by this. David Davies hoped possibly to keep L.G.
on the right lines, and when he had not the ear of L.G. (for
L.G. tended less and less to wish for his company) he would
write him letters and memoranda which, in addition to
being unhelpful, were actually upsetting. L.G. at last replied to one particularly blunt and hurtful missive by termin-
ating David Davies's appointment, after telling *him* a few
home truths.

But before matters had actually reached this pass David
Davies was naturally often in L.G.'s company, and they
would exchange stories of Wales and Welsh characters.
David Davies would give wonderful imitations of Welsh
preachers in their more amusing vein. One in particular I
remember, a sermon on the parable of the ten virgins, ending
with the appeal: 'Oh, my brethren, where would you rather
be—with the five wise virgins in the light, or the five foolish
virgins in the dark?'

Early in March 1917, soon after L.G.'s accession to the
Premiership, L.G.'s uncle, Richard Lloyd, died. L.G. was
in constant touch with Criccieth, where Dame Margaret was
helping to nurse the old man, but was unable to go down

himself until the funeral. Richard Lloyd had preached his
last sermon on the 11th February, and it was a memorable
one. He chose for his text the verse from the 23rd Psalm:
'Yea, though I walk through the valley of the shadow of
death I will fear no evil for Thou art with me; Thy rod and
Thy staff they comfort me.' After speaking movingly on
the meaning of the Psalm and its message, he concluded:

... I know that there is darkness ahead and that I shall some
day lose sight of everyone. It will be necessary to walk along
the valley of the shadow of death. Yes, it is dark, Dark, DARK,
too far from this world to get any of its light and not far enough
to see the light of the world to come; but let us not fear, little
flock, in that thick black darkness—the Shepherd will come with
us through the chasm. 'His rod and His staff shall comfort us.'

With his broad vision and his realisation of the importance of the Dominion effort in the war, one of L.G.'s first
acts was to summon an Imperial Conference. The heads of
all the Dominions and Colonies assembled in March in
Downing Street. Such arresting figures as General Smuts,
Mr. W. H. Hughes of Australia, Sir Robert Borden from
Canada, Mr. Massey from New Zealand and the Maharajah
of Bikanir from India—all these came to place their contri-
butions of wisdom and sympathy at the disposal of Britain
in her need. At the last session L.G. proposed that it should
be established as the Imperial War Cabinet and incorporated
in the machinery of the British Empire. In the Second World
War Churchill had the benefit of L.G.'s example and lost no
time in following it. The help that the representatives of the
Empire gave us in both wars was inestimable and beyond
praise.

The most able of these representatives were General
Botha and General—later Field Marshal—Smuts.

L.G. had told me about Botha's presence at the Imperial
Conference in 1907, when he represented South Africa as
Prime Minister, and he went on to talk of his breakfast with

him in 1911, when terms were being negotiated between
Britain and South Africa. Botha expressed a very definite
opinion that sooner or later there would be war with Germany. L.G. said to him: 'If there is trouble what will you
do?' He replied: 'I will keep my word and stand by the
Empire. As soon as war is declared I will lead 40,000 horse-
men into German South West Africa and clear out the
Germans.' L.G. knew he meant it, and when the occasion
came, Botha stood by his word. He not only cleared the
Germans out of South West Africa, but helped us in the East
African campaign and moreover sent a contingent to Europe
to fight.

It is strange that I have no recollection of my first meeting
with Smuts. But at the time when he first entered the Councils of Empire the war was approaching its most perilous
stage, and the march of events was so swift, so kaleido-
scopic, the picture so packed, that it is difficult in retrospect
to single out individual incidents and memories.

But what I do remember strongly is the eagerness of L.G.
to persuade General Smuts to stay on after the close of the
Imperial Conference and become a member of the War
Cabinet. There was a deep understanding between the two
men, strengthened beyond a doubt by the fact that L.G. had
sympathised with the Boers during the Boer War, and had
gone in peril, not only of his political future but of his life,
for the views he then held.

There was, indeed, something romantic about Smuts's
position in Britain during the First World War and the
Peace Conference. A British general told me in 1927 that
the last he saw of Smuts at the end of the South African War
was his back when, as an enemy, he fled from the British
Army. The next time he saw him Smuts was seated at the
British Cabinet table as a member of the War Cabinet, and
as such having access to secrets that were withheld even
from members of the Cabinet!

I used to think at that time that Smuts still had in his eyes the look of the man who has been in a tight corner, who is ever on the watch for a potential enemy. You might be on the most friendly terms with him. He would talk with a frankness and sympathy that were disarming. But always at the back of it, at the end of all the paths that you thought were leading to the man, there was a barrier with the words: 'No Thoroughfare'.

I think it was in the quality each man had of *not giving himself away* to anyone that made Smuts and L.G. very much alike. No one ever knew what either of them was thinking, though both had an uncanny capacity for knowing what the third man might think or do. He and L.G. thoroughly understood each other, but still, it seemed to me, had reservations about each other. Perhaps the Dutchman and the Celt were unable to follow completely the working of each other's mind.

It was during the Rapallo Conference that I came to know Smuts well. During this crisis I became more familiar with the working of his inventive mind in an emergency, his grasp of a situation, and his calm courage. The party was, however, by no means a dismal one, for L.G. and Smuts could both go from grave to gay in a flash. No one was grave for very long in their company, but when they vied with each other in gaiety, L.G. was sure to win. Smuts lacked the Celtic touch!

During these difficult days I was able to see the quality of Smuts at close quarters. My admiration and affection for him deepened, and I discovered how at once simple and complex he was, how truly lacking in pride and self-love, how kind and understanding even to the humblest. I came to see him as an idealist, a man of complete integrity, and he honoured me with his friendship and often his confidence.

My room was adjacent to the Cabinet Room, with huge double doors dividing an entrance to it. It was usual for Ministers or others who were waiting to go into the Cabinet to come to my room for a few minutes. Or sometimes L.G. would bring in someone with whom he wanted to have a private chat before joining the meeting. Sometimes people came who wanted an opinion conveyed through me to L.G., if they were unable to get an opportunity for a conversation with him.

General Smuts was a frequent and always welcome visitor. He formed a habit as time went on of dropping into my office at Downing Street during intervals between Cabinet meetings, or before or after a meeting, and talking informally—'off the record' as we would say now. He would often open his heart to me when troublesome matters arose on which he did not see eye to eye with some of the other members of the Cabinet—including L.G. himself! Sometimes he had misgivings about the course of the war. Sometimes he was impatient and unhappy, as when decisions were delayed. I think it did him good to air his doubts and distresses in this way. To me his friendship became a precious and unfailing thing. I was profoundly touched when, writing to me after L.G.'s death, warmly supporting the memorial for which I was attempting to get help, he said:

Dear Lady Lloyd George,
    I have your note.
    You are quite free to use my name in any way you please in connection with your Appeal for a Memorial to L.G.
    His name will of course never be forgotten and is part of the story of our terrific times. But even so, I think a small token of gratitude and remembrance is not out of place. We owe so much to him in peace and war. As a social reformer, and as a grand fighter in the cause of men he has his assured place. I was deeply attached to him both in admiration and affection, as you know. . .
    My warm personal regards and best wishes to you yourself, who so often put up with me and showed me unforgettable kindness.
                    Ever yours affectionately,
                                        J. C. Smuts

    The compliment in the last sentence rather took my breath away.

Another outstanding personality who used to come and talk to me was Ernest Shackleton. He fired me with a deep interest in his polar expeditions, and later on in 1920 I tried to help him to find money for his last one, not very successfully, I fear. I sought the interest of a *very* wealthy Conservative Member of Parliament, who, after we had explained to him the romance and the desirability of the expedition from all its points of view, asked, 'And just what do I get out of all this?' We explained that if it was publicity he wanted that could be arranged, but he evidently decided that the cost of this would be too high according to his business standards. Nevertheless, the expedition was launched but did not fulfil its object, and poor Shackleton died . . .

Lord Northcliffe came occasionally, and presented me with an autographed copy of his book *At the War*. I liked him, but found him just a little sinister. I enjoyed far better seeing the cheery and mischievous face of Lord Beaverbrook, and hearing his broad Canadian accent. A great deal of fuss was made at the time about Northcliffe's part in the overthrow of the Asquith Government, but Max Aitken (shortly to become Lord Beaverbrook) had a far greater hand in the shaping of the events which thrust L.G. in the Premiership. He remained my friend until the end of his life and I received courtesies and kindnesses from him which I shall never forget. That he was mischievous and amoral no one can deny, but neither can anyone deny his power, his tenacity, his deep love of Canada and all Canadian things; and, above all, his devotion to his friend Bonar Law, whom he succeeded eventually in making Prime Minister. I remember when we (Beaverbrook and myself) were reading through the proofs of Beaverbrook's book *The Decline and Fall of Lloyd George* at Cherkley one week-end (it is a bad title and I would never have agreed to it had I known in time) I said to him: 'You *did* love Bonar, didn't you, Max?' and he replied unhesitatingly: 'I loved him more than anyone else in the world.'

Beaverbrook had admiration and I think affection for L.G., but the latter could never depend upon him. I remember when one day L.G. and I were discussing Max, and his seeming disloyalties, L.G. said, 'Max likes to strike down the tall poppies'. But he liked their company, nevertheless. At Cherkley he gave the most exciting parties, where people of all shades of politics and caste and occupation came together, and argued strenuously—sometimes too strenuously, for bitter things were said which were surely regretted. I remember at one of these dinner tables, while Max was having a fearsome personal row with one of his columnists, Lord Castlerosse, L.G. was trying to persuade the company that Cromwell was a Welshman. 'His real name was Williams', asserted L.G., and H. G. Wells, who was sitting next to me, said in a loud undertone: 'I suppose we shall one day have to refer to Williams the Conqueror.'

There was another awkward dinner party at Cherkley when Lady Cunard and Sir Thomas Beecham arrived *very* late—the other guests were all seated at the dinner table—and received a muted welcome from Max, who considered their behaviour lacking in courtesy, as indeed it was. They proceeded during the whole of dinner to nag each other as to which of them was really responsible for being late.

Lady Cunard—'Emerald' to her friends—was a woman without manners. On a day when I went to luncheon at her house a young, lame writer and poet was sitting opposite the door of the drawing room. When she came in (one would not expect her to be there to receive her visitors!) she crossed over to him, shook hands, and said: 'I had forgotten that I had invited you.' I could see that it was like a slap in the face to him. At the luncheon table she called across to me: 'I have a friend, a patron of music, who wants a baronetcy. How much would it cost? Would £30,000 be enough?' The baronetcy was not given during L.G.'s Government, but I believe it was given later. Lady Cunard was a persistent woman.

H

At this point I should like to make it clear that I never had any interest or activity in the honours question. Any requests or recommendations for honours were sent straight to the office of the Whips, who drew up the final honours list for submission to the Prime Minister, who then presented it to the King for approval. I didn't know—I was never interested in—whether any question of payment arose. I knew that payments *were* made, as I suppose everyone did: details were given in a later, impassioned debate in the House of Commons, when L.G. made it clear that any funds for the sale of honours were divided during his Premiership between Liberals and Conservatives, and managed by their respective Whips. The custom was an old one, and like so many other old political customs I imagine it is dying out, or is perhaps already dead.

One of my bugbears during the whole of L.G.'s time as Prime Minister—and indeed afterwards—was being cross-examined by curious and inquisitive people. I think in my desire not to disclose anything I should not, I often erred on the side of being *too* uncommunicative. 'People must think I am extraordinarily stupid,' I remember saying to L.G., 'at the number of things I do not know!'

8

Unity of Command:
The Maurice Debate

As soon as L.G. became Prime Minister, the era of Conferences began. He considered that nothing was so important or so effective as the personal touch in settling difficulties, and as he himself was at his best sitting at a table and talking things out, conferences were his natural method of procedure. They were, moreover, the only method of unifying the war direction.

His short stay at the War Office had shown him how many had their hands against him and how deeply entrenched was the hostility of the military against the politicians. L.G. had written several strong memoranda on the subject of war policy, but none of his recommendations had been implemented with the exception of the promise of an overwhelming supply of munitions, and in that process there had been many casualties amongst the heads of military departments. L.G. had definitely come to the conclusion that the most pressing decision to take was that of unity of command, so that one campaign should not be prepared or decided upon to the detriment of another. He knew how the High Commands on both the French and British sides would fight against this. The French had already prepared their plans for the campaign of 1917, and expected us to fall in with them.

In the New Year, therefore, a conference was arranged at Calais with a view to sorting everything out and making a grand plan to try to end the war during the year without vast casualties. We now know how futile that plan was, with its continuation of the Somme, and then its Passchendaele campaign. L.G. has described it in his own memoirs in his graphic style.

If he could have replaced Haig with a more suitable Army chief he would have done so. But there appeared to be no one with the necessary experience and vision. Robertson, Haig's Q.M.G.,[1] was critical of L.G. and his methods, and willing to work in with L.G.'s enemies. He was a dour, hardworking Scot of the kind that laid the foundation of the British Empire. He should have appealed to L.G., with his humble origin—if he had shown more sense. He had risen from the ranks, but he had no gift of speech, and all the obstinacy of his good qualities. If he had had the intelligence not to allow himself to be used by others he and L.G. could have worked together. But he just could not express himself and the bottling up of his feelings made him appear even more obstinate and difficult. While the trouble over the Inter-Allied Council was on he travelled over to France with Major-General Robert Hutchison, who asked why he did not go to L.G. and have a frank talk with him and clear the whole matter up. Robertson did not reply, but a year later he and Hutchison again found themselves travelling in the same ship together. Without any preliminary, Robertson said: 'It wouldn't have made any difference, Hutch.' I had this story from Hutchison himself.

The result was that there were constant misunderstandings between the two, which could have been solved if they had been better friends and less antagonistic. But there was always the suspicion that the one was working against the other, and the direction of the war suffered.

The following letter, however, shows the difference in the outward relationship between Haig and L.G. this year. Obviously L.G. had sent Haig a pleasant letter, which called for the reply:

1. Quarter Master General.

General Headquarters,
British Armies in France
23rd September, 1916

My dear Mr. Lloyd George,

It gave me great pleasure to entertain you on your recent visit to France and I am more than pleased to learn from your kind letter that your time was agreeably spent.

The whole army appreciates to the full the stupendous task that has been accomplished under your able guidance in providing the enormous quantities of Munitions of all sorts without which our present successes would be impossible. We welcome the more personal interest you take in our doings, finding therein a further guarantee—were one needed—that our efforts here in France will be backed in the completest manner by all ranks of the nation at home.

We shall be glad to see you whenever your duties permit you to visit us; and I hope you may be able to spend a few nights at my Head Quarters. I can put you and one other up quite comfortably and without inconvenience to my staff or myself.

I thank you very sincerely for your congratulations and good wishes and feel confident that the close co-operation now existing between our workers at home and our armies in the field cannot fail to bring us the ultimate success to which we all look forward.

Please believe me,

Yours sincerely,

D. Haig

The Calais Conference was a walk-over for the French, who, under Nivelle and his staff, had all their plans *ready* for the next murderous campaign, which led to the campaign of Passchendaele, and then, as if to put the seal on all this loss and mutilation (of the spirit as well as the body), came the senseless throwing away of our precious tanks at Cambrai. They could think of nothing else, but after that even *The Times* turned, and demanded 'prompt searching and complete' inquiry. The Cabinet decided that the campaign had been 'a ghastly failure'. The whole of it has been under review by so many military writers and by so many biographers, including L.G., who has given a detailed account of all the 1917 operations in his memoirs, that I will not attempt to go into any details. Two of Haig's staff were blamed for the initial mistakes, and General Gough for continuing the campaign when it was evident that it could not succeed. The two first generals were removed from the positions they held, but Haig wished Gough to remain, and remain he did —at any rate until the German breakthrough of the Fifth Army in 1918.

But the 1917 campaign had convinced L.G. more than ever that there ought to be—that we ought to insist upon— unity of command amongst the Allies.

In the summer and early autumn of 1917 the position on the Italian Front worsened, and culminated in the disaster of Caporetto. L.G. had attempted to deal with the situation by means of telegrams and through military channels, but he soon realised that if the position were to be saved, nothing would suffice but a personal visit, and a conference between all the 'heads', as Henry Wilson called them. Accordingly, L.G. set out for Italy, taking with him General Smuts, Sir Maurice Hankey, J. T. Davies, and myself.

Sir Henry Wilson and Sir William Robertson joined the conference at Rapallo.[1] The French Government put a special train at our disposal, and in Paris M. Painlevé, the French Prime Minister, joined it, with M. Franklin Bouillon, his *fidus Achates*. M. Painlevé was a quiet, dreamy person: anyone more unlike a politician I have never seen. Franklin Bouillon, an astute and amiable character, talked all the time on every possible subject. Marshal Foch also joined us with some members of his staff. Cadorna himself was at the Front and could not leave, but the Italian Prime Minister, Orlando, and his Foreign Minister, Sonnino, were at the conference. There is a menu card in existence bearing the signatures of this distinguished gathering.

1. November 7th, 1917.

The Rapallo Conference was one of the most interesting and exciting incidents in my life. I had never been to Italy before, and the journey itself was a revelation and an excitement to me. The autumn hues were still on the mountains when we crossed the Franco-Italian frontier at Modane, but the slopes were covered in snow. I have a vivid memory of the spires of bright yellow trees springing from a blue-white carpet against a vivid blue sky, something that if you saw in a picture you would say was untrue or at least exaggerated. We got out of the train at Modane and this was my first step on the soil of Italy. I was exhilarated by the air and the occasion.

At Rapallo L.G. quickly got to work. Members of the Italian Army had joined the conference, but not Cadorna, who was fully occupied trying to stem the torrent of Germans and Austrians from overrunning the north of Italy. The Italian staff was in a pitiable state: 'We will never surrender,' said one of the generals, 'even if we have to retreat to Sicily.'

How it was done it is difficult to explain, but the tide *was* stemmed. Even as we travelled back we saw the French *camions* laden with troops and ammunition winding along the mountain roads to the Italian Front to take their stand there. But the trains that passed us coming *away* from the Front were packed with Italian soldiers—no doubt retreating to Sicily! It was a melancholy scene that we met at Brescia—soldiers and refugees mingled together in confusion.

L.G. and Painlevé and Foch and Robertson met the King of Italy at Lake Garda, and told him of the conclusions reached at Rapallo. L.G. describes the meeting in his memoirs.

The Italian disaster had one good result at least, for it enabled L.G. to advance one stage further his plan for a United Command—a plan which caused dreadful trouble amongst the British Chiefs of Staff now and for many months to come, and which only received its final endorsement after the British disaster in March 1918.

L.G. was to stop in Paris on the way home to make a speech explaining the steps that had been taken at Rapallo—a sort of pre-warning, I think, to people in Britain—and so he decided to halt on his return journey and spend two days at Aix-les-Bains preparing it.

The speech, when delivered in Paris, caused a sensation. L.G. threw all caution to the winds. This, he decided, was the psychological moment to declare openly that only Unity of Command could save the Allies. He had many a difficult corner to turn, many an adverse wind to weather, before the plan became an accomplished fact.

It required another disaster even more formidable than Caporetto to establish a supreme inter-Allied Command. This was the catastrophe of March 1918, when the Germans threw the whole weight of their forces against the Allied armies in France, and succeeded in breaking through. When the first news came through, L.G. was not surprised; neither was he daunted. On the contrary, his spirit soared: faced with difficulty, he was merely presented with another barrier that must be crossed. The word 'defeat' simply did not enter into his vocabulary. He would 'find a way'. Others have recorded how he lifted them up and encouraged them from day to day as the news from the Front grew worse and worse. His was the 'two o'clock in the morning courage'. That was why people instinctively followed him in difficulty or danger. He himself has told in his own memoirs how he decided that the one vital thing was to get trained American troops across as soon as possible; and how, having decided this, he got them across, and the situation was eventually saved. He plunged at once into a series of plans which brought over American troops at an unbelievable speed. He and Philip Kerr spent long hours drafting and re-drafting the forceful telegrams to Lord Reading, our Ambassador in U.S.A., urging, instructing, appealing, commanding. These telegrams would, I think, bear publication in a separate volume as a perfect example of diplomacy which produced *action*. There was no time now, as on other occasions, for the despatches to be sent through the normal Foreign Office channels, after having received the consent of the Secretary of State. The telegrams when completed would be rushed over to the Foreign Office to be coded and despatched. It was a magnificent piece of organisation in which Sir Joseph Maclay (later Lord Maclay), the Minister of Shipping, played a great part.

Actually, it was a situation that L.G. gloried in—obstacles to overcome, men to stimulate to greater action, something indeed for which his gifts and his vitality could be utilised to the full. There never was such a leader.

For all of us, however, these days were anxious ones, though we had faith that we would pull through. A map in the Cabinet Room had the British line marked on it in red, and each day the line moved sickeningly back and back. One day in April I saw that the Germans had reached Bethune, near to where my brother was buried. 'They will soon be trampling over his grave', I thought, as I took a last look at the map before leaving the office rather late in the evening, and then the words which the French Army had made immortal sprang into my mind: 'They shall not pass.' There is some thinking which is akin to prayer. I suppose if we attuned our lives aright all thinking would be thus. I do not remember anything more on leaving the office until I found myself approaching my parents' home at Wallington, instead of my flat in London in Victoria Street. My mother was surprised to see me, but understood that something was amiss. It is the only time in my life that I have suffered from amnesia.

Strangely enough that night marked the limit of the German advance. The red line on the map moved back no more!

The load of anxiety was lifted, but it was not till the

summer, with Foch's attack in July and the magnificent
assault by the American Army at Château Thierry, that the
tide really turned, and the end of the struggle appeared to
be in sight. Nevertheless the Army chiefs even then were
instructed to draw up their plans for 1919. L.G. was taking
no chances, for as Churchill once said of him: 'He was
always looking into the next field!'

But before then, in May, when things were going so badly
for the Allies in France, and we were fighting, to use Sir
Douglas Haig's phrase, 'with our backs to the wall', this was
the time when L.G.'s enemies at home, of every complexion,
sought to get him down. Sir William Robertson, whom Sir
Henry Wilson had superseded as C.I.G.S., McKenna, one
of the most inveterate of L.G.'s Liberal foes, and other disgruntled figures, in and out of Parliament, joined in an
attempt to overthrow the Government. A letter from
General Maurice appeared in the Press on May 7th, accusing
the Prime Minister of giving misleading information to the
House of Commons.

The whole of this story has been told by L.G. in his
memoirs, and by many other writers of varying complexion, but if another version were needed, the columns
of *Hansard* furnish all the facts in the report of the debate
on the motion put down by Mr. Asquith on May 9th:

That a Selection Committee of this House be appointed to
inquire into the allegations of incorrectness in certain statements
of Ministers of the Crown to this House, contained in a letter
of Major-General Maurice late Director of Military Operations,
published in the Press on the 7th day of May.

The Asquithians wanted it both ways. They were willing
—anxious—to put the Government into difficulties by
arraigning its members before a Select Committee, but
shrank from the odium which would attach to them by
bringing a Vote of Censure at such a grave moment.

Excitement ran high. Although Mr. Asquith denied that the motion was a Vote of Censure, it was fully realised that this was an attempt to defeat the Government and to bring the Lloyd George Coalition to an end. I am told on good authority[1] that Mr. Asquith had not been a party to the intrigues which preceded the debate, and it was obvious that he did not like his task. To tell the truth, he was not the best person to bring a charge of lack of veracity in a Prime Minister's statement, for his speech at Newcastle in 1915 on the shell situation had been a glaring example of misleading the public.

The motion was obviously distasteful to him. He began his speech by saying that he did not think that the conduct of the war should be interrupted by inquiries of this kind. He denied that he was seizing the opportunity of turning the Government out: 'There are people,' he said, 'gifted with more imagination than charity, and with more stupidity than either, who think of me as a person who is gnawed with a hungry ambition to resume the cares and responsibilities of office.'

He may not have wanted to return to the Premiership, but there were many close to him who were 'gnawed with a hungry ambition' to turn L.G. out of office, and I do not think Asquith himself would have been averse to this. He disassociated himself with General Maurice's letter: he denied any knowledge of it. But he did not condemn it. He was not happy in his attack, and when a member's interruption of 'Get on with the War' was greeted with deafening applause there seemed to be no more spirit left in him, and his speech came to an almost abrupt end. As an attack the speech was a failure.

L.G., on the other hand, was on top of his form. That cry, 'Get on with the war', seemed to rally the House against the Asquithians, and L.G. was quick to sense the tightening support behind him. He made good use of the

1. Miss Maurice.

fact that although General Maurice had attended a Cabinet meeting the day after L.G. had made the statement in question, he never called L.G.'s attention to the alleged inaccuracy, or suggested that it should be corrected. 'Was it not his business,' asked L.G., 'to come to the Minister whom he impugned, and say to him, , "You made a mistake in the House of Commons on a most important question of fact"? . . . *Never a syllable, until I saw it in the newspapers.*'

L.G. stated that the figures—the disputed figures—which he had used in his comparison between the British Forces in France on January 1st, 1917, and on January 1st, 1918, were taken from the Official Records of the War Office, for which he had sent before making the statement. And he quoted a further document which had been sent out from General Maurice's department nine days *after* L.G.'s speech of April 9th—the speech which was challenged—to the effect that:

From the statement included, it will be seen that the combatant strength of the British Army was greater on the 1st of January 1918 than on the 1st January 1917.

L.G. went on: 'If there was anything wrong in these figures, I got them from official sources for which General Maurice himself is responsible.'

Having disposed of this charge, L.G. proceeded to deal with the others—the question of the number of troops in Egypt and Palestine, and the extension of the British line in France. And he did not fail to point out that the controversy on the latter question would never have arisen had there been unity of command. 'One united army—one united command—responsible for the whole and for every part, was the only method of safety. I am glad we have got that at last.' Sir Basil Liddell Hart, a famous military historian, who has made a study of the breakthrough in March 1918 in his book *The War in Outline: 1914-1918*, has given me permission to quote a relevant passage from his book. In his covering letter to me he says:

What is really important is not these comparatively trifling arguments over figures, but the fact that Haig in his diary expressed himself quite confident of being able to repel the German offensive.

And writing in his book, he says:

The atmosphere changed when the crisis developed. And from it grew a controversy which for many years obscured the causes of the breakdown, and hindered a scientific examination of them. The result was generally attributed to the overwhelming strength of the German attack, and as the Government was able to scrape together large reinforcements to repair the losses—140,000 were sent out as drafts—it was natural that Haig should have seized on to this fact to shift the responsibility on to the statesmen's shoulders, ascribing his defeat to lack of troops. It is remarkable how long that excuse has passed without analysis of the facts. In a sense, of course, almost every defeat in history is due to the loser being too weak. But serious criticism demands a sense of proportion—and of possibilities. A commander in the field is naturally anxious to obtain as many men as he can. It is not within the normal soldier's province to appreciate the manifold difficulties and ultimate dangers of levying fresh taxes on the nation's man-power. That is for the Government to weigh. The British strength had certainly been weakened, materially as well as morally, by the prolonged drain of Passchendaele. For that weakness, the responsibility falls on Haig, since he had pursued his offensives and incurred huge losses in disregard of his pledges to the Government. Nevertheless, if this experience might be held a fair excuse for the Government, they could not escape the ultimate responsibility if in fact Haig's defeat was due to insufficient numbers when more troops might have been sent. The crux of the controversy is whether the German breakthrough was due to the weakness of Haig's forces. *On analysis this does not appear to be true.* The British forces were twenty per cent stronger as a whole, and only three per cent less in fighting troops at the beginning of 1918 than the year before, when they had to undertake the offensive—a much bigger undertaking. Before the German attack came they were reinforced by a further 167,000 fighting troops—equal to an additional fifteen per cent.

Moreover, the fact emerges that the Germans had no appreciable superiority in the total of men or guns over the Allies. Since the Germans had been able to resist the Allied attacks in 1917 despite a heavy inferiority, the statesmen were justified in assuming that the Allied armies as a whole could hold their own. And as the national Commanders-in-Chief annulled the scheme for an interallied reserve, preferring to make their own arrangements, the responsibility logically rests with them if one national sector proved unduly weak.

The question still remains whether the British sector was really too weak. The idea is not supported by the facts. For the total strength that the Germans concentrated on the British front gave them only a three to two superiority—smaller odds than the Germans had faced in 1917. That they doubled this superiority on the Fifth Army front was a matter of generalship—*Haig's sphere of responsibility*. Granting the wisdom of being stronger in the north, were the actual proportions reasonable? The G.H.Q. records show that Haig's dispositions were made and maintained in the belief, in face of ample evidence, that the attack would not fall on the Fifth Army. This shows that his distribution of strength was based on a false assumption—that he underestimated the risk it involved, through discrediting the warnings that came from the Fifth Army and were confirmed by the air reports.

Even so, in the light of past experience, odds of three to one are not sufficient to account for such a breakthrough as the Germans achieved. But the odds became greater in effect because of the new system of defence by which the available troops were divided between a Forward Zone and a Battle Zone, which lay a mile or two behind. The system was copied from the Germans, but its essential idea was changed. Instead of using the Forward Zone as a spring-buffer to absorb the initial shock, the British command held it in strength. The Official History states that no less than a third of the British infantry were posted in the

Forward Zone, so being exposed to the full effect of the enemy's bombardment. And when the attack came 'the Forward Zone as a whole was overrun at the first rush', and its occupants overwhelmed. *Thus about a third of the British infantry strength was forfeited before the battle really began. Such a fact makes it impossible for any fair critic to ascribe the responsibility for any weakness that developed to the insufficiency of troops provided by the Government.*[1] [Note: My italics.]

And more recently, in reply to a resurgence of the attack by A. J. P. Taylor on L.G. over the Maurice affair, Sir Basil Liddell Hart wrote a letter from which he has allowed me to quote:

The whole matter has been blown up out of all proportion to its military importance. For Haig's forces in January 1918 were only 3% less in fighting troops than a year before, even on the corrected figures, and the total strength was 20% larger. The very slight deficiency in numbers was due to the fact that 113,000 of the troops in France had gone to Italy to buttress the Italian collapse at Caporetto. Moreover, before the German attack on Haig's front came in March, his armies were reinforced by a further 167,000 fighting troops—equal to an addition of 15%. Yet in 1918 he had only to stand on the defensive, whereas in 1917 he had been on the offensive.

The whole argument about figures is trivial, and irrelevant compared with two principal facts, which are constantly overlooked or obscured in controversy:

(1) The much criticised decision to hold the General Reserve in England was taken by the General Staff, for reasons of convenience, and not by the Cabinet. There is no complaint of it in Haig's diary.

(2) On the contrary, the diary shows that Haig was amply confident of repelling the German offensive. At a conference of his Army commanders on March 2nd, he told them that he was 'only afraid that the enemy would find our front so strong that he will hesitate to commit his army to the attack with the almost certainty of losing very heavily'.

1. Liddell Hart: *The War in Outline: 1914–1918, pp 175–7.*

As this letter is so categorical, perhaps it will close the controversy, which has gone on for such a long time, and been revived so often.

To come back to the debate:

Having refuted 'each pestiferous charge', quoting in the process from the actual conclusions of the War Cabinet, L.G. brought up all his big guns to deal with General Maurice himself. He dwelt on the example of indiscipline the General had committed.

One of my jobs was to read through the French newspapers and bring anything of interest or importance to L.G.'s notice. In referring to the breach of discipline committed by General Maurice, L.G. made good use of an extract from *La Liberté*:

. . . No French party would admit that in the midst of a war a General on active service should permit himself to raise his voice in public to contradict the Government or to lecture it. With all respect to the British General, what is calculated to diminish the *morale* of the troops is not that a Minister should in good faith have stated what is not exact, whether in regard to the extension of the British front or the number of effectives, but that an officer, hitherto respected, should have thought it his duty to commit an act of indiscipline so glaring that in our democratic country it would be considered a real scandal. It is not for an officer to ask himself if he should place his duty as a citizen before his duty as a soldier.

General Maurice knew full well what would be the consequences of his action, as is shown in a letter that he wrote at the time to his family, knowing that he could count on their loyalty and understanding:—

I have decided to write the letter which I enclose, to the papers. . . . This is, of course, a breach of military discipline. . . . They may turn me out of the Army and you may suffer in consequence, though I will do my best to see that you don't. I hope you will think I am right. . . .

I am persuaded that I am doing what is right, and sure that it is, nothing else matters to a man. . . . It has been a difficult decision for, as you know, I love the army, and I have you all to think of, but it is made now and you must help me to make the best of it.

L.G. ended by pleading for the sake of the country, that there should be 'an end of sniping'.

How they hated him, these 'Wee Frees'! Pringle, the Liberal Member for North-West Lanarkshire, who followed in the debate, was almost spitting venom, his face distorted with hatred. (He was the same whom Hore-Belisha struck across the face many years afterwards at a meeting which had been called to demonstrate Liberal unity!)

Once again L.G. had shown his supremacy in debate. His foes had hoped at last to get him down, but he was at his best with his back to the wall. He turned this way and that, meeting every savage thrust with an even more savage riposte. He was indeed a 'bonnie fechter'. His enemies were visibly writhing with frustration and chagrin at this their final defeat. They had hoped, now that the situation was bad and L.G. in obvious difficulties, to get him down once and for all, but he emerged shining and triumphant. The hostile Asquithian Liberals had fired their last shot, and the only certain thing that they achieved for themselves was a shattering defeat at the next election.

There was a sequel to the Maurice affair. In 1934 I made an entry in my diary, which the late Lord Beaverbrook subsequently published in his book *Men and Power 1917–1918*, and I think it is best to quote from his book the passage which gives all the information:

I now quote in full an extract from the Diary of Countess Lloyd George, which is included in the Lloyd George Collection. It is dated 5th October 1934.

Have been reading up the events connected with the Maurice

I

Debate in order to help L.G. with this Chapter in Vol. V[1] and am uneasy in my mind about an incident which occurred at the time and which is known only to J. T. Davies and myself. L.G. obtained from the W.O. the figures which he used in his statement on April 9th in the House of Commons on the subject of man-power. These figures were afterwards stated by Gen. Maurice to be inaccurate.

'I was in J.T.'s room a few days after the statement and J.T. was sorting out red dispatch boxes to be returned to the Departments. As was his wont, he looked in them before locking them up and sending them out to the Messengers. Pulling out a W.O. box, he found in it, to his great astonishment, a paper from the D.M.O. containing modifications and corrections of the first figures they had sent, and by some mischance this box had remained unopened. J.T. and I examined it in dismay, and then J.T. put it in the fire, remarking "Only you and I, Frances, know of the existence of this paper." '

There is no doubt that this is what Maurice had in mind when he accused L.G. of mis-statement. But the amazing thing was that *the document was never fixed upon.* How was it that the matter was never clinched and Maurice or someone never actually said: 'The figures supplied by us were so-and-so'?

They argued round and over the point, but never did any one put their finger on it. I was waiting for the matter to be raised, and for the question to be asked: Why did L.G. not receive these supplementary figures? Or did he? But the questions never came and I could not voluntarily break faith with J.T., put L.G. in a fix, and who knows, have brought down the Government.

The only explanation is that Maurice & Co. were relying on getting their Judicial Committee, where every point would have been thrashed out in detail. When the Judicial Committee was turned down, it was by that time too late to bring up details again, and by that time also Maurice was beaten.

Lord Beaverbrook concludes his chapter with the following:

  1. Of the War Memoirs.

So it seems that the upward spiral of cause and effect, moving from one event to another and greater one, found its origin in a Secretary's room at 10 Downing Street. If the amending figures sent by Maurice's Department in the War Office had not been overlooked by the Prime Minister's Secretary, Lloyd George would not have given misleading information to Parliament. Maurice would not have been able to make the charge which the newspapers published. There would have been no Maurice Debate. And may be there would have been no exclusion of Asquithian Liberals at the General Election. The disruption of the Liberal Party might have been postponed or even averted. . . . Through the oversight of a Secretary, Lloyd George's Government—for months the target of a military junta and the butt of powerful and contentious forces determined to drag down and utterly destroy the Prime Minister—was saved and indeed strengthened immeasurably. Never again, for the duration of the War, was Lloyd George in danger from the assaults of enemies of the right and the left. The direction of the war remained unaltered. The Liberal Party was destroyed, while enemies were scattered far and wide.

The disruption of the Liberal Party at the Election could not after this have been averted. The Liberal Party was indeed destroyed—it committed suicide—by the Maurice Debate, from which L.G. would have emerged triumphant even if the amending figures had reached him in time.

I always felt sorry for General Maurice, but nothing that J.T. or I could have done at the moment that the amending figures came to light would have helped him at all. His military career was finished when he decided to appeal to the Press. He knew that his action would mean the sacrifice of his military career, but he was prepared to make the sacrifice. As I have said, his letter of May 7th to the Press was the first shot in the train of events which followed. On May 9th Asquith tabled his motion for a Select Committee, and L.G. demolished the 'pestiferous charges' and with them the prospects of the Liberal Party at the next election. For in spite of what Lord Beaverbrook says in his chapter on 'The Burnt Papers', nothing would have saved the Liberal (Asquithian) candidates from defeat in the 1918 election. After the Maurice debate their names (those who had voted against the Prime Minister in the debate) would have been black-listed in any case, whether the amending figures that were burnt reached L.G. or not. He was out to destroy his enemies, once and for all, so as to 'get on with the war', and this he did, and would have done, whatever the figures. In defence of General Maurice it is said that he was in France at headquarters and did not know that either the first or second set of figures had been sent to L.G. Was there no one in the W.O. to see that the correction was made?[1]

I do not think that any action at the point of discovery could have prevented the Liberals who had voted against L.G. in the debate from being doomed at the 1918 election. Those of them who *did* get back continued their attacks upon him and L.G.'s Whips knew that they *would* do so. In any case, L.G.'s Whips were Coalition-minded and they did not mind the demolition of the Liberal Party, even though L.G. himself was sorry for this. I was with him when the election results were coming through, and as the news came in of the Liberal holocaust and the mounting figures of L.G.'s successes, he said, 'I did not want this to happen', and he meant it.

When Lord Beaverbrook published my diary in his *Men and Power* (without informing me that he was doing so—

1. General Maurice's daughter, in a letter to the *Spectator* of November 16th, 1956, after the publication of Lord Beaverbrook's book, said that her father was no longer in the War Office when his letter was published, and had no access to War Office papers, and that 'he knew that the statement that Lloyd George had made was wrong, but without access to the W.O. records he could not prove it . . .' Miss Maurice says: 'He [her father] never knew that this correction had not reached the Prime Minister when he [the P.M.] gave the wrong figures to the House. . . .'

simply sending me an advance copy of the book and saying, when I protested, that it was too late to alter anything) there was a frenzied rush into publication of friends of General Maurice who thought that they could retrieve his reputation. The facts had been given, and nothing I said would alter them.

I must say at this point that when L.G. was writing his account of the Maurice debate in his memoirs (when I made the entry in my diary) I telephoned to J. T. Davies in London and said I thought we ought to tell him of the incident of the burnt paper. J. T.'s reply was that he had no recollection of the incident. So L.G. never knew what had happened.

9

Armistice and the General Election

That summer, 1918, Lord Riddell took a house for L.G. near Hassocks, in Sussex, so that the Prime Minister might snatch a change of air and scene whenever an opportunity offered.

Riddell came to all the conferences during and after the war. But during the Peace conference the French made a great fuss of him, and L.G. gradually formed the opinion that Riddell was becoming too pro-French. The crisis came during dinner one day at a conference when L.G. was having trouble with the French over Turkey's demands. L.G., who was tired and rather irritable with his many cares, turned on Riddell, and accused him of being pro-French and unpatriotic. This incensed Riddell, who left the dinner table, and returned the next day to London. After this he and L.G. saw much less of each other, though Riddell often turned into Downing Street when he felt like it. But he came to Churt rarely after the house there was finished (it was a long way from Walton Heath where Riddell lived) and the long friendship came to an end.

L.G. never forgave Riddell for transferring his visits to Bonar Law when the latter became Prime Minister. Lord Riddell had a lovely house in Queen Anne's Gate, overlooking the Park, and he used to entertain a great deal for L.G. Riddell had started life as a solicitor, had made a great success in this profession and had become absorbed in it.

Then suddenly, one night on his way home, he realised that he was becoming a slave to his work, and missing so much else in life. He never went back to his office, but soon afterwards bought the *News of the World* and devoted his whole life to it. It brought him a fortune, but he spent himself on one long search for news, and news that would excite people's interest. He realised that politics were news, and especially that politicians—some politicians—were news. He attached himself to L.G., and there is no doubt that his paper profited from this association, for even while playing golf L.G. was thinking and talking politics. They played golf every week-end together. The Walton Heath Golf Club was Riddell's property, and he had had a fascinating garden made around it by Miss Gertrude Jekyll. He was a good companion and an interesting talker, with lots of news and an interesting, if occasionally somewhat salacious way of telling it. He smoked incessantly and drank nothing and never seemed to enjoy his food. That was perhaps why he remained so spare.

Danny Park, the house near Hassocks, was a beautiful old Elizabethan mansion in a lovely setting. The only thing against it to L.G.'s mind was that there was no view from the house itself. He discovered the same drawback at Chequers when he went there, but later on he realised that most of the old houses were built in a depression, for that was where water was naturally found. At Danny one had to climb up to the top of a hill nearby to see the country beyond. This L.G. did every morning before breakfast, and I accompanied him. Unfortunately I became ill there early in August, with an inflammation of the kidneys, and had to remain there six weeks with two nurses in attendance for most of the time. Riddell took great care that I was well looked after, and I was very grateful to him.

In August L.G. himself was taken ill with influenza while in Manchester, where he went from Danny to receive the freedom of that city. There was a dangerous epidemic at the time, and L.G.'s vitality was lowered owing to the strain he was undergoing. He was very ill, and was taken from his hotel to the home of the Lord Mayor of Manchester, Sir Alexander Porter, who with his family showed him infinite kindness. He returned to Danny to recuperate, which fortunately he did very quickly. He walked into my room on his return holding the beautiful freedom—a breath-taking silver coffer with enamel plaques, containing the gorgeous scroll of the freedom—a happy smile on his face. But I was horrified at the mark that the illness had left upon him. He must I fear have been very near death's door. But he was exhilarated by the turn which events in the war had taken, and this helped his convalescence.

My convalescence took a good deal longer. I missed, therefore, the mounting excitement which heralded the surrender first of Bulgaria and Turkey, then of Austria, but there were long conferences at Danny Park and the news trickled through to me as I lay in bed. I could hear the drone of voices from the terrace below, as L.G. sat in the garden with Lord Milner, Lord Reading, Mr. Bonar Law, Hankey and others who came down to discuss the terms of Armistice and the prospect of Germany's surrender.

By October I had recovered from my illness, and in spite of the fact that it had left me feeling very much under the weather, I was able to resume my work.

One of my most exciting memories is of the Lord Mayor's Dinner on November 9th, when L.G. announced the abdication of the Kaiser. I shall never forget the triumphal procession that filed into Guildhall to take their places at the high table. It was one of the peaks of L.G.'s career, for it was clear that although the Armistice had not actually been signed, the war was as good as over, and the jubilant applause which followed his announcement that the Kaiser had fled and the Germans appealed for an Armistice was almost overwhelming.

Shortly before this, however, L.G. had been hurt and surprised to receive a communication from Churchill on the subject of the election which everyone assumed would be imminent. It was clear that Churchill was manœuvring for position in the nect Government. He went so far as to hint that he would really prefer to be free to take his own line at the election. L.G. keenly resented what he thought was an ungrateful action on Churchill's part, for as has been seen he had experienced considerable difficulty in getting agreement amongst his colleagues when he proposed to offer Churchill the post of Minister of Munitions in 1917. Then some of the Conservative members of the Government had threatened to resign, and L.G. considered that he had taken a risk in bringing Churchill back into the Government—a risk which Asquith had not been prepared to take.

It is not surprising, therefore, that this prospect of defection by Churchill at a critical time angered L.G. He indignantly resented what he considered to be an unfriendly action on Churchill's part in trying to free himself for the election. He was at a loss to understand the reason, unless it was that Churchill wished to range himself with the 'true' Liberals in the event of the Coalition breaking up. He drafted an angry letter in reply to Churchill's and, as was his habit, he submitted it to Mr. Bonar Law. The words in the letter were bitter, wounding words, impetuously written. But Bonar Law shook his head and proceeded to delete and alter. The wounding sentences were toned down, the tenor of the letter became less pugnacious, less offensive. L.G. tried to break away again, in a second draft, but he was led firmly and finally back to reason and civility by Bonar's gentle hand. The drafts are still in existence to illustrate this story.[1]

L.G., however, flatly refused to comply with Churchill's

1. The Beaverbrook papers.

request that he should be told in advance whom L.G. proposed to include in his next Government, and Churchill,
faced with an uncompromising L.G., dropped his demands.
He was, in fact, made Secretary of State for War and Air
in L.G.'s Government after the election.

I was incensed at this lack of consideration on Churchill's
part towards one who had gone out of his way to show him
consideration in the past. Men of genius in the political
world are rare, but it is now an agreed opinion that one of
them was Mr. Winston Churchill. The attitude of the politician is said to be one of affability to those around him—
part of his stock-in-trade. Not so with Mr. Churchill. There
was no gracious smile, no ready tactful word for the chance
acquaintance. He did not talk *to* you, he talked *at* you. You
did not feel entitled to take part in the conversation, for it
was not a conversation; it was a monologue, a diatribe, an
exposition of a case, but never a conversation.

But it must not be supposed that his talk was not worth
listening to—it fascinated and enthralled. It was then that
you realised the genius of the man. His sentences scintillated
with wit and ideas, they gripped you with their force and
power, they held you with their imagery and wealth of
language. His mind climbed from one idea to another, it
leaped like a flame from simile to simile, it piled argument
upon argument as it whipped and stimulated the listener.
In the end it did everything but convince. It compelled you
to admiration, but not to belief. It may safely be said that
there were not more than two or three people in the political
world at that time who could draw large audiences and
whose speeches were widely read, but one of these was Mr.
Churchill. Nevertheless the words of a great orator should
warm you and leave you in a glow; those of Mr. Churchill
fascinated, but left you cold. Why was it? The curse of
egoism warps and vitiates, and the divine spark which flies
with its message and kindles to action is killed before it
ignites. He did not lack emotion and was in fact quite

easily moved to tears. He would weep over a tale of woe or over a piteous sight, or over a bereavement, but the fact of his weeping would be of far greater interest to him than the cause of his grief and thus no sympathy would radiate from him. He was the complete egoist.

He was also a political paradox. With all his genius and his long experience he could command no following then in the country. His name drew in the House of Commons or at a public meeting, and yet it was anathema to the man in the street. He had been in one high office after another and had been a Cabinet Minister over many years, and yet he had scarcely a single success to record, but only a long line of *gaffes* and failures. In the Home Office he had his ridiculous Sydney Street episode; at the Admiralty there was the Gallipoli disaster. In the War Office he had his crazy Russian adventures. But though he blundered in one office after another he still continued to remain in office and to be a great political personage. He was full of ideas, great, wonderful, often useful ideas, conceived on a bold scale, for he had a big mind. There was no room for pettiness in it, no room for small things. Why did these ideas go astray? Judgment was lacking, or rather was obscured by self.

When L.G. was Prime Minister, Churchill was torn as to which part he would play on the political stage. He could not make up his mind whether he would go to the extreme right or the extreme left. And he was not getting much help from either side in the making up of his mind. Perhaps it was true, as Labouchère once said, that 'You can rat, but you can't re-rat.'

I modified some of my opinions about him during the Second World War, listening spellbound to the broadcasts of his speeches, realising his tremendous courage and determination and being convinced that without him we should probably have lost the war and been invaded by Germany.

I cannot leave my impressions of Churchill without telling

my favourite stories about him. He was seated at luncheon
one day beside the French Ambassador and was wearing
his Trinity House uniform of an Elder Brother, one which
was easy to wear and lent distinction to the wearer. It was
not one which the Ambassador recognised, and he asked
Churchill what uniform he was wearing. '*Je suis le frère
ainé de la Trinité,*' was the reply. The Ambassador, after a
pause, replied, '*Quelle belle situation!*' A second authentic
story is that of Mrs. Blanche Dugdale, Balfour's niece, who
acted as his secretary in Paris during the Peace Conference.
She found herself seated at dinner next to Mr. Churchill,
who asked her who she was. She told him, whereupon he
gave full vent to the particular feud he had on at the moment
with Mr. Balfour. 'You can tell him so and so and so and
so,' he roared, and when he had finished Mrs. Dugdale
said, 'Yes—and who shall I say said it?'

The signing of the Armistice could not fail to awake in
the hearts of all those who had suffered bereavements during the war a feeling of renewed loss and heartache: and
as I watched from the window of my office the gathering
on Horse Guards Parade as the bells rang out, I felt that
elation and excitement were strangely absent from my
mind. I found that L.G. was also suffering from depression,
due no doubt to the reaction after such long anxieties and
the demands upon his vitality. He refused to 'celebrate' in
the evening, dining quietly at No. 10 with two or three of
his colleagues, which included, I think, Mr. Bonar Law and
Lord Birkenhead.

There was a heavy load still upon his shoulders. There
was the election, and there was the Peace Conference: and
first of all, there were arrangements for both to be made.

The 'Coupon Election', as it has been called, resulted in a
holocaust of the Liberals. This was the last thing that L.G.
had wished, but he was in a dilemma. Party politics had
been brushed aside by him during the war years. As Mr.
Bonar Law himself said:

He thought of nothing, and aimed at nothing, and hoped for nothing, except the successful end of the War. That was his life and he had no other life. In good report and evil they saw what courage meant. It was not merely the courage of dogged determination, but was accompanied by a brilliant hopefulness which was an example and inspiration to everyone who worked with him.

And now fate played him a strange trick when a grateful country, by annihilating his Liberal opponents, made it impossible for L.G. ever to get into office again as a Liberal. But what could he do? In constituencies where a Liberal stood, and a Coalition Liberal, as in the case I shall quote, he must inevitably give his support to the latter; and, moreover, wherever a Coalition candidate stood, whether Liberal or Conservative, he was obliged to support him, for the Government was appealing to the country as a Coalition.

But he was not happy in his heart that he should be forced to oppose so many Liberals, even though they had done their best to destroy him earlier. The full measure of their hatred is exposed in a letter written by Maynard Keynes, an Asquithian Liberal (later Lord Keynes), to his mother in April 1918, from Mr. Asquith's home at Sutton Courtney:

	The Wharf,
14th April, 1918	Sutton Courtney

. . . Politics and War are just as depressing, or even more so, than they seem to be. If this Government were to beat the Germans, I should lose all faith for the future in the efficacy of intellectual processes:—but there doesn't seem much risk of it. Everything is always decided for some reason other than the real merits of the case, in the sphere with which I have contact. And I have no doubt that it is just the same with everything else.

Still and even more confidently I attribute all our misfortunes to George . . . In the meantime old Asquith who I believe might yet save us is more and more of a student and lover of

slack country life and less and less inclined for the turmoil. Here
he is, extremely well in health and full of wisdom, and fit for
anything in the world—except controversy. He finds, therefore,
in patriotism an easy excuse for his natural disinclination to
attack the Government. People say that the politician would
attack, but the patriot refrains. I believe the opposite is true.
The patriot would attack but the politician (and the sluggard)
refrain.

It is a letter which I think Lord Keynes' biographer was
ill-advised to quote. L.G., in asking Keynes to become a
delegate to the Peace Conference had no idea that he was
giving treachery its opportunity.

There was no doubt about the election result, but L.G.
was staggered and depressed at the size of the Government's majority. Nevertheless, he felt that he had behind
him the support of the country at the forthcoming Peace
Conference, and with the war and the election behind him
he entered with enthusiasm into the task ahead—a formidable one indeed.

In the middle of the preparations for the election I committed a terrible indiscretion. Sir Alfred Mond (later Lord
Melchett) was the Coalition Liberal candidate for West
Swansea, and one of his opponents wrote a charming letter
to L.G. asking for his support and saying that he agreed with
L.G.'s policies. Very carelessly, and without ascertaining
the real position, and certainly without realising that it was
Sir Alfred Mond's constituency, I wrote him a polite reply
and wished him well on L.G.'s behalf. This message was
immediately printed and issued in an election pamphlet
and Lord Reading, whose son had married Sir Alfred
Mond's daughter, came to see L.G. with a natural protest
from Sir Alfred Mond. I was asked for an explanation of my
inexcusable *gaffe*, and could give none except carelessness,
coupled with a most abject apology. I do not believe that
the Mond family ever believed that my action was not deliberate, and I was very *mal vue* with them thereafter. L.G., though

justifiably annoyed with me for causing him embarrassment, was, I think, secretly amused at the contretemps. He was by no means happy at this 'coupon' arrangement, which was being managed by his Whips, of whom the chief, Freddie Guest, a cousin of Churchill, had distinct leanings towards the Conservatives.

During the election Sir John Reith was busy with his broadcast programmes. He had been working hard on this development and L.G. had given him great encouragement. He sensed that Reith was a genius, though an extremely difficult person to deal with. He brought in F.E. to assess the new wireless possibilities, and F.E. pronounced strongly in favour of giving Reith his head. We all know the results.

Sir John and Lady Reith invited me with great courtesy to their flat to hear for the first time a broadcast, which was one of L.G.'s election speeches.

10

Versailles (Part 1)

After the anxieties and restrictions of the war, the Paris Conference was awaited with pleasurable anticipation. L.G. had been against Paris as a meeting-place, judging—rightly, as it turned out—that delegates would be too much at the mercy of the French press. But his objections were overborne, President Wilson himself favouring Paris, and arrangements began for the accommodation of the delegates and their staffs.

Seldom can there have been such a glittering gathering of international personalities on any occasion. Famous statesmen from every country were there at one time or another, with their political, military, and naval representatives. It was important that in this redistribution of Europe—and other continents!—the interested parties should be on the spot.

The Dominion representatives were all there, each taking his place in turn at the conference table. It was L.G.'s delight to watch Mr. Hughes, of Australia, hanging on the words of President Wilson, waiting to pounce or harry as the opportunity presented itself—pretending to be more deaf than he really was in order to rattle the President in his preachings. And, of course, General Smuts was there all the time, except when he went off on hurried missions to some spot in Europe where trouble had broken out again. As I have said, L.G. and Smuts understood each other

144

perfectly, and L.G. valued his help and advice. The jobs he gave to Smuts to do were legion—missions to headquarters, to South Wales to settle a strike, to Switzerland to investigate a peace offer, to Ireland to negotiate on the Irish Settlement, the studying of the organisation of the new Air Force; these were but a few of the tasks that the genius of Smuts tackled successfully. 'I have no hesitation,' L.G. wrote in his memoirs, 'in saying that Smuts was the ablest man that came to our help from the outside Empire. . . . He had rare gifts of mind and heart. Of his practical contribution to our Councils during those trying years it is difficult to speak too highly.'

A less self-seeking man it would be hard to find; and when he offered, as he did in a letter to L.G. in 1918, to take command of the American Army newly arrived, it was not because of any self-seeking on his part, but because he was doubtful of Pershing's ability to handle his army readily in this unfamiliar type of conflict, and he thought that the Americans, while they would not accept a British or a French commander, might be willing to accept him. It was *victory* that mattered, and if American *amour propre* could be satisfied, Smuts thought he could render a service to the Allied cause.

I don't think, however, that the suggestion ever went further than L.G., and I wonder how the Americans would have reacted to it!

A difficult man sometimes? Yes, indeed, in so far as he refused to compromise, or lower his standard, or tolerate humbug. And since the Treaty of Versailles *had* to be a compromise peace, because of the warring elements among the Allies themselves, he was difficult there. I always think that it was a protest that on the night of the signing of the treaty, when the celebrations were taking place in the Majestic Hotel, Smuts was not to be found, and eventually was discovered joining in the dance of the hotel staff which was taking place downstairs!

K

Smuts retained his affection and admiration for L.G. right through to the end. In the early thirties, when Smuts was on a visit here from South Africa, he was very anxious for Baldwin to include L.G. in his Cabinet because he saw that our foreign policy was wrong and he feared for the result. He wrote to Baldwin to that effect, but for obvious reasons Baldwin did not view the suggestion with favour. His comment was: If L.G. were to enter the Cabinet, there would be only one place for him—at the head of the table!

Ten years later, when the Second World War was in progress, and my husband was getting old, Smuts came to see us in our Surrey home, and I remember them both sitting together by the big library windows there, gloomily wondering what would be the outcome of it all. They were both pessimistic, not so much about victory, but about the world afterwards.

Smuts was that very rare person in history—a combination of the visionary and the man of action. To my mind Epstein has grasped this in his statue of Smuts in Parliament Square—in the eager, forward-thrusting figure. Sometimes I think that Smuts and Albert Schweitzer are comparable figures in their single-minded devotion to the benefiting of mankind; both scientists, both holy men, visionaries, but with a practical application of their visions to the needs of the world and their fellow creatures.

Louis Botha was another South African personality, as different as could be from Smuts physically, yet as bold, loyal and able. He was a man of striking physical appearance, strength of character and general impressiveness. Contrary to Smuts who was tall and lithe, he was broad and heavy-looking. Smuts spoke perfect and fluent English; Botha's English was heavy and halting, yet he never failed to impress and to drive his point home. He was a grand figure and a grand man, who won the respect and admiration of all who met him—a great man of Empire, but staunch to Boer traditions and Boer ways. He did not seem to fit in to the surroundings of the Paris Conference quite as easily as his compatriot, Smuts, who had spent more time in sophisticated surroundings than had Botha, and who also spoke better English. It would be difficult to find two men of the same nationality so totally different, in appearance, in outlook, in judgment. Both had been soldiers, but where Smuts had the quick intuition of the statesman, Botha had the common sense and courage of the man of action. I think that of the two L.G. had the greater admiration for Botha—perhaps because Smuts at the Peace Conference was opposed to L.G. in some of the latter's decisions, and did not hesitate to say so. Botha, on the other hand, took the broad common-sense view, realised the difficulties with which L.G. was confronted, and saw the necessity of compromise in some situations in order to get his way in others. And although Botha's English was halting, he and L.G. seemed to understand each other instinctively and enjoyed each other's company.

When the question of the German colonies was under discussion and the French were for annexation, some of the Dominion Premiers were for keeping their gains rather than transfer them to a mandatory under the League of Nations. At one time the conference appeared to be breaking up on this question, so strongly did some of the Dominion Premiers feel on the matter. L.G. begged them not to wreck the conference and, finally, Botha, in a masterly speech, urged co-operation, and begged them, by giving way on smaller things, to meet the difficulties and make the bigger ideal possible.

L.G. said to me after: 'It is difficult to convey the power of General Botha's speech by a mere summary of it. Behind it was the attractive and compelling personality of this remarkable man . . .' He went on: 'President Wilson told me immediately afterwards that it was one of the most impressive speeches to which he had ever listened.' The crisis was over.

He was a very great help to L.G. at Versailles in curbing the desires of the French for a punitive Peace Treaty. L.G. used to say: 'I never met a man who seemed to be such an embodiment of wisdom in speech and action. *He was a truly great man.* Throughout the Paris deliberations he stood for a settlement that would leave no roots of bitterness behind.'

At the end of May 1919 the Peace Council discussed modification of the terms which had been offered to the Germans and which the Germans were resisting. Botha was sitting next to Milner and he turned to him and said, 'This is the seventeenth anniversary of the Treaty of Vereeningen. On that occasion it was moderation that had saved South Africa for the British Empire.' He (Botha) hoped on this occasion that it would be moderation which would save the world.

Amongst the picturesque visitors to Paris for the conference were the Indian princes. The Maharajah of Patiala—a young man already looking middle-aged because of his beard and, possibly, the 300 wives and concubines which he was reputed to have brought with him—and the Maharajah of Bikanir, a figure out of the *Arabian Nights* with his jewel-studded turban, his exceedingly handsome countenance and upright bearing—these two were the representatives of India, stately and aloof, living in a world of their own but the objects of much deference and attention. At the other end of the scale, equally aloof because no one paid them any attention, were two lone figures—the Armenians (often referred to as the Armenian atrocities) who remained in Paris in the hope of being called before the Council to plead the cause of their ill-fated country.

Another outstanding delegate was M. Paderewski. It was obvious that he was not so much politician as patriot, and it was rather in the latter category that he attended as Prime Minister of the new Poland. But although he was present on many occasions at L.G.'s flat in the Rue Nitôt, he could never be persuaded to touch the piano. I wrote to my father:

There is a dance tonight at the Majestic and the R.A. Band at present in Paris is going to play. They gave a concert on Monday at the Trocadero and the P.M. took Paderewski there. After the performance a heavy-looking Frenchman came up to Paderewski and shook him by the hand. 'I wanted to tell you,' he said, 'that I think you have got a very good band.'

The flat which had been placed at L.G.'s disposal was used as a meeting-place for a great many of the more informal conferences, and being at the other end of the street from the Majestic Hotel, where the British delegation was housed, was most conveniently situated. Megan, who accompanied her father to the conference, was naturally expected to share the occupation of the flat, but she soon decided that life there would be dull in comparison with the conditions prevailing at the Hotel Majestic, and obtained permission to share my room there instead. It was difficult for me to add the duties of a chaperone to those of a secretary, but a chaperone was the last thing Megan wished for. She became a very popular figure at the Majestic, and enjoyed to the full the gaiety and attractions which Paris offered at that time. Later, however, L.G. decided that a school in Paris was a more suitable place for his sixteen-year-old daughter, and her contacts with the Peace Conference were continued from that quarter.

One of the most interesting of the delegates to the French people was, of course, President Wilson. At first his presence there was hailed with delight. He was lent a beautiful mansion opposite, as it happened, to L.G.'s flat. It was guarded by American sentries, and everything was supplied for his comfort. The fact that no one was allowed to walk down the path on the side of the President's house incensed the pedestrians, and there were lively disputes at the street corners between the gendarmes and irate Parisians who objected to their right of way being taken from them—and by an American! But gradually as the conference wore on and it became clear that he was not supporting the exaggerated claims of the French—that he was, in fact, opposing them very strenuously—the murmuring against him began. And before very long his popularity had decreased to such an extent that the lady who had lent him her villa demanded it back, on the grounds that the conference was lasting longer than had been expected. Wilson consulted L.G., who was indignant, and advised the President to refuse to move out.

L.G.'s popularity also waned with the French for the same reason, but when asked he refused flatly to give up the apartment, which had been lent him, he insisted, for the duration of the conference. The lady who owned it, however, retaliated at the end of the conference by sending him a large bill for dilapidations!

In a letter written to my mother as the conference was progressing I said:

The French of course are very panicky about Germany, as you can well understand, but they would like to cripple Germany for ever. *The Times* and the *Daily Mail* out of personal spite on the part of Lord Northcliffe are trying to breed bad feelings between L.G. and the French, but I hope people will understand what it means. Lord Northcliffe is at Fontainebleau and is directing his attacks from there. When the Peace Conference is over I hope the P.M. will get a little of his own back.

The fact was that Lord Northcliffe, who, it appeared, had expected to be invited as a delegate to the Peace Conference, and was furious when his repeated demands to be included were, as they had to be, rejected, began to attack its proceedings savagely and indiscriminately, with L.G. as his particular target. He had as his allies practically the whole of the French press, and so greatly did these combined attacks hinder L.G. in his peace-making that he returned in April to the House of Commons to attack Northcliffe personally in return and to defend himself. It was said that this speech of L.G.'s in the course of which, referring to Northcliffe, he tapped his forehead to indicate insanity, hastened the death of the journalist. L.G., of course did not know at the time that his enemy had already shown signs of the disease which killed him.

If the walls of the flat in the Rue Nitôt could have spoken they would have had a far more interesting story to tell than any history book. Many of the most important conferences between the Big Four were held there, and delicate negotiations which it would have been impossible to discuss in the full conferences were settled here beforehand. The four great Allied nations, as represented in the persons of L.G., Clemenceau, Wilson and Orlando, thrashed out—or tried to do so—their claims, which were frequently conflicting to points which were irreconcilable. Often the more polished forms of civilised expression were swept aside, and the raw, blunt words of men who were fighting for supremacy—amongst allies—took their place. In short, the Big Four did not shrink from telling each other a few home truths. Sometimes Britain and America made common cause against France, sometimes France and Britain against America. As often as not, all three combined against the Italian claims, and poor Orlando was often in great distress.

One day in June the conference shifted to President Wilson's house opposite. The luncheon hour arrived and L.G. did not return and no message was received. The drawing room of the flat looked straight down on to the windows of the American ground-floor rooms opposite. Our servant, Newnham, who had come to Paris to look after L.G. personally, and who acted as butler also, was looking out of the window to see if there were any signs of L.G. returning. Suddenly he called me to the window, and pointed: 'Look at that, miss,' he said excitedly. 'Would you believe it! *He's crying.*' And, true enough, there was Signor Orlando, leaning against the window, a large handkerchief pressed to his face. It was the morning of the fateful decision about Fiume, which the Italians claimed as their port. President Wilson flatly refused to agree to the claim, and after the conference the Italians packed up and went back to Rome.

All these events have been described at great length by my husband in his memoirs, and others, including Colonel House, who was Wilson's *alter ego* at the conference, have also written their accounts. L.G. has told of the intransigence of the French with which he and Wilson were confronted at every turn; of the intrigues that were carried on all the time between the French and the smaller European states, who were being 'persuaded' to support French policy in return for promises of material gains. Benes, the Austrian Prime Minister, for whom L.G. formed a dislike during the conference which was never modified, was the leader of the small nationalities who were thus persuaded to support French policy. L.G. contended that the concessions won by the French as a result of their votes helped to plant the seeds of the Second World War. Benes was to him 'the little French jackal' and when in the Second World War he was driven from his country, L.G. felt that he had only got what he deserved.

In addition to the great protagonists of the conference, the Rue Nitôt saw many other distinguished figures. L.G. loved entertaining, and here he was able to entertain to his heart's content. The diligent French cook who belonged to the flat must have been hard put to it to cater for lunches and dinners for people who numbered anything from six to sixteen —sometimes more—not to mention breakfast parties, which were something quite new to her! We discovered that she did all her own shopping, going out to the market at six o'clock every morning to find the ingredients for the lovely food which she set before us. After the short commons which we had experienced in England during the war this seemed indeed the food of the gods.

To the luncheon parties, in addition to political personalities, came such varied figures as Sarah Bernhardt, now old and almost grotesque with her great gold wig, though still full of vitality and gaiety; Paderewski, with *his* mane of hair, delightful and humorous, the artist not entirely extinguished by his political responsibilities as Prime Minister of the new Poland, although, as I have said, he stubbornly refused to play the piano for us. L.G. and he were entirely sympathetic in temperament, and a good deal of banter passed between them at first as to the exact proportions which the new and liberated Poland should assume. Poland in her chequered history had had so many partitions and so many different boundaries that the problem was: Of what did the authentic Poland actually consist?

When Paderewski became grandiose in his demands, L.G. rather mockingly agreed that 'there were few provinces in a vast area, inhabited by a variety of races, that Poland asking historically her inheritance of which she had been reft, could not claim'. It all depended, in his opinion, as to how far you were to go back in history, and, of course, if you went back far enough there would be no Poland at all!

Had it been left to L.G. and Paderewski the boundaries might have stood up to subsequent events, although later on at one session of the conference L.G. and Paderewski faced each other in angry opposition. Other personalities had intervened, notably Pilsudski, and the Poles, arrogant in their newly found independence, decided to take the bit within their teeth and assert their rights to even wider boundaries. Here again were sown more seeds for the war-that-was-to-be, and here again when Poland was overrun, first by Germany and then by Russia, L.G. felt that she had only got what she deserved. In his memoirs of the peace treaties he wrote in 1937:

I knew that a time would come when Germany would respond to the cry of its exiled people and seek to restore them to the Fatherland by force of arms.[1]

1. *The Truth about the Peace Treaties* (Gollancz) Vol. II, p. 991.

Foch was another visitor to the Rue Nitôt. Quiet and reserved, he did not care for social occasions, and L.G. did not
make the mistake of inviting him to these. But Foch and
Henry Wilson provided a company in themselves. The two
were old friends, saw eye to eye, and together had been in
the Allied victory. Both Celts (Foch was a Breton and Henry
Wilson an Irishman), they were almost each other's opposite in character—Foch solid, withdrawn, religious almost
one would think to the point of mysticism—Henry Wilson
gay, mercurial, effervescent, lovable, the best company in the
world; charming, volatile, brilliant, insincere, a born in-
triguer. They both disliked Robertson, whom Foch used
laughingly to call, 'Le Général Non-Non, because of his obstinate obstructiveness; and the supercession of Robertson
had been a necessity in order that the two great generals
should work together without hindrance.

Wilson and General Macready loved to 'play' the 'frocks'
(politicians) at the height of the Irish trouble, and would
chortle with glee afterwards if they succeeded in discom-
forting the Cabinet, but L.G. was a match for them both.
Wilson's insincerity is exampled by the subsequent revelation that while he was writing fulsome letters to L.G. and
receiving honours from him he was at the same time sneering at him in his diary. Wilson's recklessness is demonstrated
by the fact that he refused to be 'tailed' by a detective: this
was responsible for his untimely death.

Of the Americans, Wilson only came to the flat on formal
business, with Lansing and House, but Pershing and Wilson's doctor, Admiral Grayson, came for more social
occasions. The latter enjoyed the music which we sometimes
had. There were some excellent pianists amongst the British
and American delegations, and Leila Megane, the Welsh
prima donna, would sometimes delight us with her singing.
Balfour also liked the evenings when there was music, but
he preferred the smaller, more intimate occasions.

One evening Nancy Astor brought Ruth Draper, who was

then in Paris, to see us and, of course, we were enchanted with her impersonations, as also with the charm of her character. I saw a great deal of Nancy in Paris, and she was kind and helpful to me. She came with me to Annezin when I went there to visit my brother's grave.

It is difficult at this stage to remember all the personalities that came to the Rue Nitôt during those months. I remember that the Belgian King, Albert, came once, to pay his respects to L.G. Clemenceau came to tea more than once. He eschewed more formal meals, but he loved the *langues de chats* which the cook at the Rue Nitôt used to make especially for him. He enjoyed them like a child.

As everyone in every country who liked to be 'in the swim' contrived to be in Paris at some time or other during that period, it can be imagined what a continuous, if changing, galaxy offered itself. Besides the statesmen concerned and their delegations, the military and the naval representatives, there were journalists, writers, artists, explorers. I had the honour to meet Gertrude Bell during her brief visit. Of the artists, Augustus John was easily the most picturesque personality. He held court in Paris, having been appointed as one of the official artists to paint the Peace Conference delegates. His parties became celebrated, but sometimes riotous, and I was disappointed when L.G. placed a veto on them as far as I was concerned. John himself pretended to be offended when I refused his invitations, and I have a plaintive letter which I received from him on the matter.

It was during the Paris Conference that I perpetrated one of my inexcusable *gaffes*. Lord Derby, who was our Ambassador in Paris, invited me to lunch to meet Geoffrey Dawson, the editor of *The Times*, and his wife. When I arrived at the Embassy on what I thought was the appointed day, it did not take me long to realise that I was not expected, and Lord Derby explained that it was for the *following* day that I had been invited. After making a humble apology I prepared to leave, but the Ambassador, with his natural

tact, said that he would forgive me only if I came the following day also, as Geoffrey Dawson was expecting to meet me.
So I stayed, and I shall always remember the very pleasant
hour we spent sitting in the charming Embassy garden after
lunch, talking of innumerable things. Lady Pembroke was
the acting hostess at the Embassy, and she also did her best
to put me at my ease, with her charm and *savoir-faire*.

In fact, the luncheon the following day was not nearly as
enjoyable as this one. I did not 'fall' for Geoffrey Dawson,
neither did I feel that he was impressed by me. But I shall
always feel grateful to Lord Derby for his kindness and understanding, and I could realise why so many people were
on his side when L.G. criticised him for shortcomings when
he (Derby) was a Minister—such as his term at the War
Office. I think he hated hurting people, and so sometimes
gave the wrong decisions: but his bonhomie and understanding made him a most popular personality and he was
widely loved.

Many members of the delegations came to my office in the
Rue Nitôt when they were disappointed with the way things
were going, to give me messages to pass on to L.G. One day
Keynes came to complain about the financial clauses of the
treaty, and to say that he was going back to London that
afternoon; the financial terms were far too heavy, he said.
The same afternoon the Governor of the Bank of England,
Lord Cunliffe, came to say that *he* was going back to London; we were letting off the Germans far too lightly!

T. E. Lawrence came in once or twice, a boyish, friendly
figure, suffering bitterly from his failure to get his terms for
the Arabs. He would talk to me about his adventures in
Arabia, tending, I thought, to be a little conceited over them
(as he had every right to be). I longed to help him, but I
knew that there was little chance of his dreams being realised. The Sykes-Picot Agreement, of which the political
heads knew nothing until long after it had been signed, had
'put paid' to them! The French were the instigators of the

arrangement, by which the Arab world was left literally in the wilderness. Poor Mark Sykes, such an able and charming British diplomat, was the tool of the French Minister and was shattered by the result of his unsuspecting negotiations. He died young, as a result, I think, of all his cares and disillusionment.

But Lawrence never gave up hope, and King Feisal, one of the most dramatic figures at the Peace Conference, trusted him. If Lawrence by much asking could have won the day, the matter might have been differently settled: he certainly persuaded me, by the facts and by the tremendous charm of his personality. But the French were at the Peace Conference too!

Professor Paul Mantoux, who was the official interpreter at the Peace Conference, a most able man, was an ubiquitous figure, a universal friend, much courted by everyone for his personal charm as well as for the interest of his personality. He had so many opportunities for advancement, but no one was more modest or less ambitious.

Admiral Jacky Fisher was another great personality in Paris at that time and would drop into my office with ideas for solving all difficulties. He often lunched or dined with us, either at the Rue Nitôt or at one of the lovely Parisian hotels or restaurants. The Duchess of Hamilton often came with him.

I wrote to my mother in April:

. . . Lord Fisher came to lunch yesterday and was most amusing. He told anecdotes for about an hour, until everyone was crying with laughter, and my sides ached. . . . It was a memorable meal with Lord Fisher in his best form.

I had known him since the days of the Dardanelles, when he would leave notes on my desk on large untidy pieces of paper, with enormous untidy characters on them in Fisher's best abusive style. The letter continued:

The atmosphere of Paris is certainly quite different from that of London, and also the P.M. has not so many minor worries, and consequently we don't suffer quite so much!

Fisher was a wonderful dancer, and I enjoyed my gay waltzes with him around the ballroom at the Majestic. (I had some very pretty dresses which helped to act as a tonic to me!) Lord Fisher never seemed to get tired, and after one dance he said to me: 'Don't you think that is pretty good for an old man of nearly eighty?'

In another letter to my mother I wrote:

Evan Morgan is now in Paris, whither he has come from Algeria. I am going with him and some other people tonight, to see *Samson and Delilah* at the Opéra. The P.M. has not been very well, but is better now. I think he has been working too hard. He never seems to get any rest. . . .

In fact it was the last time that I accepted an invitation from the future Lord Tredegar. He had found it difficult to secure good seats at the Opéra, and it did not take me long to realise, when we arrived there, that *L.G.* was the person Evan was expected to escort, *not me!* The red carpet was down, and important officials awaited the arrival of the distinguished foreign statesman, though being Frenchmen they made the best of the situation. But I was very angry.

His mother was always most kind to me, and often took me to the opera in London. Augustus John, who was a great friend of hers, used frequently to join us, and, of course, I enjoyed these parties enormously. On one occasion when we went to the opera Puccini was in a box with two Russian ex-archduchesses and I was taken along very shy and awkward to be presented.

On Sundays no conferences were held, and everyone had a day off. L.G. took the opportunity to visit the battlefields of France and Flanders. We would set out in several cars and drive through the scenes of desolation, the heaps of rubble which had been villages, and L.G. would reconstruct, with the help of the military who accompanied him, the various battles of the war. He had an obsession for battlefields. His great interest on visiting any country was to go to whatever battlefield presented itself, of whatever epoch, and reconstruct the fight. For him they lived again, and he made them live again. Even driving from Churt to Wales he would make a detour in order to pass by or through one of the famous battlefields of the Civil War, Newbury or Edgehill or Naseby: and he would explain in detail the disposition of the Cromwellian forces and the route which the loyalist forces took between Oxford and Newbury. The struggle was enacted all over again—the mistakes pointed out—the victories analysed.

When in Brussels after the war, on the way to the Spa Conference, he took us over the battlefield of Waterloo, interspersing his military discourses with quotations from Erckmann-Chatrian's story of the battle, recounting the story of the Marquess of Anglesey, who rode with the Duke on the battlefield. Suddenly the Duke turned to the Marquess and said: 'By God, sir, you've lost your leg!' 'By God, sir!' said the Marquess, looking down, 'I believe I have.'

He amazed the military by his grasp of military subjects. Some of them thought he would have made a grand general: he certainly would not have erred on the side of cautiousness; and he might, on occasions, have taken great risks with his troops. But they would have had an inspiring leader. He would, like Napoleon, always have thought of the 'one thing more' which would turn defeat into victory.

For myself, who have never been able to understand the elements of a battle, to whom plans for the disposition of troops convey absolutely nothing, L.G.'s enthusiasm produced no answering interest. I was unable to conjure up any

realistic picture at all: I was simply incapable of understanding. L.G. would naturally get impatient with me for my
seeming lack of interest in these great historical events: but
the only facts which registered with me were *who* had won
or lost, not *how*.

When he went to the United States in 1923 one of the
things which gave him the greatest satisfaction was his visit
to the scenes of the Civil War, and the battlefield of Gettys-
burg. He spoke with and questioned a veteran who had
fought under Stonewall Jackson, and would often tell of the
emotion of the old soldier in speaking of his chief.

But now, during the conference, the battlefields were
recent ones, and, as I say, every Sunday during the dreary
January of 1919 we drove through towns and villages which
were unrecognisable but for the sign-boards which indi-
cated their names: through country intersected with trenches
and rusty barbed-wire entanglements and swathes of
poppies. The language of Gwilym,[1] who had had enough of
these scenes under the terrible conditions of active warfare,
and who was inclined to resent having to give up his week-
end to this kind of entertainment, became on one or two
occasions unprintable. But for L.G. it seemed almost an obsession and he gloried in it. Later in the year we went to
Verdun, and were taken over the poppy-covered trenches
by a French general. I was indeed moved by a row of bayo-
nets which protruded from one line of defence, marking the
spot where French troops had had orders not to give way,
but to endure to the death, and had obeyed their orders.
L.G. had visited Verdun while the battle was raging in 1916,
and had talked with Pétain in the citadel. Now we lunched
there, and L.G. recalled the battle and all the heroism of
that campaign.

On the way to Verdun we had stopped at Rhèims to see the
battered Cathedral and its environs, and the mayor took us to
the cellars in the town and we were given champagne to drink.

1. L.G.'s second son, later Lord Tenby.

Sometimes the routine would be changed, and we would take a picnic to the enchanting village of Barbizon, which was hung with lilac and carpeted with lilies of the valley; or, on more than one occasion, to a fascinating retreat in the Forest of Fontainebleau. One Sunday Mr. and Mrs. Churchill came with us for a picnic, and we had a riotous feast, L.G. and Churchill cursing the French for their avarice and intransigence.

11

Versailles (Part 2)

Early in May 1919 L.G. realised that he must take definite
action to get the treaty terms decided. The French were stal-
ling on the financial clauses in order to make them as heavy
as possible and there was a danger that Germany might resort to strong, perhaps revolutionary, measures, which
would jeopardise any peace treaty.

He was impatient to get on with the treaty-making. He
had asked me to get together for him particulars of conditions on the Continent from various sources, and the result
was frightening. Everywhere, it was said, there was hunger
and the sort of privation that would lead inevitably to disease, and certainly to disaffection. General Plumer himself,
with whom I dined and who had been in command in
Berlin since the Armistice, told me that in Germany they
were really starving and that it was impossible to get clothes,
except paper ones. The people were listless and despairing
and were beginning to doubt whether peace would ever be
signed. He was particularly unhappy about the miserable
condition of the children, and was hampered in his work by
thoughts of this. The Germans, he said, were very civil to
the British, but had reached the point when they did not
take any interest in anything. He told me he could not
be responsible for his troops if children in Germany
were allowed to wander about the streets half starved.
The Allies were piling up hatred for the future; they were

piling up agony not for the Germans but for themselves. At the conference meeting next day, in the middle of the discussions on reparations, a fresh appeal came from Plumer:

Please inform the Prime Minister that, in my opinion, food must be sent into this area by the Allies without delay. Even now the present rations are insufficient to maintain life, and, owing to the failure of supplies from Germany, they must very soon be still further reduced. The mortality amongst women, children, and the sick is most grave, and sickness due to hunger is spreading. The attitude of the population is becoming one of despair, and the people feel that an end by bullets is preferable to death by starvation. All this naturally results in great activity by subversive and disorderly elements. Apart from the imminence of danger from the situation, the continuance of those conditions is unjustifiable. I request therefore that a definite date be fixed for the arrival of the first supplies.

Actually the telegram had arrived before the conference, but L.G., with his sense of the dramatic, had arranged for it to be handed to him during the proceedings. He was roused to attack the French Finance Minister Klotz, who was trying to hold up the conference and the treaty. There was a long discussion, in the course of which Clemenceau, who supported Klotz, said that food would certainly not come from France. In a word, he was being asked to betray his country, and that he refused to do. However, 'after a little more persuasion', as L.G. says in his memoirs, and, indeed, ridicule of Klotz, it was arranged to send food to Germany and Austria.

This was only one of the many occasions on which L.G. had to fight the French. No wonder he became unpopular in France! He was always better in attack than in defence. Like Foch, he held that the *best* defence was *attack*, and he would often, knowing that an attack was impending, seek grounds for a quarrel with his opponent in order to attack him first and cut the ground from under his feet.

L.G. decided that the deadlock must be solved, and he retired to Fontainebleau to analyse the position and draw up the essentials of a peace treaty which the conference would accept. He took with him Philip Kerr, Hankey, Henry Wilson and General Smuts, and a document was framed which embodied the terms of peace to which the British Empire could subscribe. After the exchange of long documents, and some more conferences, in which Marshal Foch was very vocal on the subject of the occupation of the Rhineland by the Allies, the conference accepted the Fontainebleau Document, as it was known, and the Germans were summoned to Paris to hear the peace terms.

The meeting with the German delegates took place at Versailles on May 7th, but it was unfortunate that Brockdorf-Rantzau, the head of the German delegation, was unable to stand up to read his reply, and this was attributed to Teuton arrogance. The real explanation was that the man was so nervous that he was physically incapable of standing. His answer was that the note would be considered with all goodwill and a reply would be forthcoming. On May 29th a memorandum was sent in reply and certain amendments suggested, and on June 1st, after two days' discussion, agreement was reached and the treaty signed on June 28th.

The signing of the treaty in the Galerie des Glaces at Versailles was one of those functions which one is glad to be able to say one attended, but which for the vast number of people is little more than a crowd, with something happening at the other end of the room. For those who were near the great table where the delegates put their signatures there was drama and triumph. But for the lesser officials like myself there was the knowledge that one was attending an historical function, even if the view of the proceedings was poor. Outside in the great Park there were the rejoicing crowds, and the fountains played and the sun shone and it was a great occasion.

L.G. used to say that the happiest time of his life was the six months he spent in Paris during the conference. The worry of the war was finished, and he had helped to bring it to a successful conclusion: the framing of the peace brought out all his arts and skill as a negotiator—he enjoyed the fray of the conference table: and in addition he was able to indulge to his heart's content in entertaining, which he loved and for which, almost for the first time in his life, he possessed complete and unrestricted facilities.

The Versailles Treaty has had rough handling over the years since it was framed, and even yet I do not think it has had a fair deal. It has been alleged that it was too vicious, that it was too lenient, that it was responsible for the rise of Hitler, that it was in fact responsible for all the evils that have since befallen Europe. None of these things is historically true. They have been denied categorically from time to time by serious contemporary historians and thinkers such as Sir Harold Nicolson, Sir Charles Webster and other unprejudiced writers.

But it is an extraordinary thing that the allegations persist until they are almost a legend. To misquote the old proverb: 'Give a treaty a bad name and hang the framers of it.' Nothing you can say or in this case *prove* to the contrary will alter the conviction: the treaty was denounced as a bad treaty. And this, as my husband said in his memoirs, was usually by people who had never even read it.

It is true that the treaty is not infallible. The framers of it were far too diametrically opposed in temperament and in their demands to secure anything but a compromise over many of the important issues. But in the first place there is one clause that the critics never refer to, and that is the one which provides machinery for amending any defects which might become evident in the course of time.

L.G. himself would not have denied that some of the decisions embodied in the treaty would sow the seed of future war if not corrected in time. He protested, but he was overborne. Later in the House of Commons L.G. defended the treaty in the following words:

I do not claim that the Treaty is perfect in all respects. Where it is not perfect, I look forward to the organisation of the League of Nations to remedy, to repair, and to redress.

The first blow which the treaty received was the defection of the United States of America from their undertaking to support the League of Nations. The other Allies had gone out of their way to agree to President Wilson's demand— for it *was* a demand—that the matter of the League of Nations should come first on the agenda, and the first month of the conference had been employed on this, much to the annoyance of Clemenceau, who did not disguise his contempt for the measure, or, for that matter, for the President himself. The old man was a complete realist, a natural cynic and there seemed to be no point of thought or outlook upon which he and the President could meet. When Wilson was pleading the cause of right against might, Clemenceau retorted: 'Might *is* right.' Clemenceau considered Wilson to be the essence of a humbug. He had no illusions even about his beloved France. He was aware, even then, I think, of the downward path that his country was treading. Once, when talking to L.G., he expressed a doubt as to whether the Revolution had been good for France in the long run. 'It destroyed,' he said, 'a great part of the cultured aristocracy —and it brutalised France.'

One felt sorry for this lonely old man until one began to be afraid of him. For through the haunting sadness of that look was the undaunted challenge of the warrior. He had a will of iron, he could be ruthless and unbending even with himself. The stories of his cynical agnosticism were many. A nun who nursed him with devotion during illness asked him to say a prayer for the soul of the Archbishop of Paris, Archbishop Amette, on his death. The reply to this request was: 'If the good God does not know what to do with the soul of Archbishop Amette without asking Georges Clemenceau, I am afraid I cannot help Him.'

But the laugh in these matters was not always on Clemenceau's side. Next to his house in Paris stood a convent, and in the garden of the convent stood a large tree, which Clemenceau disliked, for it blocked the light from his windows and he could not see the sky. One day he saw that the tree had been cut down, and the Mother Superior was thanked on M. Clemenceau's behalf but asked why she had made this sacrifice. 'Well,' was the reply, 'we could not bear the idea of anything standing between M. Clemenceau and Heaven.' Clemenceau, in sending a reply of thanks to the Mother Superior, was unable to resist beginning his letter as follows: 'Holy Mother—for so I think I can now describe you since it is you who have shown me the light . . .' Nevertheless it was the Church which largely contributed to his downfall and his levity upon religious matters doubtless was remembered.

After the Treaty of Versailles had been signed L.G. returned to London immediately. The King sent his own carriage to meet the train at Victoria Station, and L.G. had a triumphal progress to Downing Street. Someone flung into the carriage a wreath of bay leaves, and this now hangs in the little museum at Llanystumdwy.

*   *   *   *   *

L.G. needed a holiday, however, and a house was taken for him at Deauville, overlooking the sea. It was not an ideal place for a Lloyd Georgian holiday, and he never once went to partake of the particular brand of gaiety which Deauville provided. He had, however, his own friends at the villa, and there was no lack of gaiety there, in the intervals of work—for although the treaty with Germany had been signed, the other treaties, with Austria, Turkey, etc., were still in course of preparation. At home, too, the troubles of peace were becoming apparent. It followed, therefore, that the house party at Deauville (Manoir de Clairefontaine) included many of L.G.'s Ministers—Mr. Balfour, Sir Eric Geddes, Sir Robert Horne, Sir Hamar Greenwood, and others. Mr. Bonar Law came over for a short stay. Nancy Astor was also of the party, and Lord Riddell, of course. In the evenings everyone relaxed. We had music—solo and chorus—and everyone was obliged to contribute something. Geddes' *chef d'œuvre* was 'Roses of Picardy', which he sang with much gusto and enjoyment, and gave L.G. the opportunity for a great deal of teasing. I think Mr. Balfour was the only one who was excused a contribution, but it was a delight to watch his detached figure gazing with curiosity and amused tolerance on the efforts of the other members of the party. His astonishment reached its climax when Nancy Astor and Ernest Evans (one of L.G.'s staff) performed an apache dance, which ended in Nancy flinging herself, after a series of cartwheels, into the lap of Lord Riddell.

Lord Allenby, his Palestinian laurels still fresh upon him, also visited L.G. here to discuss the mandates and treaties for the Near East which had yet to be settled.

The happy tenor of our holiday was somewhat disturbed by a grim incident. We were seated one day after lunch on the terrace when a woman, draped heavily in black, ascended the steps and approached L.G. She was, it appeared, the owner of the house (the name had not been divulged, as the renting had been done through intermediaries) and her son had been condemned to death for traitorous activities. She had come to plead with L.G. for him to intervene with the French Prime Minister, M. Millerand, to pardon her child. He was young, very weak, and had no doubt been the dupe of more able men than himself, but he had nevertheless been tried and condemned as a traitor. One word from L.G., said his weeping mother, could save his life. It was, of

Frances Stevenson at Churt, 1936

Constable of Carnarvon Castle

On the farm at Churt, 1938

Orchard scene, 1943

At Churt, after marriage, 1943

Churt, 1944

course, impossible for L.G. to intervene in the matter, but
it shook him a good deal, and we did not remain at Deauville for very long after that. On his return to England L.G.
went up to Wales to finish his recuperation from the arduous
six months of peace-making. He returned in the autumn to
an accumulation of domestic (political) difficulties.

One of L.G.'s chief worries at this time was the attitude
of Mr. Churchill on the Russian situation.

It was inevitable that two men, both moulded on so grand
a scale, and with such different backgrounds and outlook,
should disagree strongly on many things and many policies.
It had been apparent in 1911–12, before the First World
War, when Churchill was for a big Navy, and L.G. wanted
to spend money on the social services. Now it became acute
over the vexed question of Russia—and history alone will
decide which of them was right, for L.G. and Churchill
were constitutionally and politically poles apart in their
thinking on this matter.

L.G. had thought that the War Office, *once the war was
over*, would be a safe department for Churchill, and he had
not foreseen the possibilities which Russia would offer for
Churchill's warlike propensities. It soon became apparent,
however, that the latter was contemplating warlike operations on behalf of the anti-Bolshevik forces in Russia. After
all, what was the use of being Secretary of State for War
with no war? Churchill could see no reason at all why we
should not link up forces with the White Russian General
Yudenitch, and conduct a war for liberating Russia.

From the beginning of the Russian Revolution in 1917,
L.G., with his capacity for long-term thinking, had realised
that once the new regime had established itself there was
no hope whatever for the White Russian Army. He did not
share Churchill's fine opinion of Yudenitch. He took the
view that the Russians did not want to be liberated—that
the greater part of the population were enthusiastic for the
new regime. The old order had changed once and for all,

and had given place to the new, and L.G. considered that
we should remain true to our traditional foreign policy, and
recognise the right of other countries to choose their form
of Government, even if it were a Bolshevik one. He considered the anti-Bolshevik obsession of Mr. Churchill
wrong and dangerous, and that any further military adventures in Russia would be waste of time and money that we
could ill afford.

When, therefore, he received while he was at Deauville a
long memorandum from Churchill outlining fresh enterprises in Russia he became angry. We had already spent
since the war £100,000,000 in Russia, with no results.
It was time to give Churchill a good rap over the knuckles
for his warlike schemes, and to remind him that the Secretary
for State for War had in fact other functions than conducting
wars. What the country wanted was to cut down military
expenditure, not to increase it. Let the Russians fight it
out amongst themselves; it was not for us to intervene.

L.G. and Churchill remained diametrically and obstinately opposed to each other on Russian policy, and on the
question of the recognition of the new Russian Government. L.G. continued to work,with many setbacks, for an
understanding with Russia, realising the vital importance
of not quarrelling with this vast country, and the folly of
trying to stem the flood which had been let loose by Lenin.
But he was hindered and opposed at every turn by his own
colleagues and by his Allies the French. And when, in 1922,
L.G. announced his intention of attempting to treat with
the Russians at Genoa in the hope of furthering the peace
of Europe, Churchill did his best to wreck the plans for the
forthcoming conference, and Poincaré succeeded by subtle
means in torpedoing the conference itself.

After the Peace Conference there was naturally a desire
to return to pre-war conditions—those days which have
never returned. Some of the reforms which L.G. contemplated were in fact carried out—Women's Suffrage, Home

Rule. But he met with bitter disappointment in other directions: his programme for land reform was cut down drastically, much to the chagrin of his Minister of Agriculture, Lord Lee; and his education plans were severely curtailed, to the disappointment of Mr. H. A. L. Fisher, the Minister for Education. The Geddes Axe did its work ruthlessly, to the delight of the Tories and the dissatisfaction of the Liberals.

Meanwhile London hostesses were also striving to bring back pre-war conditions into a post-war world. The great houses were thrown open again, there were balls and house parties, but a certain vulgarity and lack of discernment crept into entertaining, due perhaps to the large fortunes which had been made during the war, and partly perhaps to the emancipation of the young.

L.G. was in much demand by the hostesses of Mayfair, and was regarded all the more as a prize because he was so difficult to 'land'. But much as he loved pleasant companions, L.G. could not and would not bring himself to attend the large evening parties which were being given at that time. He preferred to arrange his own society, which invariably consisted of colleagues with whom he could discuss current problems. This did not rule out wit and laughter and badinage. But late nights did not suit him, and he was completely out of his milieu in grand assemblies. I found, too, that I could not stay up till the early hours of the morning, and, much as I enjoyed being invited to these parties, and meeting interesting people, and being generally made a fuss of (not, I realised, for my *beaux yeux*, but because I was the Prime Minister's secretary and supposed to have influence with him!), I found that I must limit my party going.

At one of these great parties, the coming-out dance of Lady Alexandra, the youngest daughter of Lord and Lady Curzon, I found myself sitting at the same supper table with a dark, shy young girl whose quiet beauty and grace

of bearing distinguished her from her gayer companions—
Lady Elizabeth Bowes-Lyon, a future Queen of England.
It was rumoured that the Duke of York had fallen in love
with her, and that his suit was favoured by his parents.

At one dance to which I was invited in 1920 I was introduced to the Prince of Wales and danced with him. He was
naturally much in demand by hostesses, and there was
great heart-burning because he displayed a preference for
certain houses rather than others. Sir Philip Sassoon, who
became L.G.'s Parliamentary Secretary, entertained him a
great deal, to the annoyance of certain more established
families who considered that they had a prior right to
royalty. But the Prince, then as always, knew what he
wanted, and refused to be dictated to in these matters.
Philip was an admirable host, gay but self-effacing, amusing
but thoughtful. He filled his houses with interesting and
prominent people, and entertained a great deal for L.G.,
both at Park Lane, his London home, at Trent Park, near
London, and at Lympne on the Kent coast, a house in an
unusual and beautiful setting. Philip's sister Sybil, now
Lady Cholmondeley, was often his hostess in these houses.
She was a wonderful and experienced hostess and the foreign statesmen who came to these conferences were greatly
helped by her understanding.

I was so frequently invited to Philip's parties and house
parties that this became a matter of discussion in the Lloyd
George family, none of whom were invited there. L.G.,
who came into the unpleasantness and was obviously
intended to do something about it, suggested that I should
ask Philip to invite Megan to some of his parties. I did so,
as I thought it would ease things at home for L.G. But
Philip was adamant. ' I ask to my parties,' was his reply,
'the people whom I enjoy having. I will *not* ask Megan.'
It would, of course, have been the thin end of the wedge.
The next demand would be that I should *not* be asked, if
she were there, as happened on some other occasions.

There were many criticisms of Philip's lavish hospitality, mostly, as I have said, by disappointed people, but having received much kindness from him I would like to defend, if defence is needed, a man whom it pleased to give pleasure and who did not rank self-advancement nearly as high as did some of those who criticised him. He was a host *par excellence*, and while he had many hangers-on, he had many real friends who greatly deplored his early death. Nancy Astor was a hostess who resented very strongly Philip's entertaining of L.G., and of the Prince of Wales. She herself gave large parties, in St. James's Square and at Cliveden, but L.G. would not attend them as Nancy would invite guests of her *own* choosing, not of L.G.'s. And the Prime Minster did not *want* to be entertained by Nancy, whose tongue was often employed in chastising his activities—and his friends! As to L.G., she clearly wanted advancement for her husband, Waldorf, a man of whose capacity L.G. did not think very highly at that time. And Nancy also wanted a step-up in their title. 'I am a viscountess,' she used to say to L.G. 'Why can't I be a countess?' But L.G. would not be bullied.

I was sorry for the rifts that Nancy created for herself. She was a stimulating person, a fearless politician, and she was extremely kind to me, especially helpful in my ignorance of London Society. I spent a lovely week-end at Cliveden, and began to understand how gracious entertaining could be combined with political manœuvres! But she never conquered her jealousy of Philip Sassoon's successful and very enjoyable parties.

Once the King's three sons were guests at one week-end party to which I was invited. The Prince of Wales was, I think, genuinely fond of Philip, whose houses provided him with the freedom which he so much enjoyed, and of which he was so often deprived elsewhere. Here he could relax and be an ordinary human being. He gave me a photograph of himself at that time. His photographs were almost always serious and wistful, but I asked him if he had one with a smile, and the photograph he gave me was taken, I think he said, during his visit to Australia: he said it was the only smiling one he had!

Philip Sassoon studied the tastes of his guests, and, being a perfect host, catered for them. For L.G. he often arranged to have music.

There was a party given by him at his house in Park Lane at which Chaliapin sang for us; and another at which the Prince of Wales was present and Ivor Novello played and sang his newest songs. At another party L.G. found himself talking to a most attractive red-headed woman, and was obviously greatly impressed by her. The conversation at an end, he came over to me and said: 'Who is that to whom I was talking?'

'Lady Lavery,' I replied. 'You know her.'

'Yes,' he said testily, 'but the last time I met her she had *black* hair!'

And one other dinner party I remember well, for I sat next to J. M. Barrie. I had heard tales of his extreme shyness, and, being shy myself, wondered how the conversation would go on this occasion. To my surprise he showed no trace of shyness, but talked gaily and amusingly the whole time. Some time afterwards I approached him asking him to help, if he could, a lovely young actress, the sister of a colleague (the late James Henderson Stewart), afterwards a Liberal M.P., and received the following reply from him:

Adelphi Terrace House,
Strand, W.C.2
31 March 1927

Dear Miss Stevenson,

Sad that you should think I may have forgotten you and the dinner where I was on your right hand and the table cloth was yellow and our host was Mr. Sassoon and I followed you about in a marble hall terrified lest I should be left all alone with rousing singers all around me. I have been to a concert since then, but otherwise all is quiet. Though you sadden me I am also rather elated to note that you don't know that I died long ago and am not one for ladies of the stage, who also frighten me very much, but I'll see Miss Stewart with pleasure though I'd rather you came yourself. I am going away on Saturday till just after Easter, when she will perhaps send me a line of reminder and the historic affair will take place.

With kindest regards,

Yours sincerely,

J. M. Barrie

The historic affair did take place and a large public enjoyed the acting of Sophie Stewart in her many roles.

12

More Conference Personalities

Early in 1920 L.G. decided that the next conference should be in the sun, and San Remo was chosen. We went in April by boat to Marseilles, and motored along the Riviera coast. Megan and I shared a cabin, and the voyage was very rough—so rough that L.G. himself, who scarcely ever succumbed to seasickness, was forced to keep in his cabin. Megan and I were prostrate and L.G. would send Newnham along to our cabin to inquire how we were. On one occasion Newnham returned to L.G. with the news: 'The young ladies are still in the perpendicular.'

At San Remo L.G. was joined by the other Prime Ministers and officials, and also the service chiefs. Briand was there with his Foreign Minister, Berthelot and Marshal Foch accompanied them. And as matters affecting Greece were under discussion, M. Venizelos also came.

Venizelos was a magnificent type of Greek, cast in the classical mould mentally and physically. L.G. and he took to each other from the first, by reason of their Liberal outlook, and by the fact that Venizelos recognised L.G.'s Gladstonian-cum-Byronic attitude to Greek problems and naturally welcomed it. L.G., having been bred in this tradition, supported Venizelos through thick and thin, and they remained firm friends, even after they both fell from office and power. Venizelos came to Churt to see L.G. when they were both out of office, and they afforded each other comfort in their mutual misfortunes.

On Megan's birthday (her eighteenth) L.G. gave a dinner party to which the distinguished delegates were invited. I remember that I sat next to Berthelot and talked to him almost for the first time at any length, and I quickly fell under his spell, for he was a fascinating talker.

We met a good deal at subsequent conferences. He would entrance me with his stories of his own personal experiences and his flights of fancy; and his French was a delight to listen to. He had travelled extensively in China, and his descriptions of his experiences there were enchanting. He wooed me mentally, weaving an exquisite web from mind to mind, speaking no word of love but taking infinite pains and being entirely indifferent to any onlookers. He was profound, amusing, cynical, erudite, provoking. No Englishman could possess this especial power of attraction: no Celt would be able to subordinate himself so completely to the task. The Frenchman is supreme in this art, and Berthelot was a master.

But I became alarmed, especially as lunching one day with two French journalists, Philippe Millet and André Géraud (Pertinax), the former said impertinently so that I could hear: '*On dit que Berthelot a fait une déclaration à Miss Stevenson.*' This, of course, was meant to draw me, but I passed it off with a joke. I realised, however, that we were being watched, and that the French, at any rate, would never believe that Berthelot and I only met in public. Fortunately the conferences were becoming too few and far between for matters to become embarrassing. I think Briand, the French Prime Minister and Berthelot's chief, must have sensed the position, for one morning, when the French had departed rather suddenly owing to disagreement at a conference in London, I found on my desk when I entered my office a large sheet of paper which was written in Briand's bold characters: '*Les Conférences Interalliées ne*

M

sont pas les champs de batailles les moins dangereux. Aristide Briand.'

The two French journalists I have mentioned, Philippe Millet and André Géraud (Pertinax), and their wives, were friends of mine. They obtained information available to no other journalists, but sometimes I was angry with them for their persistence and, as I judged it, unscrupulousness. They were both great admirers of L.G., if not of his policies, and I enjoyed meeting them at the conferences, although we pretended we were sworn enemies. Poor Philippe Millet died in Germany at a conference soon after the war (there was a suggestion that he was poisoned), but 'Pertinax' continued to attend the inter-Allied meetings. In spite of his annoying behaviour and his preposterous methods, I think 'Pertinax' was really Anglophile. Even after L.G. went out of office we always met when he came to London. We would argue violently, but I have a treasured little snake-skin belt which he shyly offered to me one day, with a note pinned to it: 'A piece of the skin of the snake "Pertinax".' I was sorry to lose touch with him during the second war, but I heard that after the fall of France he went to Canada.

In the summer of 1920 L.G. went with a small party of friends to the Villa Haslihorn on Lake Lucerne, lent him by the King of the Belgians when he heard that L.G. was going to Switzerland for a holiday. It was a pleasant villa, with room to house a number of people, but we were unfortunate in the weather, for it rained a good deal of the time. Maurice Hankey brought his young son Robin with him, a boy destined for high office in world affairs. The King of Greece, recently deposed, and his family were staying at an hotel in Lucerne, but they did not visit the villa, though we used to meet them in the town. The Mayor of Lucerne was invited to dine one evening, and it was a merry meal. Gwilym was also of the party, an amusing member. He had just become engaged and was in a particularly happy mood.

In the intervals we went for expeditions up the mountains, for picnics along the shores of the Lake, and we had lively amusing evenings. It was, nevertheless, a busman's holiday for L.G., for despatches were sent to him daily on the progress of home affairs, prominent amongst which was the condition of the Lord Mayor of Cork, who was hunger-striking to the point of death. If he died, L.G.'s life would, they said, be in danger. He did in fact die, and the guard around L.G. was strengthened, but the Irish menace remained and was not entirely obliterated by the treaty which was signed at the end of 1921, as was proved by the subsequent murder of Sir Henry Wilson on the one side and Michael Collins on the other.

During the Peace Conference members of L.G.'s family had procured for him a country residence near Esher, instead of the somewhat small and inadequate house at Walton Heath. The new house was commodious and comfortable, but it lacked a view. He did not remain there long, however, for very soon Sir Arthur Lee (later Lord Lee) made his generous gift of Chequers, in Buckinghamshire, to the Prime Ministers of Britain for an official country residence. It was a handsome gesture and a handsome property.

Arthur Lee was a quietly ambitious man of great persistence and a good deal of ability. Cultured, fastidious and individualistic, he had come to the Ministry of Munitions in its early days to help L.G. as liaison officer with the War Office and to co-ordinate the departments of the Ministry of Munitions, itself a very essential thing. When L.G. became Prime Minister, Lee became First Minister of Works and, after the War, Minister of Agriculture, which he still was when he presented Chequers to the nation. His wife Ruth, an American, was lovely and gentle and gracious. Her wealth, I think, had helped her husband along the paths he desired to pursue. It was she who had made Chequers the splendid home that it now was, perfect in all its appoint-

ments. She had intended it as a home for life for herself and
her husband, and at first, so we understood, was passionately opposed to parting with it during her lifetime. But
her husband's persistence won in the end and the transfer
was effected early in 1921.

Arthur Lee believed in wearing-down tactics. He reminded
me of a tag I had heard in my childhood, 'Constant dripping
wears away a stone.' If he wanted anything he would proceed
to wear away any barrier which stood between him and the
object of his ambition at that particular moment. I do not
suggest that his ambitions were not completely laudable and
legitimate. As often as not he would be seeking to improve
the efficiency of his department, or to devise a measure which
would help his chief. The Agriculture Bill which was
brought in under his auspices in 1920 was an admirable
piece of legislation, and had it been possible to carry it
into effect would have benefited agriculture enormously and
permanently. But the cost of its operation, like so many
other schemes at that time, ran counter to the necessity for
economy and the Geddes Axe reduced the proposals to
such an extent that Lee resigned from his post in despair.

Lee was made a peer after the gift of Chequers had been
completed. It was said that part of his object in giving
Chequers to the Prime Ministers of Britain was to ensure
that the Labour Prime Ministers of the future should have
surroundings which would have a civilising effect upon
them. I do not think that the Labour Prime Ministers who
have inhabited Chequers up till now stood in any need of
being civilised, but possibly Chequers had a civilising effect
on their guests. The thought, nevertheless, was a worthy
one, springing as it did from love of his country, one of the
most endearing characteristics of Arthur Lee. There can
be no doubt that Chequers has added to the amenities of
the Premiership. In L.G.'s time it enabled him to entertain foreign visitors under the most charming conditions,
for the house was endowed with an adequate income for

running it. Foch, Briand, Berthelot, the Crown Prince of
Japan, were amongst the distinguished foreigners who
stayed there, while there were constant gatherings of Cabinet
Ministers during the trying days of the Irish negotiations.
And as a sample of the kind of loyalty and affection which
L.G. could call forth I should like to add this document
which Arthur Lee of Fareham sent to *The Times* (though
it was not published) on L.G.'s death:

As one of the few surviving Members of Lloyd George's last
(Coalition) Cabinet, and the only survivor of the 12 Conservative Ministers who stood by him after the Carlton Club Meeting
in October 1922, may I respectfully controvert the apparently
prevalent misconception that his leadership was unanimously
repudiated by the Unionist Party at that time. There was, it is
true, a successful Palace Revolution against him, organised
mainly by aspiring Under-Secretaries and the adherents of
Bonar Law, but there was a not unimportant minority, headed
by Balfour, Birkenhead, Austen Chamberlain and others of his
colleagues, who protested publicly against the ingratitude shown
to their great Pilot who had led the country to Victory, and who
did not hesitate to sacrifice their own careers in his defence.
In their signed Manifesto of October 19th, 1922, they said:
'There has been no difference between us on matters of
principle or policy. Our personal relations with him have
throughout been close and intimate, but we are nevertheless
expected to say to him in effect "We do not differ from you at
the present moment; we have not differed from you during the
period of our co-operation. Your prestige greatly assisted at the
last election; we made the fullest use of it, but we have considerable differences in our Party. Your value to us is much less
than it was even a few months ago. We therefore propose to
you, in the most civil language at our disposal, that you should
relieve us of your embarrassing co-operation."
'We think it necessary to make it plain to our friends that we
cannot and will not consent to carry such a message to the
Prime Minister.'
One other misconception I desire to correct, after listening

to Dr. Thomas Jones' somewhat arid 'tribute', broadcast by the B.B.C. last night. He said in effect that while Lloyd George evoked admiration he seldom inspired affection. That to my knowledge was patently untrue. Although admittedly a hard master at times, and intolerant of inefficiency or failure, he was strangely forgiving of personal disloyalties and seemed never to harbour resentment against his political enemies, of whom he naturally, and fairly, made many in the course of his tempestuous career.

In his private life, however, and apart from his obvious love of home and family, he was capable of deep if discriminating friendship for those in whom he believed and trusted. At times, it is true, the swift reactions of his Celtic sympathies might prove somewhat disconcerting to his more stolid English intimates. As Lord D'Abernon once remarked 'Ll.G. is a grand man to go tiger hunting with, were it not for the possibility that, at the critical moment of the chase, he may conceive of the tiger as the underdog and go over to his side!'

Speaking for myself only, and after more than 30 years of close association, I can testify unreservedly to the warmth and sincerity of his friendship; to his all-pervading sense of humour which made him quite incapable of pomposity or self-importance, and to the deep but touching simplicity of his religious convictions and loyalties.

To him not only his countrymen, but lovers of freedom throughout the world, are now hastening to pay that tribute of gratitude which was too often begrudged him in his life-time, but let these human and endearing qualities of the man also be held in remembrance.

But we had our excitements at Chequers. One week-end, when the Hamar Greenwoods were staying there with us, it was discovered that there were I.R. slogans chalked on some of the small buildings in the grounds—but near enough to the house to arouse alarm amongst the Scotland Yard detectives who were very much concerned with the safety of L.G. from the Irish revolutionaries. They—the detectives—scoured the place and found a small band of young Irishmen who denied having anything to do with the chalked slogans, but whom the detectives locked up for the night. The next day it was stated that inquiries revealed that they were medical students from Dublin who 'wanted to see Chequers'—being in England on holiday. They were released and sent home, but L.G.—and certainly Hamar Greenwood[1]—were not convinced of their innocence. And when our chief detective stated that he had made a plan of Chequers for Scotland Yard, and that the map could not now be found, everyone was convinced that the young men had been up to mischief and were members of the I.R.A.

But although L.G. appreciated the facilities which this beautiful country house afforded him, he was never entirely happy there. For one thing, there was no view. The house—like so many old houses—was built in a hollow, and one had to climb up the hill behind to get the superb view over the Buckinghamshire plain. L.G. liked a view from his window. Moreover, he did not care for old houses. His spirit resented the atmosphere of preceding generations which seemed to cramp and encroach upon the essential independence of his nature which refused to be contained. It was something instinctive and innate and primeval which made him recoil from anything resembling the shackles of the past.

His feeling that Chequers was haunted by the spirits of previous occupants was endorsed by the rather peculiar behaviour of his Chow dog, Chong, who when L.G. was resting in the long gallery in the afternoon used to lie down beside him. L.G. was constantly roused by frantic barking from Chong, who would sit erect with her eyes fixed to one spot in the gallery. L.G. was convinced that it was a ghost that the dog could see, but in spite of his efforts to locate it, was never successful in proving its presence.

1. The Secretary for Ireland.

13

The Irish Treaty

In the spring of 1921 Mr. Bonar Law was forced to resign through ill-health. This was a great blow to L.G., whose affection for Bonar was real and deep. The partnership between the two men had been a perfect one; they were entirely complementary. I have in my possession a note placed on my desk at that time by Bonar Law in which he says that nothing but illness would have allowed him to leave L.G. I am sure that Bonar Law was reluctant to step into L.G.'s shoes later on (there is, indeed, record of this) when the Coalition Government fell, but it was expedient for the sake of his party and he was over-persuaded.

Now Austen Chamberlain took Bonar Law's place as Conservative leader, but there was not the same sympathy between him and L.G. as there had been with Bonar Law, and L.G.'s task was made that much heavier by the loss. Austen Chamberlain was a pale imitation of his famous father, but nevertheless a man of great quality and high principles. He concerned himself with the smaller and narrower points in the political landscape rather than with the larger view. He was a man of complete integrity, but totally lacking in inspiration, and as one of his colleagues put it, 'always playing the game and never winning it'. He was conscientious to the point of dullness, and his meticulous deliverances bored his colleagues. He was a faithful and dependable second to L.G., who, when Bonar Law resigned, missed Bonar's company, his sad sense of humour and his lovable characteristics.

By the time the summer recess approached in 1921, L.G. was tired out. Lord Dawson 'did not like the look of him', and advised a long holiday in a remote spot. L.G. demurred at this, saying that it was impossible for him to be away from the heart of things for any length of time, that he would worry all the time. 'Nonsense,' said Dawson, 'a holiday *must* last a month at least to be any use to you. The first week you will be quite certain that things cannot go on without you; the second week you will be a little less certain. The third week you will have come to the conclusion that they can; and the fourth week you will not care a damn whether they do or not. That is when you can feel quite sure that your holiday has done you good.'

Lord Dawson went even further, and found for L.G. a house near the sea at Gairloch in Ross-shire. Although in a lovely setting, opposite the island of Skye, and amidst that most beautiful scenery, it was thirty miles from the station, over a narrow winding road. That summer was dry and sunny everywhere else, but at Gairloch it rained every day. We got wet through playing golf, and one after another of the party went down with chills and temperatures. In addition, L.G. developed an abscess in his tooth, and a high temperature resulted. The local doctor, a charming Scot, did not feel equal to the emergency of tackling the Prime Minister's mouth, and Dawson, who was also in Scotland, was asked to come along. A visit to the dentist at Inverness ensued, with Dawson in attendance, and the raging toothache was cured. Dawson stayed on for some time, to keep an eye on L.G., and also on one or two other patients. I had a high temperature and had to remain in bed for several days. One morning, suffering from the depression which influenza drags in its wake, I was ruminating on my equivocal position in the house party, some of whose members inevitably regarded me with disfavour; and dwell-

ing on my sins in general, I decided to settle down and have
a good cry. I was in the middle of it when the door opened
and in walked Lord Dawson. He was a marvellous psy-
chologist, and took in the position at once. He could sum
up in a moment what was the trouble with anyone, and
prescribe the right treatment. I said I would like to go home,
but he said that was impossible, and would not help L.G.
at all. I was soon feeling that my troubles would quickly
disperse, and I was filled with gratitude to Lord Dawson—
as so many people must have been over the years. He was
a keen student of human nature, and of politics also. L.G.
had the highest opinion of him as a man, and often discussed politics with him. He thought Dawson's speech in
the House of Lords in support of birth control, and his
attack on Mrs. Grundy, showed great bravery.

L.G.'s troubles, however, were not at an end, for the
unemployment crisis, and the ever-present crisis of Ireland,
followed him to Gairloch. There was a deputation of
London mayors who insisted upon waiting on L.G. at
Gairloch to place suggestions regarding unemployment
before him: there were urgent despatches and correspondence on the subject of British proposals for an Irish
settlement, and of a conference in London between the
Irish leaders and the members of the British Government.
These culminated in a Cabinet meeting at Inverness, after
which L.G. went over to report to King George V, who
was staying at Moy Castle with the Mackintosh, and who
was naturally deeply interested in the Irish negotiations and
anxious to learn of their progress.

There was also a visit to Inverness to receive the freedom
of that borough—a wonderful address in a lovely casket
adorned with amethysts and cairngorms, now in the museum
at Llanystumdwy. There were visits from General Macready,
Sir Alfred Mond, and Sir Hilton Young (later Lord
Kennet) to advise on their respective responsibilities in
Ireland, on unemployment and on finance. The house was

not a big one, and the resources of the local hotel had to be called in. Dame Margaret, who would much rather have been amongst the Welsh hills than the Scottish, had her hands full, with these goings-on, in a strange house, especially as none of the visitors was particularly pleased at having to undertake this very long journey to the wilds during the summer recess.

And now, as an additional worry, once again Churchill assumed the role of critic of the Government, and wrote to L.G. complaining of the lack of progress on housing, unemployment, and of the cutting down of expenditure on Government schemes, especially housing. It was true that the expectations of the Coalition Government on trade expansion, which in 1920 seemed to be justified, had not materialised, and as a result unemployment had increased by leaps and bounds. As a result of the coal strike in the early spring the position had continued to deteriorate, but the Cabinet committee at Gairloch had been outlining measures which were destined to bear fruit towards the end of the year. On the heels of these decisions came Mr. Churchill's critical contribution.

It was not suprising that L.G. was not best pleased to receive this belated criticism from his colleague who had never shown any great interest in social reform, and who was now urging action which had already been decided upon.

In spite of these interruptions to L.G.'s holiday, he remained at Gairloch well into September. I do not think it was quite the holiday which Lord Dawson had visualised for his patient, but the latter seemed to derive sufficient benefit from it to deal with the arduous negotiations on the Irish Treaty which opened on his return to London.

I was able to return to London before the others because at this time L.G. was anxious to acquire a country home of his own, and we had for some time been looking for a suitable house in the right spot—that is, within easy reach of London and with a good view. L.G. *must* have a view, and this he did not have at Chequers. Moreover, he sensed that the Coalition could not hold together indefinitely—indeed, he thought it would come to an end much sooner than it did—and he wanted to be provided with a country home in that event that was not so far away as Wales.

But he realised already that there was no such thing as the right house in the right spot, and that it would mean finding a good site and building on it. We had heard, through the kind offices of Sir Howard Frank, of an estate that was to be sold in Surrey, and it fell to me to investigate the possibilities. I found myself on a glorious afternoon at the beginning of September on a Surrey hill-top, with pine and bracken and heather around, and it seemed to me that this was the appointed place. The auction was to take place almost immediately and I wrote to L.G. giving him full particulars and waxing eloquent on the advantages of the piece of land upon which I had fixed. He wired back asking me what was the aspect of the site and I, very rashly, and without proper investigation, but feeling certain that everything was perfect, replied that it faced south. Whereupon the order was given to go ahead, and the hill-top with its sixty acres of heath and bracken and pine was purchased.

Immediately on his return from Scotland, L.G. set out to view his latest purchase. Alas! the day was raw and misty—so different from the glorious afternoon on which I had first seen the property. The view was almost obscured by the mist, and when I pointed it out to him he took out his watch, which he always used for a compass, and said, 'It is due north.'

I was reduced to the verge of tears, and hurriedly considered whether I should be able to muster enough money to buy the land back from him, and leave him free to go on with the search; but my discomfiture was so great that he burst out laughing, and immediately proceeded to plan for the building of the house. 'We will call it "Bron-y-de",' he said, 'which means "breast (slope) of the south".'

That autumn, however, the whole of his time and energy were occupied in the negotiations which led to the signature of the Irish Treaty in December. These events are described in great detail in Lord Beaverbrook's book *The Decline and Fall of Lloyd George* (a title which I very much dislike). I should like to quote an extract from my diary at one of the most difficult moments of the negotiations (p. 115):

The note is being sent to the Ulster people who are coming to London today. D. (Lloyd George) feels that their resistance is hardening, but this makes him all the more pugnacious and determined to get a settlement *in spite of* Ulster if he can. He says he is inclined to get the S.F.'s (Sinn Fein) to accept Ulster's attitude of remaining separate and then point out to them (Ulster) that as they are not participating in the proposals which affect the South, they are not entitled to the lower taxation which Southern Ireland will obtain under these proposals. If the S.F.'s will agree to this, D. will put it up to Ulster and he thinks they will climb down.

D. is frightfully hurt about Bonar Law and the attitude he is taking. This is all the more extraordinary as Beaverbrook is fighting for D. and a settlement for all he is worth. D. says he knows he can only get him (Beaverbrook) for a short run, but it is worth while. *D. is seeing F.E. (Birkenhead) and Winston and Beaverbrook almost every night, so as to keep them on his side.* F.E. is fighting splendidly but D. says that Winston is contributing nothing and he is just not going over to the other side.

L.G. had a unique advantage in dealing with the Irish in that he himself was a member of a small Celtic nation whose aim, like that of the Irish, was Home Rule. His first appearance on a political platform was in company with Michael Davitt, the Irish champion of Home Rule, and Home Rule for Ireland had always been one of the chief planks in L.G.'s platform throughout his political career. He was therefore in strong sympathy, in the true sense of the words, with the men whom he was confronting, and they in their turn, though still suspicious and ever hostile, seeing that L.G.

was Prime Minister of Britain, must have sensed that L.G. understood their feelings and their case better than could any other member of a British Government.

These negotiations are a perfect example of L.G.'s determination to carry a matter through to a successful conclusion once he had embarked upon it: in other words of his supreme ability to get what he wanted, of his refusal to be beaten in face of overwhelming odds, of his inimitable art of negotiation. I know of no other man who would have continued even to hope for a settlement in view of such insuperable difficulties as were presented to L.G. in the summer and autumn of 1921; who would not have been daunted by the repeated setbacks. But he played his men with consummate skill; and while sticking to his point that the negotiations should take place on the British Governments terms, and not on those of the Irish, he gradually inveigled them into the conference room at Downing Street. Once there he continued to weave his spell until the treaty was signed. In the words of one of his friends, who presented him with a lovely piece of silver on the signing of the treaty, he was 'the solver of the insoluble'.

I remember sitting in my room next to the Cabinet Room through the night when the last stages of the treaty were being agreed to, and the signatures appended: wondering if even at this last moment the Irish representatives would not draw back, and all L.G.'s efforts be wasted. L.G. has himself told how Michael Collins signed 'like a man who was signing his own death warrant', as indeed he was. (He was murdered (in Ireland) the following year.) My colleagues, J. T. Davies, Geoffrey Shakespeare, and Ernie Evans, came in from time to time for a chat and to report any progress which they had gleaned.

Just before 3 a.m. L.G. himself came into my room, exhausted but triumphant, and handed me the treaty document with its historic signatures and seal.[1] 'Lock it up care-

1. December 6th, 1921.

fully,' he said, and I did so, in a despatch box. There it lay for many years, until I unlocked the despatch box on going through L.G.'s papers after his death, and discovered it again. The amazing thing was that during all that time it had never been asked for!

The achievement of the Irish Treaty revealed in full what it was that L.G. possessed which other men lacked, in the understanding of human nature, in the art of tenacious negotiation, to a degree which few men in history have exhibited. If one way closed, he opened up another: he was not afraid to *'reculer pour mieux sauter'*.

14

Cannes and Genoa—Lloyd George's Liberalism

After the signature of the Irish Treaty, the inter-Allied conferences began again, for the question of reparations still continued to be a vexed one, and the Turko-Greek conflict was becoming more serious. L.G. conceived the idea of calling a full-dress European Conference in the spring of 1922, where every nation would lay its cards upon the table, and the peace of Europe become, with a superhuman effort, an established fact. L.G. was over-optimistic, as events turned out, for the Germans and the Russians played a game of their own before the conference opened, and other adverse forces combined to wreck any prospects of the Utopia which L.G. planned.

It was decided that Genoa should be the venue for this final gathering of the nations and in the meantime a conference was arranged at which the agenda for the Genoa Conference was drawn up.

L.G. disliked conferences in Paris: he was too much at the mercy of the Paris press—a press which was for the most part notoriously unscrupulous and subsidised. I remember H. A. L. Fisher telling us the story of a Spanish statesman who, when he went to Paris, was received with torrents of abuse and insinuation. Hurt and surprised, he complained about this to the French Foreign Minister, who asked him whether he had seen the heads of the big newsappers, and suggested that it might be worth his while. The

statesman took the hint, and one gathers the abuse ter-
minated.

In any case, the South of France in January was more
delectable than Paris, and certainly than England, and the
conference was fixed to take place in Cannes. In order to
avoid staying in an hotel, the late Sir Albert Stern arranged
that the Villa Valetta should be put at the disposal of L.G.
and his Secretariat. Other members of the delegation
included Lord Curzon, and Sir Robert Horne, who was
then Chancellor of the Exchequer, Mr. Churchill and Sir
Laming Worthington Evans. Briand was the French Prime
Minister, and so well did he and L.G. understand each other
that L.G. was very sanguine about the success of this conference, which was to pave the way for the conference at Genoa.

All went well for the first part of the conference, in the
gay, sunlit town. It is true that the French delegates were
somewhat outraged when the British Chancellor of the
Exchequer appeared at a French Finance Conference in
flannels. He had been playing tennis and had had no time
to change, but the French sense of propriety was not easily
propitiated, and the event was regarded as something of a
scandal.

The parrot at the Villa Valetta introduced a note of merri-
ment into a British delegation conference held there, by
his unexpected interruptions from his unnoticed cage in the
corner of 'Stop it, Horace', and 'Shut up, you old fool',
at extraordinarily well-timed moments. As Sir Laming
Worthington Evans (Horace was the name by which he was
called by his friends) was presiding, the parrot's remarks
were somewhat embarrassing.

A young Italian journalist named Mussolini, the new
editor of the *Popolo d'Italia*, asked for an interview with L.G.
But his name was unknown to the British Prime Minister,
who in any case deemed it unwise to give an interview to
the editor of a Socialist journal while sitting in conference
with the Italian Prime Minister. So it fell to the lot of Tom

N

Jones, who was on L.G.'s secretariat, to take Mussolini out to dinner.

It was obvious that the usual intrigues were going on in Paris, but L.G. was happy in that Briand showed no sign of wanting to resign. So well did L.G. understand the Frenchman that he knew in advance when he was getting weary of office, and could recognise the symptoms. But now these were absent, and spirits were high, and L.G. judged it not amiss to take his friend on the golf course with him and play a comic game of golf. Alas! the mischievous elements in Paris saw their opportunity and unbelievably a crisis suddenly arose from this harmless fooling. Briand was obliged suddenly to leave Cannes. '*Don't resign,*' L.G. pleaded with him as he saw him off at the station. This time Briand had not intended to resign, but the intrigues between Poincaré (now President) and Barthou (Briand's Foreign Minister) against Briand were too strong, and Briand resigned. Coming out of the Council after his resignation, Briand turned to Barthou and said: 'Can you tell me, M. Barthou, what is the equivalent of thirty pieces of silver at the current rate of exchange?'

And so the Cannes Conference came to an abrupt end, but not before a series of resolutions had been passed for discussion by the Allies at the forthcoming conference at Genoa. A plan was drawn up on which the establishment of peace in Europe was to be founded at the conference: another for a Franco-British Agreement in which Germany was to be invited to join, and by which eventually all countries should associate themselves in an undertaking to refrain from aggression against their neighbours. In order that it may be seen how comprehensive and even prophetic was the memorandum I should like to quote its concluding paragraph:

. . . It is moreover their particular desire that this Entente between Great Britain and France, so far from excluding other

nations, should form the basis of a wider scheme of international
co-operation to ensure the peace of Europe as a whole. They
look confidently to what can be accomplished by collaboration
between the Allies in this purpose. The last of the conditions
laid down in this Memorandum as the basis of the proposed
Economic Conference[1] propounds a simple condition of International accord 'that all nations should join in an undertaking
to refrain from aggression against their neighbour'. The hope
of Great Britain is to secure this undertaking from all the nations
of Europe without exception. It is essential that the division of
the European nations into two mighty camps should not be
perpetuated by narrow fears on the part of the victor nations
or secret projects of revenge on the part of the vanquished. It
is essential that the rivalries generated by the emancipation of
nations since the war should be averted from the paths of international hatred and turned to those of co-operation and goodwill. It is essential, also, that the conflict between rival social
and economic systems which the Russian revolution has so
greatly intensified should not accentuate the fears of nations
and culminate in international war.

   If the conditions created in Europe by these new rivalries and
diversions are not wisely handled by co-operation between the
Powers, peace can only be shortlived, and Europe will be
plunged by the coming generation into another fierce struggle
which may overwhelm its civilization in even completer ruin
and despair. It is for the Allies, to whom the war has bequeathed
a position of vast responsibility and far-spreading power, to
stand together against this menace, to combine their influence
in averting it, and to make sure that in the heart and will of their
own peoples, who fought and bled for civilization, the cause of
civilization prevails. Great Britain, therefore, offers to France
and Italy her intimate and earnest co-operation in building up
a great system of European accord, which will put the main-
tenance of peace between nations and the reduction of national
armaments in the forefront of its aims; for only so, in her
belief, will Europe secure that sense of safety amongst nations,
great and small, which through the many centuries of its political
history it has never yet attained. If the Economic Conference

1. At Genoa.

is agreed to, it will create an opportunity for the great Allied Powers—France, the British Empire and Italy—to inaugurate an era of peace in their own continent, whose war-sodden fields record a history more terrible than that of any other continent in modern times.

L.G. made a stop in Paris on the way home from Cannes to attempt, in his optimism, a point of contact with Poincaré, the new French Premier, and to enlist his co-operation in the great plan which guaranteed France against aggression, but none was possible, and the delegation returned to England sad and depressed.

From this time onward the French took the bit between their teeth in international affairs. L.G. with the greatest difficulty managed to hold them for the few more months that he remained in office, but Poincaré wrecked the Genoa Conference, and no sooner did the Coalition Government come to an end than the French marched into the Ruhr, with all the dire consequences that that involved. The reconstruction of Europe, which had been so near L.G.'s heart, was doomed.

In the interval between Cannes and Genoa L.G. had been strongly tempted to resign. In addition to the intransigence of the French, his difficulties with his own Government were on the increase. Feeling that the power and prestige of the Coalition Government were weakening, he did in fact propose resignation to Austen Chamberlain on February 27th, offering him support on agreed lines afterwards. But the Tories wanted it both ways. Many of them resented the spate of Liberal measures which the Coalition had carried, but they needed L.G.'s name as a headpiece and his prowess as a supreme negotiator, at any rate for the time being, when there were still so many difficulties to be settled abroad. L.G. himself was unwilling to give up his office while there was still a chance of evolving at Genoa a plan for permanent

European reconstruction. I believe that but for this he would have insisted in resigning in February. As it was, although tired and discouraged, he remained in Downing Street.

He was tempted again the following month (but only slightly) when urged by Lord Beaverbrook to end the Coalition and form a Centre Party. I think that even had the idea really appealed to him—which it did not—L.G. was too tired to undertake the vast amount of organisation and campaigning and negotiation that such a political upheaval would have entailed. And although L.G., like Churchill, in his heart of hearts was not a party man, unlike Churchill it would never have occurred to him to change his party. He was for policies rather than parties—for measures in defence of the underdog whatever party would carry them out. That was why he was so exasperating to members of his own party at times. His allegiance, however, was fundamentally to his constituency and to Wales, where Liberalism was more than a political faith, and where political instincts were deep-rooted, fundamental. Closely allied to nonconformity, Liberalism in Wales was almost inevitably associated with the people's religion. And because it was bound up with the people, the element of caste, of class, also entered in. So much the more, then, was L.G.'s Liberalism than Liberalism anywhere outside Wales. So much the more was his political faith one of the heart and the hearth rather than the hustings. To change his party would have been treason to his politics, his religion and his people. In the years that followed his fall from office it seemed many times that he would have been wise, especially in view of the cantankerousness of the Liberal Party, for him to throw in his lot with one of the other parties. Churchill had no hesitation in doing this, not once, but twice. But to L.G. it was never a serious proposition. When Lansbury wrote him in 1933 suggesting that he should join the Labour Party, L.G. replied:

'Coming over' is not the best way to help. It would antagonize millions of Liberals with hereditary party loyalties who otherwise would gladly support any Government from another party provided it carried through a bold programme for the reconditioning of Britain. . . .

Despite the 'opportunities' which is one of the temptations and necessities of office, and now and again deflects every man from his course, I have always sincerely striven to do my best for the class from which I sprang.

And so his constituents returned him to Parliament for fifty-five years as a Liberal and he did not disappoint them.

He was cast on too great a scale to conform to any orthodoxy. His genius was not of the kind that could be moulded. Although a staunch nonconformist, he did not really conform to nonconformity, and often misled or shocked his faithful Free Church followers by his policies and sometimes by his actions.

His Liberalism was engendered by nonconformity and by the sense of grievance caused by real wrongs with which he was surrounded when young, and which kindled his imagination and his pugnacity. I often wonder what would have happened had L.G. been brought up in a different setting, in another part of the country. But then the Lloyd George that we knew might never have emerged.

In my diary of May 30th, 1936, I find the following:

L.G. was discussing with me the dislike of the Liberal hierarchy for him. 'As a matter of fact,' he said, 'the aristocracy have always been far more partial to me than these people—more even than they have been to Bonar Law or Baldwin. When the Coalition broke up in 1922 the majority of the Conservative leaders stuck to me—Balfour, Chamberlain, F.E., Crawford, Anglesey, the Devonshires, the Salisburys. Actually Ormsby-Gore was the only member of an aristocratic family that went with Baldwin, and when I asked someone the other day the reason for Ormsby-Gore's promotion I was told that it was because he went with Baldwin at that time.'

L.G. did his best after the 1929 election, with his pro-grammes for dealing with unemployment, to resuscitate Liberalism, but although these meetings provided him with a platform, and although they were packed, the Liberal Party continued to diminish in prestige and power.

Now, in 1922, the divergence in outlook between himself and his Conservative colleagues was widening, especially in relation to the British attitude towards Russia. Churchill headed a group which strongly opposed any recognition of Russia. He made considerable trouble for L.G. before the Genoa Conference, refusing to support L.G.'s programme, while L.G. again threatened to resign if Cabinet support were withdrawn. He wrote to me from Criccieth, where he had gone for a short rest:

. . . I mean to fight on Genoa. The Diehards all loathe it. It is the real test of whether a Coalition is to be progressive or reactionary. If I am beaten on it, I retire on a Liberal issue which I can go on fighting . . . If I win, the Coalition is definitely Liberal in the real, and not the Party, sense. . . . Heavy snow showers all day, I love them and I am lying outside now on the verandah with the snow whirling around. . . .

He got his way and went to Genoa.

Through weeks of arduous negotiation he persisted in his attempts for a plan for Europe—many times he was faced with the break-up of the conference and the failure of his endeavours. He refused to accept defeat and returned again and again to the task. Even in the end he would not admit that the French had entirely wrecked the conference, and he often said in after years that he hoped someone would write the history of the conference, to show what actually was accomplished and what might have been accomplished but for the wreckers. He never doubted that Russia could be brought into harness with the rest of Europe if she were rightly approached and sympathetically treated.

I was prevented by illness from going to the Genoa Conference, but the letters that L.G. wrote to me at that time are heroic in their determination to win through to his desired ends in spite of setbacks and disappointments. And it was typical of him, too, that if he was beaten he refused to recognise it.

I quote some extracts from these letters, which convey some idea of the pace at which he was working and the obstacles he was encountering:

Villa d'Albertis
Genoa
(19 April)

. . . The Conference is once more in serious peril. Damn German stupidity!

I am working as I never worked in my life to save it. Every art and device my simple nature is capable of. You ought to know all about it. . . .

(23 April)

. . . Had to sacrifice my Sunday rest to smooth over another French crisis. I am so glad you are not *all* French otherwise you would be difficult to handle. As it is, I get a French crisis now and again, don't I? Even with our *entente*!

The Conference is still labouring heavily and without a boast, I am the only man who can put it through—but it is going to take a lot of life out of my frame. If my health holds out, I shall win. So far I am holding out, but I have had a fortnight of nerve-wracking work. . . .

Wednesday (26 April)

. . . I have had a simply diabolical day, all work and worry. The Conference is trembling on the edge of a precipice and I am doing all I can to save it—and I am just now very tired . . . I am still sanguine.'

(30 April)

. . . The French I could overcome were I certain of the Russians. But I am far from sure of them. They are fanatical Orientals. Benes thinks they do not mean to settle and no doubt he knows

them well. Never mind I will go on fighting as long as the muzzle
of a gun is out of the water. Then I shall have nothing to reproach
myself with . . .

I have come to the end of my shilling shockers. The consump-
tion is unparalleled! Can you send some Byron's poems (unex-
purgated please) and such Ridgwell Cullum as I have not read—
and any other tales of adventure? . . .

L.G.'s light reading was always somewhat of a problem.
The supply of 'shilling shockers', as he called them, was not
inexhaustible, and though he would re-read his favourites
with great pleasure, there were sometimes crises when the
supply gave out.

Ridgewell Cullum was a favourite author, and fortunately
a prolific one, and there were many American 'Wild West'
stories that he enjoyed, and Hodder & Stoughton, the publishers, often came to our rescue when supplies were short.
A novel that always filled a gap was Davies's *A Victor of
Salamis*, an exciting and extremely well told story fulfilling
all requirements of a 'thriller'. I should not like to say how
many copies of this novel we bought over the years, but it
never failed to please him.

A few British authors gave him pleasure too. A novel by
Jeffrey Farnol was seized upon as soon as it was published,
and his *Amateur Gentleman* was read over and over again.
Warwick Deeping's romantic novels were also in demand.

There were no contemporary Welsh writers to give him
the same pleasure as some of the English ones, though there
were always his favourite Welsh poems to dip into. Dafydd
ap Gwilym was his favourite. But Byron was his favourite
English poet, especially the more erotic passages. Milton's
Paradise Lost he found the best poem ever written, and
Burns also, for the erotic quality of some of his poems, and
for his tilting at the rich and his defence of the poor, he
would often quote, loving the rebel in him.

He found tremendous satisfaction in reading Macaulay's
works, and would often turn up a passage to illustrate a con-

temporary point, or to show what style really meant. He envied Macaulay his deadliness in dealing with a political enemy, or a backslider of any kind.

Dickens he would read over and over again. He asked for his novels when he lay dying, and I have in my possession the little, tattered, spoilt volumes (on India paper—they were easier to hold)—*Martin Chuzzlewit*, *Pickwick Papers*, *Oliver Twist*.

(2 May)

. . . I am having the struggle of my life. Foot to foot and face to face. But I am still on the hopeful side. In a few days I can tell you whether I am off next week or whether I am booked for another three weeks. . . .

No cloud without a rift—if you wait long enough! Just had one little patch of blue this morning. Rothermere sent his confidential man to me (I had already had a pleasant talk on the boat with Rothermere) to place the whole of his papers at my disposal to support and defend me! . . . He has come to the conclusion there is no one else worth backing up!

. . . The Villa Albertis is beautiful—lizards crawling on the balcony. Grigg encountered one in his bath. I like the little fellows.

Wednesday (3 May)

. . . Don't you ever apologise again for sending too long a letter. . . .

I want *all* gossip, political and otherwise. The political news is valuable to me—and the rest is most entertaining. . . .

After a desperate struggle I got the document through to the Russians. It is substantially mine. I kept out of it most of the obnoxious stuff the French and others wanted to insert in it. . . .

I see from the *Sunday Express* that the attacks made upon me by the hostile Press both in France and England are specially vicious—'and of a personal character', 'on my honour and integrity'. What are they? I have not seen them. They are out to down me if they can—they are getting desperate. . . .

(4 May)

. . . What warm days we have had! Hot fly-infested days. Eaten with flies. I am waiting for the return of Barthou and the reply of the Russians. This morning I had a couple of hours with the German Chancellor, Von Rathenau. Germany is in a mood of despair and it is too early to predict what the Russians will do. They do not know themselves. They are very divided and distracted.

F.E. came here last night. His eyesight is still very bad. Rothermere left early this morning. He is most friendly. He told me some illuminating things about the intrigues of the past few months.

Chamberlain was undoubtedly at one time tempted to try his luck. 'There is no friendship at the top.' I am enveloped in intrigues. I hate this waiting. . . .

I am in a mood to chuck politics altogether and retire to Italy like Byron and Shelley who told the world to go to the devil. I pass Byron's house every day . . . I am in a very bad temper with everyone round me. . . .

Sunday morning (7 May)

. . . I am off to Kirk! No time to write!

Had two hours with the German Chancellor—after three hours with the American Ambassador and several interviews before that.

The struggle is *acharné—à la mort*. I am not done yet, although beset by enemies of all kinds. Many more enemies, open and secret, than friends—at least that is the case here. . . .

Tuesday (9 May)

. . . It is very hard to go through all the worry and perplexity without you. . . .

I have no one here who thinks it is worth their while to cheer me up when I am oppressed and almost overwhelmed with anxieties.

The Russians difficult—hesitating—with their judgment warped in doctrine. The French selfish—Germans impotent—the Italians willing but feeble—the little countries cowed. *The Times* devilish!

The Russians are replying tomorrow. I have no notion—not after several interviews with them—what they mean to say, but I am far from hopeful. The French are seeking every chance to break the Conference. There are many others who would like to join them. But they are still rather afraid of me. I have a certain hold on Liberal opinion throughout the world, and I can thus make trouble for them in their own countries.

I am fighting the most difficult battle of my life—and the most decisive, for better or for worse.

Your letters give me a strength you can hardly appreciate.

(11 May, 1922)

. . . I am working so hard so as to get back as soon as possible. . . . I had a real success yesterday. Saved the Conference by a 'bantering' speech. . . .

Saturday night (13 May)

. . . Very hard day but a very good day. Beat French hip and thigh. Looks as if we were going to get something substantial after all. It has been, and still is, a terrible fight. . . .

(15 May)

. . . The fight is still desperate but I am hopeful of saving my last scheme. That means the Conference will go on at the Hague. The fight for peace will continue. Next week I shall have to make a speech in the House. That bothers me. . . .

End of the Coalition

After Genoa, Turkey. Problems and worries seemed to be piling up during the summer for an overworked Prime Minister, and his enemies, at home and abroad, took advantage of his predicament. The rise of Mustapha Kemal in Turkey produced a new threat to peace.

As long as Venizelos had been in power, Greece had been able to hold her own in Asia Minor and Thrace; but on the accession of King Constantine to the Greek throne, after the death of King Alexander from the bite of a monkey, Venizelos was driven out of office and out of Greece, and the position changed completely. The French made a secret treaty with Mustapha Kemal, the Italians reinforced the Kemalist Army, and in England the whole of the Tory Ministers in the Coalition Government were pro-Turk, with the exception of Mr. Balfour (Mr. Churchill was still nominally a Liberal).

The old adage of the Conservative Party that 'the Turk was a gentleman' was again quoted. There was a marked lack of sympathy for the poor Greeks whom the Turks were massacring as they drove them from the region which the Peace Treaty had allocated to them. With L.G. the old Gladstonian tradition allowed him no doubt—he was for the Greeks, and the Turks were still the 'mad dogs of Europe' and reinforcements were rushed to Harington, who was in command in the Straits.

One morning towards the end of September my door opened and L.G. and Churchill walked in from the Cabinet Room. L.G. asked me to take down from Churchill the text of what I realised was to be a telegram to the Dominion Governments asking for their support in the event of a war with Turkey. I was horrified at the unwisdom of the message, conveying as it did the prospect of renewed warfare on a grand scale. L.G. and Churchill took the draft back into the Cabinet Room, where the meeting was in progress. Shall I send L.G. in a note warning him against such an action? I thought. But then again I thought, he will never agree to such a telegram being sent.

The next thing I knew was that the telegram had gone. It was one of the factors which helped to bring the Coalition Government to an end, and within a fortnight it had fallen.

The story of the meeting at the Carlton Club, engineered by Baldwin (L.G. said he did not recollect him ever opening his mouth at a Cabinet meeting), is well known and it is not necessary to re-tell it. The great figures of the Conservative Party—Balfour, Crawford, Birkenhead, Milner, Austen Chamberlain, Horne—would have nothing to do with the manœuvre: they were anxious still to keep L.G. in office for the good of the country. The manner of the coup disgusted them, for the organisers of the meeting were still members of L.G.'s Government. The proper procedure was for any who were in disagreement with L.G. and his policy to resign. To hold a conspiratorial meeting before doing so was, to quote Balfour's words, 'the sort of thing that gentlemen do not do'. They sent in their resignations *afterwards* in a spate of letters—short, formal notes, with no word of gratitude or regret. I could not help wondering at the time if they did not feel a little ashamed of their behaviour. I was talking to L.G. in the Cabinet Room while the meeting at the Carlton Club was in progress, and I remember the door being flung open by Sir Austen Chamberlain, and his words as he strode into the room: 'We must resign, L.G. Baldwin has carried the meeting.'

The most humiliating and shattering thing about adversity is that it gives one's enemies an opportunity for triumph.

L.G. had enemies on every side.

Not only was the Coalition dissolved, but there was no unity in the Liberal Party. The election which followed was the 'Coupon Election' in reverse, but the Liberals suffered just as much. L.G. knew he was fighting a hopeless battle, but he fought well, addressing huge meetings all over the country in the dreary November weather. Enormous crowds came to see and hear him, and then, as was the fate of Churchill in 1945, voted against him.

On the night that the election results came out we dined at Philip Sassoon's house in Park Lane. Lord Birkenhead was there, and, I think, the Churchills. By the end of the evening it was clear that it would be a Conservative victory, but there was no exultation among the Conservatives there, who, loyal to L.G. as they were, would have preferred to go on working with him.

One day in the spring of 1922 Dr. Ethel Smyth (as she then was), whom I had met once or twice, came to see me in my office. She had a favour to ask, and the favour, I need hardly say, was not for herself. She put forward the claim of Dan Godfrey, who had done so much for music while directing the Bournemouth Orchestra, for some sort of recognition—a knighthood, perhaps. I said I would tell L.G. of her request, and L.G. and I subsequently talked the matter over. He was quite willing to submit Dan Godfrey's name to the King for a title, and then we talked about Dr. Smyth —what a remarkable woman she was, how much she herself had done for British music, and for the cause of women's suffrage. 'What is wrong with submitting her name for a title?' he asked. 'She is certainly the kind of woman who would adorn an honours list.' And so it came about that the names of both Dan Godfrey and Ethel Smyth appeared in the next Honours List, and no one was more surprised to be offered the honour than Dr. Smyth herself, who thereafter became Dame Ethel Smyth.

I used to meet her from time to time, and she stimulated and terrified me. One day we had been lunching at the house of a mutual acquaintance, and Maurice Baring, who was also there, asked Dr. Smyth and myself to join him in a visit after lunch to an exhibition of extremely modern art at the Goupil Gallery. There was a hush in the Gallery when suddenly the other visitors were electrified as Ethel Smyth, after examining a few of the pictures, remarked at the top of her voice: 'Maurice, I might just as well cut a piece out of your trousers, stick it on a piece of paper, hang it up there and call it a picture!'

I preferred, however, not to be involved in the honours business. I found it very difficult to be polite to people who came to press their claims to recognition. There was one man who came regularly before each honours list to ask for a title—not for himself, he said, because he was not interested in titles, but solely for the sake of his wife. Then his wife died, and I thought well, we shall hear no more of this title. I was mistaken. Quite unashamed, the man turned up before the next honours list, saying that his wife would have wished him to do so!

I am afraid I do not suffer humbugs gladly.

During the last period of L.G.'s Premiership it had become known that *The Times* was for sale. Some of L.G.'s friends suggested that a syndicate should be formed for the purpose of acquiring the paper and putting it in L.G.'s control. There was indeed more than one scheme and such divergent personalities as Lord Rothermere and David Davies of Llandinam, who had the money with which to make the purchase, busied themselves in competing for the paper. By the end of June L.G. himself had become interested in the project. He realised that the Coalition could not last much longer. If and when he left office he would have to look about for some means of earning his livelihood, but he had received offers of vast sums for his memoirs, and this would normally have been his first task.

'I would not mind resigning,' he said one day to me, 'if I could become editor of *The Times*, at a decent salary and with a decent contract.'

Nevertheless I was quite sure that he had no serious intention of accepting such an offer. He appeared to toy with the idea, and to encourage its proposers, even as later, during the Second World War, when he was offered first office by Churchill and then the Embassy at Washington. He never had any intention of accepting either of these offers, although he went through all the pretence of considering them. I have known him talk around a project, even a most ridiculous one, with every appearance of favouring it but without the slightest intention of accepting it. I have seen him go right up to the threshold of acceptance when he knew that he would not enter, though many would have sworn that the matter was settled.

I grew to learn, though there were many who did not understand this, that until L.G. actually said 'Yes' to a proposal there was every prospect that he would say 'No'.

There was obviously a great temptation to control the policy of *The Times* which had attacked him so remorselessly and so vindictively during recent years. But I am quite sure that he never seriously entertained the idea of working under the aegis of Rothermere, still less of David Davies, whatever opinion there may have been to the contrary.

After the election he was exhausted and depression set in. One day at Churt we were walking and he said to me, 'I am old; I am nearly sixty.' We decided that he ought to get into sunshine for Christmas, and a holiday at Algeçiras was arranged.

The sunshine did a great deal to cheer him, and later Lord and Lady Birkenhead and their family joined the party and it was a gay company.

o

We returned to our new office in 18 Abingdon Street to take up the threads, and to adapt ourselves to the new conditions. L.G. had been in office for seventeen years, with all the aids to living that that implied, officials to help him, messengers to wait on him, secretaries to look after him, an official residence to live in. At one fell swoop all this was removed. When it was known that L.G. was going out of office Sir Warren Fisher, who was head of the Civil Service at that time, offered to make me a permanent civil servant in the First Class. I think I would have been the first woman to receive this honour. But this would have meant parting from L.G. and there was no question of it.

J. T. Davies, my colleague, who was now a K.C.B., was still nominally with us, not being a permanent civil servant. But L.G. had made him a director of the Suez Canal Board, and it was obvious that he would no longer continue his work as Principal Secretary to L.G. Actually, he continued to come to the office in Abingdon Street a great deal, and to help L.G. in manifold ways, chiefly in looking after L.G.'s finances, which included the Political Fund.

A. J. Sylvester, however, had remained at Downing Street in Mr. Bonar Law's Secretariat. He had been responsible during the latter part of L.G's Premiership for matters relating to church patronage, and I believe that he continued in this capacity under Mr. Bonar Law.

While L.G. was still Prime Minister he had been approached by Curtis Brown, the doyen of literary agents, who persuaded him to accept a proposal that as soon as he was free from office he should write his memoirs. However, while the 1922 election was still in progress, I was approached by Mr. Keen, the London representative of the United Press Associations of America, with a request that L.G. should write a series of regular articles for their organisation which would be syndicated throughout the world. Keen offered him extraordinarily good terms. The prospect of expressing his views on current events in the way thus

proposed to him, which would in effect give a world platform, appealed to L.G. enormously, and he accepted the
offer. Curtis Brown was rather offended at the time, holding
that L.G. was committed to settle down to his memoirs.
But L.G. was, I think, reluctant to embark forthwith upon
this task so soon after leaving office, with all its exigencies
and fatigues, and he reassured Curtis Brown that he would
in fact write his memoirs as soon as he could. Meantime, he
agreed to write a fortnightly article for Mr. Keen's United
Press Associations on a fifty-fifty basis, reserving the British
rights for himself. He asked me if, in lieu of salary, I would
like to have ten per cent of the net profit on these articles,
and I need hardly say that I was amazed and delighted to
receive at the end of the year a cheque for £3,000.

L.G. continued to write these articles for many years, and
I have very pleasant recollections of my association with
Mr. Keen over the selection of subjects, and other points
arising out of the contract.

When his contract with the United Press Association
ended he signed another with the Associated Press of
America. This was not quite so lucrative, and it was also unpopular, owing to the fact that Randolph Hearst was one of
the proprietors of the agency, and L.G.'s political enemies
made the most of this, though it was quite clear that L.G.
never wrote to order, much as Hearst would have liked him
to do so. He continued to write his articles for world circu-
lation until after the outbreak of the Second World War.

I soon discovered that the work in our new office was
going to be more than I could manage, for I was the only
secretary left out of the little band at Downing Street, and
now that the resources of official departments were no
longer at our command the work really became very heavy
indeed. One of L.G.'s weaknesses was that he was quite incapable of comprehending how much work one person
could do in a given time, however willing, nor could he
grasp how long any given job would take. There was no

one who was the obvious person to step into the secretarial gap, and I struggled on through the spring and summer in an endeavour to cope with an almost overwhelming variety of responsibilities. I had a very competent staff of typists to help me, but when we closed down for the summer holidays, L.G. going to Criccieth and I to stay with some friends in Scotland, I was nearing the end of my tether, and L.G. realised it.

Meantime an invitation to visit the United States and Canada had been accepted by L.G. and the question arose as to who was to accompany him as secretary. Obviously, it must be a man, and experienced at that, and one who knew L.G. well; and I could think of no one better than A. J. Sylvester, who had worked close to L.G. for many years, and who was not afraid of hard work. The difficulty was that he was a civil servant, and if he gave up his official job he would lose his pension; L.G., however, offered to commute his pension for him, as well as to give him a salary a good deal higher than the one he was getting. One thing more, however, Sylvester demanded, and that was that he should be known as 'Principal Private Secretary'. I demurred, thinking that at least we should be on equal terms, since he was the last comer to the secretarial staff at Downing Street. I thought there was no necessity for the word 'Principal' to appear at all in the notice of his appointment! But Sylvester was firm that this should be a condition of his joining L.G.'s staff, and L.G. gave way. There did not seem to be anyone else who fulfilled all the qualifications for accompanying L.G. on his trip, which was imminent, and on his return Sylvester would be able to look after all the business connected with the House of Commons, which J. T. Davies had previously managed.

I knew of no one—after Philip Kerr—who worked harder than A. J. Sylvester. He had enormous application and determination, and if he was after something he would not stop till he got it, and he never spared himself.

As an example of his behaviour, I give the following story. During the Second World War, when Field Marshal Smuts was over here, L.G. invited him to lunch in a private room in the House of Commons. I was there too, and Sylvester, having arranged everything, decided that he also would be a guest. (This often happened.) Smuts began to talk very freely, which was what L.G. wanted. Suddenly he stopped, and dried up completely. He had noticed that Sylvester was taking down in a notebook on his knees what he was saying. L.G. realised what was happening and sent Sylvester off on a message. The lunch proceeded in the friendly way that L.G. had intended.

Sylvester would give a helping hand to anyone in trouble. He was an unselfish and kindly person, and I was sorry that after L.G.'s death Sylvester wrote a mean and unlovely book about him. He certainly had his living to make, but as L.G. had provided generously for him, it was not necessary for him to get money in that way.

The American visit was an enormous success. L.G. was fêted everywhere, and his reception acted like a tonic to him, and a tonic of which he stood very much in need. He wrote me from the States that if he had still been Prime Minister no greater fuss could have been made of him. He was almost killed with kindness, and in the middle of the tour he developed a temperature and a bad throat and was obliged to rest for a few days. He was front page publicity all the time, and the press notices of the visit form a large, large tome, now housed in the Lloyd George Museum at Llanystumdwy.

I think one of the things that gave him most pleasure during his visit was to meet veterans of the Civil War, and especially one old soldier who had fought under General Stonewall Jackson, one of L.G.'s heroes. The Americans who were with him on this occasion were amazed to learn how accurate and detailed was L.G.'s knowledge of the battles and the campaigns.

Dame Margaret and Megan were also fêted, and I think it

was a tonic to them also. They had felt keenly the change from Downing Street to an unofficial home.

I also decided that it was time for me to have a holiday on my own, and a woman friend and I went to Paris and Florence together. At the Opéra we went to a concert of Stravinsky's *Sacre du Printemps*, the first performance in Paris, and conducted by Koussevitsky. I thought the music terrifying, though I have since grown to like it. Then we satiated ourselves with the sight of the treasures and loveliness of Florence, grasping greedily all that she had to offer us. We had intended to go from there to Naples, but we could not tear ourselves away, and the fortnight that we spent there has always been one of my most cherished memories. We visited San Gimignano, driving through the vineyards where the harvest was in progress, and that part of Italy became to me a beloved spot, and remained so.

In mid-Atlantic on the way home L.G. received news that Baldwin was not doing well in his Premiership. He had suddenly announced in a speech at Plymouth on October 25th:

I have come to the conclusion myself that the only way of fighting this subject [unemployment] is by protecting the home market. I am not a clever man.

The result was that a General Election was imminent on a clear-cut issue—Protection versus Free Trade. L.G. was greeted on his arrival at Southampton by members of his organisation who presented him with the plans for fighting it.

The Asquithian Liberals had their office in 21 Abingdon Street, a few doors away from ours, and it was inevitable that there should have been already tentative advances on both sides by their less bitter members for an understanding which would give the Liberal Party some sort of future. Now, on his return to England, the negotiations were accelerated, and on November 13th (three days before the Dissolution) L.G. met Asquith, Sir Alfred Mond and Sir John Simon, and a statement was issued, signed by Asquith and L.G. The manifesto was a truculent and trenchant one. It stated amongst other things 'that in a single year the Government's conduct of foreign policy in great matters essential to our livelihood has signally and disastrously failed . . . and for the past year its blindness, indecision and impotence have been such that it has ceased to exercise any guiding influence upon European affairs'.

To my mind this indictment of the first Baldwin Government epitomised the downward trend of British influence which continued (under Baldwin's influence for the most part) until it culminated in the Second World War.

I firmly believe that had it been left to Asquith and L.G. the breach in the Liberal Party would have been safely closed and unity firmly established. Each had an admiration for the finer qualities of the other. Asquith had upheld L.G. in the fights in the Cabinet in 1909 when L.G. had been pressing his new taxes.

L.G. enjoyed full sympathy and support from Asquith in the series of bold and original measures he brought forward to make war on want and to lighten the lot of the helpless poor. The first of these was his Old Age Pensions Scheme, a reform he had studied and urged for years. He persuaded the Liberal Cabinet to approve it, and Asquith, as Chancellor of the Exchequer, actually had the task of framing the bill, which he then passed over to L.G., who succeeded him as Chancellor in 1908. L.G. hammered it through Parliament in the teeth of bitter Tory opposition, and the country rightly acclaimed him as its true father. For years afterwards old people talked of going to draw their 'Lloyd George'! In recent times some voices have been heard claiming the paternity of the measure for Asquith himself; but when it was enacted, England knew perfectly well that its conception as well as its triumphant passage was due to L.G. But for him it would never have been framed, still less carried.

L.G. had told me how the struggle in the Cabinet was far more difficult than his fight in the country. Harcourt was the most inveterate of all in obstructing L.G.'s proposals, while posing all the time as an ardent Radical. Crewe, while not liking them, said very little. Grey said nothing. But at heart they were against him, all except Asquith, who was helpful, at any rate when it came to a vote. Once, when nearly everyone around the table had raised objections to a certain proposal, Asquith passed it, and summed up with the words: 'Well, I think there is substantial agreement on this point.' (At that time, as I have said, there were no minutes taken of the proceedings, and no votes recorded.)

Later, at the time of the Marconi trouble, Asquith stood firm for his Chancellor of the Exchequer, not listening to those who urged that now was the time to get rid of a dangerous rival.

And in spite of the intervening bitterness of the years 1916–22 I still think that these two men could have come together—with what different fortunes to the Liberal Party! As it was, Lady Oxford (then still Mrs. Asquith) made no secret of her hatred of L.G. She had never liked him—he had never heeded the imperious and mischievous notes she had poured out to him from 10 Downing Street. A study of these (still in existence among L.G.'s papers) would serve to convince anyone of where the mischief lay which wrecked any chances of a reconciliation.

The result of the 1923 election was the first Labour Government in this country. It was a minority Government and hampered at every turn by this fact. It was fair game for L.G., who with every pretence at keeping them up to the mark, made life very difficult for them.

16

Two Labour Governments Collapse

Although L.G. would willingly have helped the Labour Government had the Liberals been given any encouragement to do so, he found that Ramsay Macdonald's vanity made any kind of co-operation difficult. Accordingly L.G. became more and more truculent and before long he made a violent attack on the Government and on Shinwell, who was Minister of Mines, in particular, for their failure to deal with the mines problem.

On August 7th, 1924, L.G. attended the Liberal Summer School at Oxford, where he was due to speak. Just before he rose, a message came to say that the question of the Russian Treaty, lately concluded, with the promise of a loan to Russia, by Ramsay Macdonald, was to be raised on the adjournment of the House that afternoon. L.G. cut short his speech and motored straight from Oxford to the House of Commons. We prepared the notes for his speech in the car, and he delivered a powerful attack which gave another shake to the already tottering Labour Government. His attack was not on the grounds that he was against helping Russia, but that the proposed loan threatened to divert resources which were badly needed for dealing with unemployment at home.

When the House met on September 30th the Government, rather than meet a challenge on the Russian loan, took the one on the withdrawal of judicial proceedings against Mr. Campbell, the editor of the *Worker's Weekly*, for an article he had written inciting mutiny in the Navy and the Army.

The Government was defeated, and although it actually fell on the Campbell case, it was generally recognised that the real cause of its downfall was the manner in which this country had been committed to a loan to Russia.

The election was decided in no uncertain manner by the publication of the 'Zinovieff letter'; the Conservatives were returned to power for five years. Asquith was defeated, and the number of Liberals returned to the House of Commons was reduced to forty-two.

After the 1924 election, and when it was clear that the Tories were safely in office for another five years, L.G. canalised his energies into a vast enquiry into the 'State of the Nation', and into preparing schemes for putting the national economy on a surer basis. Land, coal, finance, and industrial relations all came under review. Time, money, experience were all poured out in this outstanding effort. Money became available on a large scale as a result of the sale of the *Chronicle* which L.G. effected in 1925-6.

The *Chronicle* was bought by L.G. for the Party in 1918. The story is told by Frank Owen in *Tempestuous Journey* (pp. 692 *et seq*.). After L.G. bought the *Chronicle* Gwilym had been made managing director with a salary. Charles McCurdy was the chairman, and he thought it would be a good thing to have a woman on the Board. He discussed this with L.G., and said he thought I would be a suitable person, and L.G. agreed. The Lloyd George family was incensed, and in 1926, when L.G. was in low water politically and many people were out for his blood, his family decided to tackle him on his relations with me. A joint letter was written, signed by his wife and all his children, demanding that I should be removed from his secretariat . . . or else . . .

L.G. was enraged by the note which he had received from his family. He then wrote a terrible letter to Dame Margaret, upbraiding her and the children for attacking him and offering her a divorce, which he said he would welcome. I knew nothing of all this until L.G. handed me the letter which Dame Margaret had returned to him, obviously accepting defeat. This was one of the many hurts I experienced, inevitably, in my confrontation with the L.G. family. While L.G. was in office it was necessary and simple for me to remain in my official office and not to run across them. They came to my room individually to talk to me, and Gwilym was always friendly, or so I thought. But I think there were people around who were always ready to try to breed bad feeling, and they certainly succeeded with Megan, who became less and less friendly in her attitude. It was not surprising, as she clearly took the line that I was a rival to her mother, whom she used as a weapon when she wanted support from her father. And after she entered the House of Commons she knew that she had, so to speak, a blackmailing advantage.

L.G., after consultation with Beaverbrook, decided to sell the *Chronicle*.[1] He had been greatly helped in all the negotiations by Sir Alfred Lewis, the head of the National Provincial Bank. We all, including the L.G. family, had shares in the *Chronicle*, and, as the original shares were sold at an enhanced price, became a good deal richer as a result.

In the course of the preparation of the scheme for dealing with unemployment, and for drawing up a programme for the next election, Bron-y-de was very busy. Conferences were continually in progress, of one kind or another, and experts constantly at work drawing up memoranda and briefs for L.G. and his committee to examine. Amongst those who were helping L.G. and who joined the discussions were C. F. G. Masterman, now reconciled to L.G., but, alas, in failing health (he died in 1927) and Maynard Keynes, also, as L.G. thought, again his friend, but who was soon to publish another attack on L.G. even more bitter than the first, in that it was more personal. But now, to all ap-

1. For a detailed account of the *Chronicle* negotiations, see *Tempestuous Journey*, by Frank Owen, p. 394.

pearances, he was heart and soul in the schemes which L.G. proposed to put before the country. When questioned at a meeting about his attack on L.G. in 1918 in *The Economic Consequences of the Peace* and his present attitude, Keynes replied: 'I oppose Mr. Lloyd George when he is wrong and support him when he is right.' But L.G. liked his followers to support him through thick and thin! Seebohm Rowntree was again in the forefront of the new proposals for reform, and Mr. E. D. Simon (Lord Simon of Wythenshawe) and Lord Layton also were on the committee. Colonel T. F. Tweed, whom L.G. had brought from an organising post in the North to join his staff as chief organiser, was in charge of the campaign. He was a man with strong Liberal principles and a splendid war record—and sometimes uncompromising in character. There were often clashes between Colonel Tweed and L.G. on principles and tactics, for the former was fearless in expressing his opinions; but the common cause of Liberalism usually settled their differences. I wish it had been possible for someone to report the brilliant conversations around the table at Bron-y-de on the occasion of these conferences—the wit, the gay repartee, L.G. gayest and most brilliant of all, the company hanging on his words.

It was inevitable that during those years I should find work in the office a little dull after the atmosphere and excitements of Downing Street, especially when L.G. was away campaigning as during this time he often was, or when he went abroad in the winter to the Mediterranean or to other sunny climates, sometimes leaving me behind. I therefore set myself a task of going through L.G.'s speeches right from the beginning of his career, and extracting epigrams and outstanding passages. This was subsequently published, with a foreword by Philip Guedalla, under the title of *Slings and Arrows*. I had previously edited two volumes of L.G.'s war speeches—*The Great Crusade* and *Through Terror to Triumph*.

But at the 1929 elections the Liberals, for all the gigantic efforts which had been put forward, and all the colossal amounts which had been spent, only returned fifty-nine members. L.G., nevertheless, was very satisfied with the Welsh results. He had fought hard, not only in his own constituency but in those of his son and daughter, the latter being returned to Parliament for the first time—strangely enough, at the very same age that her father was returned—twenty-seven. There was naturally great rejoicing in the Lloyd George family, and their success softened the disappointment which L.G. felt at the failure of the Party itself to return more members.

Another fact which compensated for this failure was that *no* Party had an over-all majority, and this produced a situation after L.G.'s heart, for now the Liberals were again holding the balance of power. Ramsay Macdonald once more became Prime Minister of a Labour Government and L.G. again did his best to keep him up to the mark. Had the Prime Minister been any other than Macdonald it might have been possible for L.G. to make some headway with his schemes, but Ramsay seemed to be constitutionally and temperamentally unable to take any action. He was vain and jealous, and there never had been any love lost between him and L.G. He probably realised that L.G. was a better Socialist than he was! A handsome figure as he sat on the Treasury bench, he was nevertheless a figure of fun, with his rolling vapourings and empty sententious phrases. Nothing was accomplished, and his own followers were in despair, but impotent.

One of L.G.'s first visitors at Churt after the election was Sir William Jowitt (later Lord Jowitt). He rang up and asked if he might come down to see L.G. immediately. L.G. had a pretty good idea of the object of the visit. Jowitt was due to arrive about six, but was detained in London and arrived at Bron-y-de just as dinner was served. He asked L.G. if he might have a word with him privately. 'You may not want me to stay to dinner,' he said.

The rest of us, including some guests, went in to dinner

and soon L.G. and Jowitt came in. I knew what had happened, as L.G. had warned me. Jowitt had announced his
resignation from the Liberal Party and his secession to the
new Labour Government, which had offered him the post
of Attorney General.

I have seldom sat through a more uncomfortable meal.
L.G. talked animatedly on every subject but politics. One
of our guests said he had no notion that there was anything
wrong, but Jowitt was obviously ill-at-ease, and as soon as
the meal was over departed hastily.

'He was a guest in my house,' said L.G., 'and I had to
treat him as such.' Personally I think it showed great courage on the part of Jowitt to come down and face L.G. He
could easily have written a letter. But I don't think he an-
ticipated that dinner party!

After two years of manœuvring and faced with increasing
unemployment, owing to the crash on Wall Street and its
repercussions here, Ramsay Macdonald was toying, very
unwillingly, with the idea of a National Government, of
which he would be the head, and in which L.G. would inevitably be included. In the early summer L.G. had many
talks with Ramsay from which nothing definite emerged,
and L.G. became impatient and irritable. I thought it was the
disappointment and frustration that was telling on him, but
in fact he was a sick man at this time. And now fate dealt
him a cruel blow, for he had suddenly to undergo a serious
operation which would put him out of action for months. I
was alone with L.G. over that August Bank Holiday week-
end when he was taken ill. His family had, as usual at these
times, departed to Criccieth, leaving a skeleton staff at
Addison Road, where L.G. now lived. I found that Lord
Dawson was away, but managed to cope with the invalid
with the help of Sir Thomas Carey Evans, L.G.'s son-in-
law, who came up from the country, until Dawson returned
on the Monday. He (Dawson) diagnosed a prostate condition needing an immediate operation, which was carried

out by Mr. Swift Joly, an eminent surgeon, at L.G.'s house in Addison Road. Dame Margaret and the other members of the family came back from Wales on the Tuesday, and I was obliged to leave Addison Road for my flat in Westminster. I waited for news from time to time. L.G. came through the operation well. The surgeon said that as L.G. was recovering from the anaesthetic a cup of tea was handed to him by the nurse. 'This isn't China tea,' L.G. grunted.

Ramsay Macdonald for once acted quickly; he seized the opportunity to form the National Government, from which obviously L.G. must be excluded. From that time onwards L.G. had no chance, to my mind, of returning to office until the war—and then he was too old. In the intervening years Britain went from one disastrous foreign policy to another, and Hitler gained in power correspondingly.

Sir Herbert Samuel and Lord Reading represented the Liberal Party in the new National Government. The former, never a close friend of L.G.'s, was no doubt relieved at the exclusion of L.G., but Lord Reading, I think, must have been grieved, for these two were bound together by close bonds of long political association, and of personal regard. But the change wrought a final break between L.G. and the Liberal Party as such. The tide of Government swept on and left him stranded as far as party politics were concerned. He accepted the inevitable, not, however, without soundly rating, to the point of insult, the Liberal members who, having joined the National Government, further committed themselves to a General Election on a Tory programme. L.G. was furious.

The invalid was not allowed to see me and, as a result, succeeded in persuading his doctors to let him travel to his beloved Bron-y-de ('I shall never get well in London,' he told them) for the rest of his convalescence, where I was able, with the help of a nurse, to look after him. He received the offending Liberal members, who came to Churt in the hope of receiving his blessing. He let forth the whole blast of his wrath upon them and, exceedingly hurt, they left awkwardly and, he hoped, ashamed. This episode set L.G. back several weeks in his recovery.

L.G. had been in the habit for some years now of going abroad for the winter. When the gloom of November began to close in he would say 'Where shall we go now?' He sometimes prophesied that the day would come when the whole population of this island would close down for the winter months and seek the sun, leaving the place, as he put it, 'in the hands of caretakers'. I wonder!

Personally, I thought that even the few flawless days one gets in December and January, days of crisp and exhilarating sunshine, with their sparse harbingers of another spring, were worth the other dreary winter days. Indeed, I rather superstitiously thought that these latter were the price one had to pay, under the law of compensation, for the incomparable glories of an English spring, however short. One is not entitled, I feel, to behold the dazzling glory of such a spring and to see the daffodils shouting 'Hallelujah', if one has not been present in the dark days to witness the first green tips pushing their way through the earth. And I disliked the upheaval and the long journeys which took us to foreign hotels, where one endeavoured to ensure for L.G. the same comforts and conditions that he was accustomed to have at home. But L.G. thought, probably rightly, that as he grew older his health might suffer from the cold and the damp, and so abroad we went.

The winter of 1931–2 was a special case. Because of his illness Lord Dawson thought that L.G. should not remain in England at all for the whole of the winter, and a journey to Ceylon by sea was arranged. Dame Margaret and Megan went with him. And now it was L.G. who was reluctant to start and bewailed the departure. He was confirmed in his conviction that the voyage was a mistake by the roughness of the first part of the journey. 'What made me leave my comfortable home at Churt?' he wrote me. But his reception

at Bombay cheered and rallied him. 'I might still have been
the Prime Minister of Britain,' he reported. Nevertheless he
was anxious to return, and could not wait to finish the journey back by boat, coming overland from Marseilles and thus
gaining a few days. He was often like that with his holidays:
we used to say, in the early days, that if he said he was going
away for three weeks he would be back in ten days. But as
he grew older he was more reconciled, for health purposes,
to staying out his term abroad, in a more clement climate.

When L.G. left for his journey to Ceylon after his illness
in 1931 he instructed Malcolm Thomson and me to prepare
material for the first volume of his memoirs. We had plenty
of stuff to work upon, but what a task! Poor Malcolm was
glued to the typewriter for hours on end, digesting and dis-
entangling the memoranda and other documents with which
I fed him. But, even so, when L.G. returned it was not
enough. We *really* got down to work on the memoirs. My
time, of course, was all L.G.'s, but he did not understand
that Malcolm ever wanted to go home to his loving wife
and child! Malcolm Thomson had been on L.G.'s staff since
the early twenties, when L.G. began his schemes for curing
unemployment, and he helped to write the briefs for the
various pamphlets which L.G.'s committees published, e.g.,
the Green Book (on land reform), the Brown Book (on
urban reform), the pamphlet 'We Can Conquer Unemployment'; and 'Organising Property', which was published in
the thirties and known as 'The New Deal'. He now prepared the chapters for the memoirs, and dug into the masses
of files and papers which L.G. had accumulated, to find relevant data for the book. As may be imagined, he worked
terribly hard and was a very unselfish member of the staff,
always ready to help and never grumbling—well, hardly
ever! He was a mine of general information, and I never
knew him to fail to answer any question that was put to him.

He had a fund of sympathy, too. One day during these
years, when L.G. was striving to carry the Liberal Party with

P

him, he received a letter from Tom Jones, who was then helping Baldwin. The letter was full of flattery under which lay a request for a favour. I was furious, and thinking I could see through all the wiles of this other Welshman, told L.G. so in no uncertain terms. He turned on me and drove me to tears with the bitter things he said. Malcolm came in and found me in distress and I told him the cause. 'But I'll never retract what I said or change my opinion,' I wailed . . . 'Even if he slays me!'

'Yet I will maintain mine own ways before him,' murmured Malcolm sympathetically.

There were many visitors to Bron-y-de while the memoirs were being written, for L.G. found that there were so many people whom he wanted to consult on the events of so many years ago. Admiral Richmond came to talk about the sinking of ships in 1916–17, and gave L.G. relevant figures which he wanted. Basil Liddell Hart describes in his own book how he sometimes became critical of L.G.'s handling of the war story, and how one day L.G. turned on him and said, 'Who's writing these memoirs—you or I?' But Basil always stuck to his guns, and was a tremendous help to L.G., who knew he could always rely on Liddell Hart's facts. Between the wars Liddell Hart did his best to guide the military machine along the right road, though when the second war came those in charge were not prepared for it. Basil had been a constant visitor to L.G.'s home in Churt and in Wales, and the copy of the memoirs that L.G. inscribed to him says: 'I regard him as the highest and soundest authority on modern war whom it has been my privilege to meet.'

And speaking of inscriptions, my own copy of the memoirs is inscribed on the fly-leaf in L.G.'s handwriting: 'To Frances, without whose sympathetic help and understanding I could not have carried through the burden of the terrible tasks whose story is related in these volumes. D. Lloyd George.'

During the years after the 1929 election L.G. went less

and less to London, and became more disinclined to attend public functions and even private ones. But people wanted to see him, to visit him, to get his views on world affairs; and so they would seek an invitation to Churt, and L.G. was not averse to entertaining them in this way.

I think the most important and interesting of these visitors was Mahatma Gandhi. In 1931 he was staying in London with the two Lester sisters, who knew him well, at their settlement in the East End at Bow, and they asked if they could bring him down one evening to Churt to talk with L.G. The latter was eager to see and talk with the great man, who sat for three hours cross-legged on the sofa in conversation. We had, of course, prepared dinner for him, but he said that he had had his meal in the car on the way down —dates and raisins, as was his habit. (One or two other members of his party, however, were glad of food.) I think Gandhi did most of the talking, and of course L.G. encouraged him with searching questions. L.G. said afterwards: 'Well, Gandhi may be a saint, but he is certainly a first-class politician.'

Before he left, the Mahatma asked to meet the kitchen staff. He seemed to sense that they would like to meet him as indeed they did. A strange little incident occurred during the evening: a completely unknown cat came into the room and jumped on to Gandhi's lap. When he departed, so did the cat.

Amongst the distinguished people who came to visit L.G. was Einstein, in flight from Nazi Germany. He had had to leave all his belongings, including his beloved violin, behind in Germany and he was travelling in a white cotton suit. L.G. was no scientist, but the two fraternised very quickly, L.G. being naturally sympathetic to the sufferings of the Jews under Hitler. Another German visitor (not a refugee) was a grandson of the Kaiser, Prince Frederik, who was earning his living as an engineer in this country, a charming young man, obviously bearing no grudge against this country for its victory in 1918.

Lindbergh came too, shortly before the Second World War showed signs of breaking out. He did not stay long, however. He had been to Germany and was much impressed by the German strength and confidence, and having no doubt heard of L.G.'s opinions and criticisms of those in this country who had become warmongers, he pressed L.G. to take a firmer pro-German line. L.G. turned on him in such anger that Lindbergh took his leave, and L.G. did not even accompany him to his car.

I need hardly say that William Beveridge was always a greatly welcome visitor. He had sat at the feet of L.G. since the days of the Health Insurance Act, and was imbued with all L.G.'s determination to improve the lot of the working classes, especially as far as health and medical benefits were concerned. L.G. could always depend upon him for information and advice on any social schemes. Beveridge moved about a good deal in the course of his work—to Oxford, to the School of Economics, to Northumberland (between the wars), to Wiltshire, where he had a hideous bungalow among the historic earthworks of Amesbury. But wherever he was he was always available for L.G. whenever necessary. He and Mrs. Mair, later Lady Beveridge, would turn in at Bron-y-de to discuss the political situation—and personalities—or we would meet at a London restaurant. Sometimes Beveridge would dine with me at my flat in Morpeth Mansions of which I had been lucky enough to get the lease after the 1929 election and which faced on to Westminster Cathedral, which, when touched by the setting sun, flung a rosy hue on to the walls of the flat. One memorable evening Beveridge took me to see Paul Robeson and Peggy Ashcroft in *Othello*, a great and unforgettable experience. He had taken what he said were 'the best seats in the theatre', the two middle seats in the front row of the dress circle, and I remember his saying—a human touch—that if he were rich enough he would take these seats in every London theatre all the year round, so that he could be sure of having them for any play he wanted to see. I thought that here was a touch of royalty which accorded strangely with the Beveridge outlook on life.

He could not help inspiring affection and respect, but he did not plan for it—he did not know how to plan for it. One of the most prized volumes which I possess is a small one called *The Price of Peace*, which he sent me just before L.G. died and which is one of the most inspired pleas for the understanding of peace and security. He was coming down to Wales to talk about it in March 1945, but L.G. was so ill that I had to put him off and we never met again. He inscribed it to me: 'This book is not quite as it should have been, but the best I could do alone.'

To my mind Beveridge was an example of greatness without the power of influencing. But he was a very delightful personality and a man of complete integrity, which is rare in political circles. He telephoned me when the new National Health proposals were about to be introduced and said to me: 'They are not what L.G. would have wanted, Frances.'

Lord Beaverbrook often came over from Cherkley, usually bringing a guest—on one occasion Tallulah Bankhead, beautiful and husky-voiced.

Lawrence of Arabia was brought down by Basil Liddell Hart. The latter indeed was a constant visitor, and he and his charming wife are dear friends of mine. (L.G. and Basil saw eye-to-eye on the second war as it developed, each regretting the lack of foresight on the part of the Government in supplying adequate defence measures, especially where tanks and other armoured vehicles were concerned.) Lawrence, I felt, was never very much at ease with L.G. He was still critical of and disappointed with the Versailles Treaty in its dealings with the Arabs, and was writing his criticism in his famous books.

Churchill and members of his family turned in to see L.G. on many occasions; Sir Archibald and Lady Sinclair (now Lord and Lady Thurso) loved to look in for a talk, both charming people and very fond of L.G. One day William Randolph Hearst and Marion Davies lunched with us. It was a gay meal, L.G. and Hearst teasing each other over politics and the articles that L.G. had written for the American press; Marion Davies at her most alluring, sitting next to H. A. L. Fisher. She did, in fact, in the course of the meal arrange for her nephew to be allowed to come as a student at New College!

Maisky, the Russian Ambassador, would come from time to time for a talk with L.G. Madame Maisky sometimes came with him, and gave me a book of Pushkin's poems translated into English, which I did not know. The book includes some delightful short stories. M. Maisky gave L.G. a charming lacquer cigarette box, saying that he wished to show L.G. that the modern Russians had artistic gifts and could produce beautiful things.

There was a long argument one day between the two men about *Mein Kampf*, which Hitler had written. L.G. said it omitted any reference to the invasion of Russia, but Maisky contended that it was there. L.G. produced his copy, which had no reference to Russia in it, and Maisky said that an edition had been prepared specially for England *without* the chapter on the Eastern campaign. He said he would send L.G. the complete volume, but I am not sure that he ever did this.

I always felt that Maisky's friendship with L.G. might have been judged in Moscow as being bad for his soul, but L.G. was sorry when he was recalled to Russia. We were asked at the end of 1943 to lunch with his successor, M. Gousev, who did his level best to find out from L.G. what the prospects were of a 'Second Front' in the coming year, but L.G. was not to be prompted. Madame Gousev taught me how to drink vodka without being overcome, and this was much more pleasant. We were not invited to the Ambassador's house again.

Lord and Lady Snowden and the Fishers often came to

Sunday supper, when we frequently watched a film after-wards—usually a 'Wild West'. Sometimes there would be singing, choruses and hymns, and we would end up with Snowden singing 'On Ilkley Moor 'baht 'at'.

There was music too, when L.G. was helping to compile a new hymn-book. Sir Richard Terry, the organist at Westminster Cathedral, would come for the week-end, Sir Walford and Lady Davies, and Sir William Hadow and L.G. would sing his favourite hymns. The book was published under the title *Hymns of Western Europe* with a preface by L.G.

Wilfred Grenfell, the famous missionary, came from Labrador, He advised us to get jackets of the famous wind-cheating 'Grenfell' cloth—we did so and realised their worth. Grenfell was much impressed by our piggery at Bron-y-de, and L.G. offered him a boar and a sow for breeding in Labrador. These were duly sent, Lord Rothermere very kindly helping us to arrange for their journey.

The Guedallas, Philip and Nellie, were frequent visitors at Bron-y-de. Philip had stood as a Liberal for Parliament, on several occasions, unsuccessfully. Although a fervent Liberal, and witty, he did not show his talents to advantage on a political platform. But he was an engaging member of a house party. A brilliant conversationalist, he possessed the unusual gift of drawing out his companions so that they, too, felt they could sparkle. One never quite knew when his next sally would come. One morning at breakfast L.G.'s latest acquisition, a not very well-bred St. Bernard dog, appeared outside the window. 'What do you think of him?' L.G. asked. Philip took a long look. 'Well,' he said, 'my own opinion is that any self-respecting traveller, being dug up by that dog, would immediately ask to be put back again.' I used to enjoy going to spend the week-end with them at Dunmow. One would travel down with them from the most ghastly station in London—Liverpool Street—with

hampers destined for a return journey full of vegetables
and flowers, but now containing London dainties. Philip
took with him a P. G. Wodehouse novel, in which he would
immerse himself, that is to say when we were not walking,
or eating, or sunning ourselves in the charming garden.
They had lovely and sophisticated dinner parties every week
in their spacious house in Hyde Park Street, gatherings of
literary people whom it was a delight and privilege to meet—
Wells, Max Beerbohm, E. V. Lucas, Rose Macaulay, Ronald
Fraser, G. B. Stern, and others.

When L.G. realised that the National Government had
no intention of making it possible for him to join them,
and that he really had no wish to do so in any case, he
resolved himself to draw up his own proposals for dealing
with the country's difficulties. With the help of experts and
friendly politicians the document known later as 'The New
Deal' was framed and with great difficulty placed before
the Government.

It has since been realised that this scheme, if carried out,
would have been of enormous benefit to the country, both
before and after the war, and would have alleviated the
bitterness caused by the permanent unemployment during
the thirties. There would have been no such thing as
'distressed areas', and Britain would have been better
equipped in every way to deal with her post-war troubles.

L.G. himself was asked to meet the Cabinet to explain
his document. As was expected, the schemes were politely
but firmly returned to L.G. without, as far as I remember,
any comment. What became increasingly obvious at the
meeting was that the Cabinet had never at any time any
intention of interesting themselves. 'The meeting was
studiously pleasant,' L.G. remarked to me afterwards, 'but
they knew in their hearts they were about to knife me.
What they did not know was that I too had a dagger in my
sheath for them.' The dagger was the organisation afterwards

Season of harvest

Harvest home

The warrior

At peace: the grave beside the Dwyfor, Llanystumdwy

known as the Council of Action which he resolved to set up for putting his proposals before the public, in preparation for the forthcoming election. Later in the year, when he was voting in the Opposition lobby, a Welsh Socialist member said to him: 'Well, have you thrown away the scabbard?' and another Socialist standing near said: 'There never was one.'

One would have thought that at his age—he was now seventy-two—with his memoirs and his farm to occupy him, he would have been loath to enter upon another strenuous campaign. But the call of politics was hot in his blood—neither the book nor the farm sufficed—and the 'Council of Action' was initiated. It meant the burning of his boats as far as the National Government was concerned, but in my opinion there was at no time any chance of his joining that ship. A Tory friend who still had hopes that L.G. would be asked to join the Government complained that Baldwin was now angry, thinking L.G. was out to wreck the National Government. 'That is precisely what I am out for,' was L.G.'s retort.

From the start I was apprehensive about the whole plan. It was obvious that the heads of the Free Churches, upon whom L.G. had hoped to rely, as he had done in the old days, were not enthusiastic. Colonel Tweed, the head of the organisation, was very doubtful about the campaign, and I fear gave L.G. little encouragement. He was reckless and indiscreet in his criticism. And although at the beginning of July the proposals burst upon the public in a blaze of publicity, since it was obviously impossible to ignore anything emanating from L.G., the organisation never really got a sufficient hold upon the country to fire the nation.

On July 20th I noted in my diary:

A string of 'regrets' in to-night's bag [sent down from London every day] from people who had promised to support L.G.'s

Council of Action, but who are now crying off because they do not want to attend a wedding feast which looks like being a frost. L.G., however, is not daunted and continues preparing his plans. He is confident that he is going to smash the power of the National Government at the election.

In fact, at this time the dissensions in the Liberal Party had already become a subject for jokes and sneers in the House. In the course of an attack upon the Liberals, Marjoribanks, a Conservative member, said: 'In the Liberal Party are many mansions,' but his equilibrium was somewhat shaken by L.G.'s quick retort: 'And in the Conservative Party there are many flats.' Will Rogers, who was present at the debate, was very pleased with L.G.'s *mot*. 'I wish I had said that,' he said to L.G. afterwards.

In July 1935 the question of the Speaker's seat was revived by the resignation of Mr. Whitley. Whitley was a Liberal and the author of the Whitley Report. To L.G.'s mind he was an unfair Speaker. His own party was now suffering partial eclipse, and L.G. considered that Whitley made things even more difficult for them by his partiality to the Tories (perhaps caused by over-anxiety to be impartial). L.G. never forgave him for the snubs which he (in L.G.'s opinion) inflicted upon the Liberals and upon L.G. himself. After his resignation Whitley came down to Churt to take leave of L.G. and, as L.G. thought, to put himself right. But although L.G. treated him with scrupulous courtesy ('As I did Jowitt when he came here to tell me he had betrayed me,' L.G. said) the meeting was a strained one and Whitley went away, I fear, left in no doubt of L.G.'s feelings towards him. So bitter indeed was L.G. about the incidents in the House under Whitley's Speakership that he did not attend Whitley's funeral when he died.

During this summer L.G. saw a good deal of some of the younger Conservatives, including Mr. Harold Macmillan and Waldorf Astor. They came to Churt several times for talks. They were dissatisfied with the leadership of the Party, both on home and foreign affairs, and would have welcomed L.G. in the Government. They themselves had prepared a programme of reform entitled 'The Next Five Years', and it matched very nearly the programme outlined in L.G.'s 'Organising Prosperity', so it was thought that the two might be combined, and some campaign organised on common grounds. But the negotiations became rather sticky—the Conservatives, I imagine, fearing that the movement would mentally swamp them and become an entirely L.G. campaign, and put them in an awkward position at the election—as indeed it would have done. Nothing therefore materialised, except the fact that this section of the Conservatives saw almost eye-to-eye with L.G. in their ideas on social questions. Indeed Seebohm Rowntree, a Liberal, and Waldorf Astor worked with each other subsequently on plans of social reform.

By the end of August it was quite clear that the non-conformist leaders were running away from the Council of Action—Dr. Scott Lidgett and Mr. Sam Hughes and other members of the Free Church Council made efforts to withdraw. L.G. turned on them and rent them. 'Gideon knew how to distinguish between the funks and the brave men,' he flamed, 'I wish someone would give me that power.' 'He had only 300 left at the finish,' ventured Hughes. 'But he won,' retorted L.G. L.G. must have felt just as I did, ten years later, when I wrote asking men of reputation who had known and worked with L.G. in the past to support a memorial to him, and received from many of them cold letters of regret.

L.G., however, succeeded in rallying them temporarily, and a heavy campaign was embarked upon preparatory to the General Election which was imminent. My misgivings were somewhat reassured by the fact that Lord Lothian was backing L.G. He had indeed helped wholeheartedly to formulate the 'New Deal' scheme, but even Philip, I

think, began to have his doubts as to the ultimate success
of the Council of Action. With true Scottish loyalty, however, he would not have it on his conscience that he had
failed to come to the help of his old chief when expected
to do so.

17

Quiet Days in Churt and Morocco

The 1935 election approached, and L.G.'s depression deepened as the international situation worsened. He felt that the election had come too soon for him. The forces behind him were unorganised and unreliable. 'I feel,' he said to me, 'as the Abyssinians must be feeling, knowing that all the guns and ammunition are on the other side, and the poison gas, too.' He spent a great deal of time making calculations as to the probable state of the parties after the election, and inviting his friends to give their forecasts. His own was a majority for the Government of fifty-five. It seemed a foregone conclusion that the Government would win. L.G. realised that the election had torpedoed his plans. Physically he was in excellent form. We would go for long, long walks over the surrounding commons, and I often found it difficult to keep pace with him. Certainly at the end of these walks he was much less tired than I was. He would finish exhilarated and refreshed. Dr. Anderson, the Scottish beekeeper, who lunched with us one day at this time, said that L.G.'s vitality was phenomenal. L.G. recalled his Queen's Hall meeting in Boer War days, when he dealt with a very rowdy crowd and made a most effective speech. W. T. Stead, who was there, prophesied a remarkable future for L.G.—'If only his fragile physique is equal to the demands upon it'.

L.G. had been brought up on long walks, often as a

young man making the journey from Criccieth to his office at Portmadoc (six miles) on foot. All his life he attached the greatest importance to exercise and fresh air, and to deep breathing exercises.

The farm at Churt, as it expanded, gave him ample opportunity for exercise, and we walked over it sometimes twice a day, keeping an eye open for anything that needed attention, and making a note of it. He would enjoy talking with the men. One of them had, rather naturally, a vendetta against the blackbirds and the finches which were making havoc amongst the plums and the cherries. But L.G. stopped him from shooting them, saying: 'We've got to pay the birds for their song, you know, Jim.' It was the same man who, when L.G. asked him what was the strain of his attractive dog, replied: 'Well, her mother's a spaniel, and her father's somewhere between Churt and Thursley.'

It had been L.G.'s life-long ambition to grow fruit trees, and he embarked upon planting many acres of orchards. Very early in the orchard development L.G. made contact with the West Malling organisation in Kent, and the head of it, Sir Ronald Hatton, became a great friend and adviser, coming over often with his wife to Bron-y-de to plan our plantings of apples and pears and soft fruit. The trees are still there, though the orchards have been broken up, as L.G. always said they would be after his death, by his family. But in spring the sight of the blossom is still breath-taking.

The project and the progress of the farm itself and the walks over it, the delight of the discussions and the subsequent care and development, were good for L.G.'s body *and* soul, and often revived the visitor as much as they revived him. When the fruit was developing we would walk through the orchards sometimes twice a day, morning and evening, *counting* the blossoms, *counting* the fruit set, then working out the quantities of fruit that we could expect. (Of course, when the weevil and the scab and the frost had finished with it there was but a small proportion of fruit to be gathered.)

He tried many experiments on the farm—bells for frost warning, which meant that some of the men had to spend the night under cover in the orchards to be ready for the warning bells and light small containers of paraffin placed under the trees, when the smoke would drive the frost away. I do not know how successful this venture was, or how much it added to the crop of fruit, but it certainly provided L.G. with a new interest, interrupted, alas! by the war, when the metal containers were commandeered by the Government, in spite of protests.

There were journeys over to West Malling, too, when L.G. wanted some special help, and he was grateful for the willing courtesy extended to him on these occasions. There was a group of young naval officers who planted an orchard colony with their war gratuities at Kirdford, nearby, under the auspices of Sir Ronald Hatton, and we got the benefit of their experience. The orchards, I think, still exist.

Our local agricultural committee also supplied willing experts on fruit and other farm crops and on improving the land.

Thus we would spend hours in discussing the development of the farm, especially the orchards, and in contacting and interviewing people who would help and advise. There was one sad incident later in the development of the plum orchards. L.G. had obtained his first batch of plum trees from an old-established firm and the result had been so satisfactory that when the owner died L.G. invited his son to come over to Churt for luncheon and discuss the orchards with him. Luncheon time came, but no nurseryman. We waited a long time, delaying the meal until our visitor should arrive, and finally he turned up very, very late, and full of excuses. L.G. listened, and then said: 'Your father would not have been late.' The discussion on the orchards lacked spirit, and when the trees that L.G. ordered also arrived late for planting he decided to go elsewhere for his orchard material.

One of the first jobs on the farm was the building of cottages, and L.G. entrusted me with the plans for the first pair of cottages for the farm workers. They had a large kitchen where the family could sit for meals, hot and cold water (the first cottages in Churt with such a supply) and half an acre of land. But the tenants said that half an acre was too much to maintain, and the next cottages were only given one-third of an acre, which they said was ample. He built a number of cottages on various patterns, but I think the first two were the most attractive. A moderate range of farm buildings was also added, and a farm office, the hub of activity; and while all this was going on, L.G. was buying up parcels of land as they became available, and small farms, all of which had lovely storage barns, from the days of Waverley Abbey.

In one of the barns a herd of pedigree pigs was housed and a trained pig manager looked after them. Some of the pigs were given free range over derelict land, which, when ready, was ploughed with a deep plough, and in due course orchards were planted. These orchards are now bearing splendid fruit.

We had setbacks, of course. One day in spring, when the blossom was fully out, we found that a large percentage of it had become brown and shrivelled, and the manager said that the blight was spreading and might destroy all the fruit blossom. L.G. got busy at once, to see if there was an antidote spray. He was told by I.C.I. that they were working on a spray for this particular pest, but it would not be ready until the following year. It was the now famous D.D.T., and L.G. realised that if he could survive this spring his crops would be safeguarded in future—at some expense, of course.

We weathered that year, with a considerably reduced

crop, and had reason to be grateful to the chemical firms for their help over other pests which appeared with regularity and were regularly dealt with. The use of these new sprays meant new machinery, which also added to the expense of running the farm. To help us, Mr. Harry Ferguson stepped in with his new little tractor, one that could operate easily between the comparatively narrow alleyways of the orchards, and for which we were truly grateful. Mr. Ferguson came down himself to demonstrate the tractor and was most helpful in getting it launched in the orchards.

The final building, when the fruit harvests began to come in, was an enormous fruit store, with an electrically cooled storage section for the fruit after it had been packed. H. A. L. Fisher called the building 'a blot on the landscape', but it provided employment in the fruit season for a large number of people in and around Churt. Nowadays this is the accepted equipment for a fruit farm, but then it was the kind of pioneer work that L.G. greatly enjoyed.

L.G.'s pioneering work was in the early days of fertilisers, and he was liberal in his use of them. This did not always meet with the approval of his staff, and one day when he was discussing with one of them the application of a concentrated fertiliser to a potato crop, the gruff remark came, 'I don't 'old with these consecrated manures, sir'.

All this development entailed the laying-on of water and electricity and a large outlay in expenditure in many other ways. He also, helped by the experience of Mr. F. Secrett, who had a market garden nearby, sank an artesian well, with the aid of a neighbouring water diviner, and the local excitement was great. L.G. was writing his articles and then his memoirs, and this provided him with the money he needed.

At a later date L.G. decided to introduce a herd of sheep into the Bron-y-de economy, thinking they would be good for the orchards. They did not prosper, owing, we under-

Q

stood, to faulty management, and they were sent to the Farnham market. At a Sunday supper party Philip Snowden said rather viciously, in that rather sneering manner which was characteristic of him: 'I saw some sheep of yours in the market yesterday, L.G. I've never seen such a poor lot of animals.' L.G. was furious, the more so as Ethel Snowden had, at a previous supper party, accused L.G. of having put Philip in prison during the (first) war. This was, of course, untrue. Philip had been put in prison at the beginning of the war together with other conscientious objectors, and I think it was L.G. who helped to get him released.

The Snowdens had bought a large house on the Tilford Road below Bron-y-de, and we saw a good deal of them, especially when Philip was in office, and liked to talk things over with L.G. Ethel Snowden was enjoying her social status and as she was an excellent speaker she was in demand. Queen Mary made a great fuss of her. But L.G. was very much against the Coalition Government and made no secret of this, and there were many arguments which often became heated. However, Philip did not stand up to the strains of office, and his life-long weakness became worse, especially when a local doctor diagnosed his illness wrongly. This became known when Philip, calling in a specialist, had his malady properly diagnosed, and improved in health. The first doctor afterwards called and said, 'I don't suppose you will want me any more'.

'Oh, I may as well have one damn fool as another,' was the testy reply, in his strong Yorkshire accent.

In spite of all the pain he suffered throughout his life he was at heart a sweet-tempered person. I used to go down to talk to him when he was bedridden during his last illness, and derived instruction and spiritual example from his unselfish attitude to life and his philosophical counsels.

About October, L.G. ran into Ramsay Macdonald in the House and scarcely recognised him, he was looking so changed and ill. Ramsay told him he was feeling ill, and that he began sentences and forgot what he had been going to say. 'You have never had that, have you?' he asked L.G. anxiously, almost appealingly. L.G. realised too late that Ramsay had hoped to be reassured by him and said that he had not. It was pitiful to see the present condition of the man who four years before had been so full of pride and power, and was now treated by his colleagues with insolence and contempt.

There were many attempts to bring L.G. and Herbert Samuel together before the election, and one night L.G. received a message from Lord Reith to say that Samuel had offered to give L.G. one of the Liberal broadcasting dates. This showed how completely L.G. was now severed from the Liberals, in that Samuel would appear to be making a concession in offering this. L.G., however, sought out Samuel in the House and they dined together. L.G. was not so much interested in the broadcast as in an effort to get Samuel to make a statement before polling day advising Liberals in constituencies where there was no Liberal candidate to vote for the candidate who supported the Council of Action questionnaire. Nothing came of this.

In the election campaign L.G. virtually won three seats— his own, Gwilym's and Megan's. He was pleased with the Welsh results, but in one or two cases the candidates failed to get in because, according to L.G., they insisted in clinging to the fetish of Free Trade. He advised one of them to leave Free Trade alone. 'I must stick to my principles,' the candidate objected. 'Do you want to go to Heaven or Westminster?' was L.G.'s cynical retort.

L.G. returned from the campaign in good spirits and full of plans for the future. But the following week-end was a very quiet one, and his spirits ebbed somewhat. There was not a single telephone message from any source, political or otherwise. It was as though he had suffered a total eclipse. Nevertheless he began to make plans for the Council of

Action activities for the next two years. It gave him a sem-
blance of activity and as long as he had this he was happy.

But he went less and less to Westminster now, and
more and more around the farm. The time was coming, he
felt, when every scrap of food that could be produced
would be wanted, and he resolved to warn the nation, in
speech after speech, of the coming necessity. Whatever
subject he spoke on, he would always, if possible, end on
this note of warning. But members did not heed him. Even
his own friends would shake their heads and say: 'What a
pity it is that L.G. must *always* drag in agriculture. The
speech would have been a good one without that.'

It seemed indeed as though he had merely to advocate a
policy for it to become taboo not only to the Opposition
but to many of his friends. From my place in the Gallery
I watched members on the Opposition benches sneering
and mocking at him when he broached the subjects which
were near to his heart, and, as he deemed, vital to the safety
of the nation. Those who were not engaged were bored.
For the first time, members left the House before L.G. had
finished his speech when he spoke on agriculture and food
supplies. His own friends though the had a bee in his bonnet.

That winter (1935) we went to Tangier, and on to
Marrakech for a holiday—so-called, though L.G. was working hard at his memoirs, and there were several of us helping him. Francis and Jessica Brett Young also came with
us, and added greatly to our entertainment during the non-
working hours.

We found Marrakech enchanting, with the gorgeous
range of the Atlas Mountains in the distance, the picturesque
old Arab town nearby, the sun and the palm trees. There
was even a golf course laid out by the Sultan, and we were
invited by him to use it whenever we wished. As a golf
course it left a great deal to be desired, but it was a glorious
place to walk over, bordered by wonderful trees, and every
now and then a flight of storks overhead.

On Christmas Day a telephone call came for L.G. from Churchill, who was in Tangier. 'What was the weather like at Marrakech,' he asked, 'and what sort of a place was it? The weather in Tangier was vile.' L.G. gave him a suitable description of Marrakech. 'I'm coming along,' said Winston: and shortly afterwards he arrived with his son Randolph, his daughter Mrs. Sandys, and her husband Duncan Sandys, and Professor Lindemann, who was, even at that time, Mr. Churchill's constant companion. Churchill was also busy on his history of Marlborough, so that the mornings for both men were taken up with work. Sometimes Churchill would resort to his painting, and a beautiful picture which he painted of the Atlas Mountains from the hotel balcony he gave to my husband.

Randolph Churchill left the party to fly back to Scotland to contest—unsuccessfully—a by-election at Ross and Cromarty, much against his father's advice.

It was a very happy party. There was a wonderful dinner at the Palace of the Glaoui—the local Arab chieftain—where sumptuous Arab dishes were served to us in Arab fashion, and we helped ourselves with our fingers. One course required a very deft movement to convey the morsels, which were covered in rice, from the platter to the mouth, and L.G. emerged from it with his coat and even his hair covered with rice. There were magnificent black servants at hand, however, with towels and bowls of water, to help the guests in such an emergency, and to lave their hands at intervals. It was a marvellous feast.

Jessica Brett Young and I were invited to tea with the Glaoui's wives in his harem. As we set out we met Mr. Churchill and Randolph and we told them where we were going. 'Can't Randolph go too?' asked Winston with a twinkle in his eye. I shook my head. 'They won't even let L.G. go,' I replied. This seemed to amuse him a great deal.

At Marrakech rumbles reached us of the Hoare-Laval battle. At the height of the crisis Sylvester tried to telephone

to L.G from London urging him to return. But although the
call came through, fortunately not a word of what Sylvester
said could be heard, and we remained at Marrakech. L.G.
could have done nothing in any case, for the trouble was
quickly over. He might have made a moving speech in
the House, but he could not have moved the Government
or events at that time.

L.G. told me that Joseph Chamberlain once said to him:
'Take care always to have the Party machine behind you.
Nothing can be accomplished without this.' When L.G.
quarrelled with the Liberal Party during the first war, he
forgot about this. He thought only of the war. And when,
in the Coupon Election of 1918, he severed himself from
the Liberal Party machine, the prospects of his returning to
office were doomed. He thought he could create some sort
of Party machine for himself, but it was built upon sand,
and the forces behind him were too diverse and ramshackle
for him to forge any lasting machinery. The large resources
of his fund were poured away to no purpose, unless it were
so to undermine the power of the Conservative Government as to give Labour its great chance. And so, all through
the thirties, he continued to remain in the wilderness.
Churchill was also in the wilderness—blackballed by the
Tory Party; Churchill, too, as long as he lacked the support
of the Conservative Party machine, was powerless to imple-
ment his ideas for strengthening the forces of this country.
And so he and L.G. remained in their separate wildernesses,
until war brought the younger one back into full power
and age forced the older one into permanent retirement.
(L.G. was nearly twelve years older than Winston.)

We returned from Marrakech earlier than we intended,
owing to the death of King George V. The sudden change
from heat to the miserable British weather gave L.G. a
chill from which he took some weeks to recover.

One day, when he was convalescing, we sat and discussed Mirabeau, whose biography by Sudder L.G. had

lately read. Incidentally, Louis Barthou, discovering in November 1917 (after the Rapallo Conference) that L.G. was an admirer of Mirabeau, gave L.G. a copy of his own biography of that statesman, and inscribed it thus:

A Lloyd George, le grand homme d'état, pour lui dire de l'admiration que m'inspire son eloquence imagée, son courage clairvoyant et sa force d'action.

L.G. however, on reading this book came to the conclusion that Barthou did not understand Mirabeau any more than he understood L.G. (How different was Barthou from Briand, the 'brother-Celt'. He and L.G. had understood every trick and feint of the other, knowing when each was in earnest and when he was bluffing.) L.G. himself considered that he did understand Mirabeau, although he judged him, to quote his own words, 'the greatest *carrière manquée* in history, with the possible exception of Hannibal'. In L.G.'s opinion Mirabeau would have saved the Revolution from many of its horrors and mistakes. If he and Lafayette had worked together, argued L.G., another story would have been written. (And, I thought to myself, if L.G. and Baldwin could work together they would get the country out of its troubles and muddles.) But Mirabeau, because he was not entirely against the Monarchy as such, and because he did not believe either in the old order or in every aspect of the Revolution, was accused of insincerity and treachery. 'There is a danger,' he said, 'of making the Revolution abortive by expecting too much of it.'

Sometimes L.G. would discuss the old Welsh preachers. This was a favourite topic with him. He was steeped in Bible lore, which he had received from the lips of his uncle in his childhood. The little nonconformist community in Llanystumdwy, like so many others in Wales, gave their chapel pride of place in the village—it was the social centre, as well as the seat of judgment for local backsliders. The

Sunday School was attended by adults as well as children, and thus L.G. while very young became acquainted with Bible teaching and Bible phraseology. In many of his great speeches he drew upon the Bible for an illustration. Many of his most apt quotations were from the Book.

One morning during L.G.'s Premiership he was entertaining—at breakfast, as was his wont—the Rev. Philip Jones, a famous Welsh preacher. The conversation was absorbed and prolonged—so much so, indeed, that a secretary who had entered the room remained there several minutes before the pair observed him. 'I am sorry to disturb you, sir,' he said to the Prime Minister, 'but the Cabinet have been waiting for you for ten minutes.'

The conversation had been on the subject of the old Welshmen who had achieved fame as preachers in the eighteenth and nineteenth centuries, and there was no subject more dear to L.G.'s heart. It had been his intention to write a book about them, and to this end he had collected a quantity of material. His special favourites were, I think, Christmas Evans, John Elias, and William Williams (Wern). But their merits would be debated in comparison with Edward Matthews (Ewenni), John Jones (Talsarn), Robert Roberts (Clynnog), Herber Evans and many others. In L.G.'s youth there were many men still alive who had heard these men preach, and were able to tell of their performance.

One of the sermons which L.G. was most fond of reproducing was the sermon of The 'Little Lantern'. It was preached by Herber Evans on the subject of the 'Higher Criticism'—the 'New Theology', which found fault with the Bible on the ground that its history was poor, its influence failing, its theology full of holes and its meaning in places very doubtful. To illustrate his story Herber Evans described an old preacher who had come a long way to address his congregation, and who had to return home that night along a dark road beset with danger and difficult to follow. As he was leaving, a woman in the congregation put a small lantern into his hands with the words: 'It is only a small lantern, Mr. Evans *bach*, and it is full of holes and very old; but it will light you home, Mr. Evans, it will light you home.' And lifting up the great Bible from the lectern, the preacher held it aloft, and cried: 'Thy word is a lantern unto my feet, and a light unto my paths!' As L.G. retold the story we could see the anxious face of the woman as she thrust the lantern into the man's hand, we could see the little flickering lantern itself; and when his voice rang out with the final words, the thrill which it produced brought the tears to our eyes.

Another of his special favourites was the sermon on the Feast of Belshazzar and the Writing on the Wall, preached by John Elias. This was more than a sermon, it was a theatrical performance, and the stage had to be set for it. John Elias, visiting the chapel before the service, directed that the candles should be so arranged that his outstretched hand, while preaching, should cast a shadow on the white-washed wall of the chapel. 'Place that one there'—L.G. would depict him as saying to the verger. 'And this one here—no, a little farther back.' The arrangements were completed with the greatest care, and then the preacher would embark on his famous sermon—the Writing on the Wall, in relation to the sins of the present generation. L.G. would describe the terror of the congregation when, at the psychological moment, the awful message *was* actually written on the wall. And no matter how often the sermon was repeated, and it was repeated often, and by request, John Elias was able to produce the same effect upon his audience. It was the same dramatic gift that enabled another preacher to describe the Crucifixion with such power and vividness that the congregation interrupted and implored him to cease, that they might not have to witness the last agonising scene.

These men had the power of bringing the Bible to life

for their congregations, by reproducing Biblical events almost as it it were in modern dress, and recounting imaginary conversations between the characters to illustrate the theme in question. Christmas Evans, for instance, whose message was always the infinite mercy of Jesus, took for his text Christ's command: 'Go ye into all the world, and preach the Gospel to every creature.' He described the disciples questioning Jesus. 'In *Jerusalem*, Lord?' 'Yes.' 'But, Lord, it was there that Thou wert crucified. Surely we are not to preach *there*?' 'Yes, you must preach to all.' 'To the man who plaited the crown of thorns and placed it on Thy head?' 'Yes, and tell him he can obtain a crown of glory out of the shame.' 'What if we come across the man who nailed Thy sacred hands and feet to the Cross? And the man who stabbed Thy side? . . . and he who spat on Thy face?' 'Preach the Gospel to all of them, tell them there is a welcome for all to partake of the blessings of my Salvation, that I am the Lord, and generous to all who seek me.'

In the same way that these famous men held their congregations spellbound and played upon their emotions and their imagination, so did L.G. hold his hearers in thrall when he related these sermons. Indeed I sometimes wondered if the original sermons surpassed his rendering of them. Certainly, no voice could exceed his, in quality and vibration and eloquence, no eye flash more passionately, no gesture be more dramatic or compelling. Sometimes he would describe the style of these sermons. The preachers did not start off with a flourish. 'It was,' L.G. would say, 'like a ship getting out of harbour. The sermon had difficulty in getting away—there would be an occasional bump—you could hear the chain creaking but soon it came sailing out easily and smoothly on the fairway. Then you felt a speeding-up and a slight heavy roll and you knew you were being carried along into the open sea, the breeze filling the sails as you drove through the hurricane.' (These were L.G.'s own words, which I find written in his notes.) Sometimes the

preacher would make two or three false starts, and the
congregation might begin to worry, and then, suddenly,
the sermon 'broke' and they were lifted along in ecstasy by
a master hand. My husband's uncle, Richard Lloyd, would
sometimes preach in this fashion, ending on an inspired
note and with his congregation transported with joy. Thus
did I hear the other day a supreme artist of song—a son of
the people—begin his programme, softly, gently; by the
end of the programme he had the audience beside themselves and in the hollow of his hand: 'What is it?' I asked
my companion. 'The Divine spark,' came the reply.

The sermons were carefully prepared in every detail—
intonation, gesture, even to the timing of the 'breaking' of
the performance, when the congregation would often lose
control. The preacher then could mould them in his hands.
When John Elias, for instance, hurled his message at the
congregation in the form of an imaginary arrow those in
the line of the arrow moved aside! These men were more
than preachers: they were poets, dramatists, prophets, and
accomplished orators. In L.G.'s own words again: 'They
were remarkable not only for their spiritual intensity but
for their intellectual power. They aroused and wakened the
intellectual interest of the people. They informed their
people as well as inspired them. They made nonconformity
a great public school for educating the masses of the
people. . . .'

Over a period of 150 years they successively leavened
Welsh life, and it is not surprising that L.G., with his own
power of oratory and his imagination, should have studied
and admired them, and acknowledged his debt to them.
'One of the things,' he would say, 'that I would like to
enjoy when I enter Paradise is a Preaching Festival, with
John Elias, Christmas Evans, William of Wern and others
occupying the pulpit. That is how the Fathers of nonconformity appeal to me.'

The majesty of the Old Testament books appealed more,

I think, to him than the gentle teachings of Jesus. L.G.
could be kind, he could on occasions be infinitely tender,
but he could never be meek. And, yet, when he was dying
he whispered to me: 'It is the sign of the Cross.' I asked
him what his meaning was, but he only repeated: 'It is the
sign of the Cross.'

And sometimes we would discuss the theatre. For L.G.,
the two greatest figures on the stage when he came to
London as a young man were Henry Irving and Marie
Lloyd. In Henry Irving, true to the traditions of tragic
acting, L.G. found an actor after his own heart, and no
one ever matched him. Most subsequent acting appeared
to him anaemic. And the man who himself could keep a
crowd in the hollow of his hand by a look, a smile, a word,
was enchanted by the supreme artistry of the woman
(Marie Lloyd) who could capture her audience with a wink.

The only operas he cared for were the light ones, and
these he would go to whenever the opportunity presented
itself. *La Fille de Madame Angot* was a particular favourite,
and all the Gilbert and Sullivan operas he loved. Such
musical comedies as *Véronique* and the *Merry Widow*
enchanted him, but he did not care for the latter-day,
more sophisticated ones, such as *Bitter Sweet*. He liked
happy stories. And he liked *action*. He once went to see
Tristan in company, I think, with Herbert Samuel, and was
so bored that he had difficulty in sitting it out. 'He took a
whole act to die in,' was his comment on Tristan.

During all these years we used frequently to go over to
Lord Beaverbrook's house at Leatherhead to dine and to
talk politics. Here there was always good company and the
conversation in itself was an entertainment. On one occasion,
a small dinner party, Arnold Bennett and Noël Coward
were the other guests. The former I found singularly lacking in charm, but I fancy that he must have been feeling
rather uncomfortable, for, unknown to us that evening,
he was publishing the following day a book called *The*

Prime Minister, containing a not very kind pen-portrait of myself whom he had never before met.

Noël Coward, on the other hand, was charming and modest. He was easy to talk to, and entirely without affectation. It was a lovely evening with a full moon, and we walked and talked in the enchanting old garden in the intervals of listening to the Dolmetsch family playing Elizabethan airs.

There was often music at Cherkley. One evening Paul Robeson delighted us with his Negro spirituals, and on another occasion a choral party sang sea shanties to entertain the guests.

Speaking of music, L.G. could get inspiration and comfort from certain composers, and he would never miss an opportunity of going to listen to the *Messiah*, a work that the Welsh are brought up on, and can sing lustily, as they do the old Welsh hymn tunes which I used often to play to L.G.

I had gradually come to realise that L.G. would be more and more at Churt, only coming to London when official occasions, including his presence in the House of Commons, demanded it. He had no obligations in the House, being to all intents and purposes an Independent, if a very powerful member. He had no intention of again becoming harnessed to the disgruntled, divided and rapidly dwindling party to which he nominally belonged. He was engaged in writing his memoirs, and the greater part of the meetings and conferences which were held in connection with his new proposals for solving unemployment took place at Churt. And the farm itself was becoming to him more and more important and more and more of a solace against the bitterness of politics.

I had moved from London to Worplesdon after L.G.'s operation in 1931, in order to be nearer to Churt, having let my flat in Westminster to the Churchills. But I realised that in the new circumstances I should have to be still nearer to Churt.

I decided therefore to build a small house on some land I had bought adjacent to Bron-y-de. L.G. chose the actual site, giving me a wonderful view, and laid the foundation stone. The house was built by a young architect friend of mine, who has since achieved distinction in the architectural world. It was built in the modern manner, and was named Avalon, since it stood in the midst of apple orchards. We had some difficulty in persuading the local authorities to pass the plan, as with its Continental air, its flat roof, white walls and large expanse of glass, it was not at all what a conventional council would approve of. Even L.G. dubbed the style of architecture 'Neo-Abyssinian'. Would not a house of mock-Tudor style be more traditional and in keeping with the landscape? the puzzled council enquired. But we stuck to our guns, and I think the members of the council themselves were impressed by the pleasantness of the finished article, which had an atmosphere of light and spaciousness, and a unique setting.

18

Drifting into War

By the early summer of 1936 L.G. had recovered his buoyancy and his pugnacity. The Government was being carried
along in policy at the heels of French statesmen, some of
whom turned out to be little more than crooks. L.G. fumed
at his impotence to influence our foreign policy and deplored
our loss of prestige. When Britain abandoned the sanctions
which the League of Nations had imposed upon Germany,
he could keep silence no longer. In the Foreign Affairs
debate which followed in June 1936, the vials of his wrath
and contempt were outpoured:

'I have been in this House very nearly half a century, and . . .
I have never before heard a British Minister, speaking on behalf
of the Government . . . say that Britain was beaten—Britain and
her Empire beaten—and that we must abandon the enterprise
we had taken in hand.'

Referring to the Prime Minister's message to the Peace
Society: 'Let your aim be resolute, and your footsteps firm and
certain,' he went on. 'Here is the resolute aim: here is the certain
footstep—running away!

The Rt. Hon. Gentleman has boasted today and he boasted
in the last speech of his that I heard in the House, that we led
the nations. That increased our responsibilities. We led in the
imposition of sanctions: we led also in denunciation of the
aggressor. We led, too, in proposing, I think, oil sanctions in
principle!' He quoted Neville Chamberlain's words at the last

election: 'The choice before us is whether we shall make a last
effort at Geneva for peace and security, or whether by a cowardly
surrender we shall break all the promises we have made and
hold ourselves up to the shame of our children and their children's children.' He then cried, scornfully, pointing to the Front
Bench: 'Tonight we have had the cowardly surrender, and
there are the cowards.'

The speech was devastating: L.G. resurrected his old
fighting days. The House was almost hysterical. The Front
Bench seemed to cower before this onslaught, and Baldwin's
reply was pitiable. There was consternation on the faces of
the Tory back-benchers at Baldwin's impotence to tackle
L.G. After the speech a young Tory member went up to
Churchill and said that he had never heard anything like
it in the House. 'Young man,' Churchill replied, 'you have
been listening to one of the greatest Parliamentary per-
formances of all time.'

But L.G.'s test of a great speech was whether it would
move to action or not. And nothing could galvanise Baldwin
to effective political action, save the prospect of securing
the abdication of a King whom he did not like.

In July L.G. lunched alone one day with Maisky, with
whom he was on excellent terms. Maisky was upset to hear
that L.G. was contemplating a visit to Germany. He said
that Moscow was convinced that Germany intended to
have a great Mittel-European state—that she would attack
Czechoslovakia, and take the Corridor, Lithuania and Latvia,
and then, with the help of Poland, attack Russia. He was
not very far out in his prognostications!

But L.G., in spite of Maisky's protests, visited Germany
in September. Great pressure had been put upon him to do
so, though many of his friends were doubtful of the plan.
But it is not surprising that L.G. was anxious to meet the
man who had surmounted Germany's economic difficulties,
and in accepting the invitation he was only following the

precedent of many others in high places here who had visited Germany and formed a high opinion of Hitler.

Much has been written of this visit, and of the impression which Hitler made on L.G. It is not suprising that this should be so, for L.G. and his party were shown all the perfectly legitimate schemes which Hitler had carried out for the welfare and resuscitation of his country. Many of these schemes were comparable to those which L.G. had been advocating in Britain to deal with unemployment—agricultural schemes, electrical development, road and railway development, and many others—schemes which L.G. had failed to bring into being. It is not surprising, therefore, as I say, that he was full of admiration for one who had done what he had failed to do, especially when he saw the advantages that were accruing to Germany as a result.

There was no doubt that on Hitler's side there was also admiration for L.G. He remarked to Lord Lothian, who visited him later in the year, that after making the acquaintance of L.G. he understood why Britain had won the 1914–18 war.

And I still believe that had L.G. been given a say in the affairs of Britain during these years preceding 1939, with power to approach Hitler and negotiate with him, the Second World War would never have happened. I think this view has gained ground. L.G. would have bargained with Hitler, giving back to Germany some of the territories which had been taken from her against L.G.'s advice in the Peace Treaty of 1919, and which had remained a source of grievance during the years which followed. And no one could ever touch L.G. in negotiation—he was indeed superhuman in the art of persuasion and in understanding the mind of his opponent, and I know that he would have put forward all his strength to come to some understanding with Germany. It would have not been all persuasion: there would have been threats as well: but if L.G. had threatened, Hitler would have known that there would be the wherewithal to enforce the threats.

R

I thought even at this time that it might be possible, if L.G. continued to press his attacks upon the Government, for him to get them down. I said this to him one day, but he replied that he did not wish to do this now; that he would not take office if it were offered to him, because he did not feel equal to it, and he was constitutionally incapable of undertaking anything unless he flung himself whole-heartedly into it. I think that this was the first time it dawned upon me that he really would not be able to take a strenuous job again—one that meant continuous and unremitting work, which a Cabinet post would inevitably mean to him.

We went in November in search of sunshine to Jamaica, and to continue the work on the memoirs.

When we left there was no sign of the crisis that was to break. But, soon after, the new and as yet uncrowned King made his historic visit to the South Wales distressed areas, and the whole situation quickly changed. By December 4th the story of the King's proposed marriage had broken, and what happened subsequently is part of the history of our country.

The moment the trouble began Mr. Churchill sent a message to L.G. to return at once, and we booked passages on the next ship home and packed our things. But before we could leave, another message came to say that it was no use; that everything was over and the King was abdicating. Like so many others we listened to his abdication speech with wrung hearts.

I fully believe that the crisis was purposely engineered while L.G. was out of the country; and I believe that had L.G. been in England, he and he alone could have persuaded the King where his duty lay. Baldwin knew what an influence L.G. had always exerted on the young Prince. 'But for the Abdication,' L.G. would say, 'Baldwin would never be heard of in history.' He contemplated writing an article on Baldwin, entitled 'Tomlinson'—after Kipling's poem—the story of the man who was fit neither for heaven nor hell.

L.G. held the view very strongly that a public man had no right to put his private desires before his job; that if he did so, he was betraying the people who had given him their trust and their support.

L.G.'s theory was that so long as a man, or woman, kept the conventions outwardly, the public would excuse or ignore his private behaviour; but that Mrs. Grundy was a merciless person when her codes were openly challenged. It is a cynical point of view, and not exactly a moral one. It does not speak very highly for the intelligence or the morality of the 'public': but I think it is nevertheless true, and that L.G. was right. As I say, L.G.'s theory went one further, for he held that once a man or woman had accepted a public position and the support of his followers, then he had no right whatever to let them down. It was, in a way as strict a code of behaviour as any moral law.

'If love were all' . . . says the Princess in a romantic novel which has become a classic and captured the imagination of all English speaking people. 'If love were all' . . . she says in renouncing her dear lover. So many of the King's subjects had been obliged to place duty before love in the service of their country that they felt that they had surely a right to expect him at least to *follow* their example.

In March L.G. decided to go again to Antibes, to finish off his volumes on the peace treaties, and he arranged to meet in Paris *en route* certain important French politicians. He had a feeling that the sands were running out, and he was appalled at the inefficiency of the British Government and the weakness of successive French Governments. He did not know at that time that there was also corruption in high quarters in France, and he sought to bring home to people like Leon Blum the urgent necessity for France and Britain to combine in an effort to curb the two dictators, Hitler and Mussolini. Daladier, the French Prime Minister at the time, excused himself from meeting L.G. and the latter felt that he had made little impression in Paris in Government quarters. And now it was Etienne Mantoux, the son of our old friend Paul Mantoux, who accompanied us; Etienne, gay and intelligent and kind, who, after writing his famous book *The Carthaginian Peace*, was to die for his country in the coming war.

We proceeded to the South of France, where we found that the Duke and Duchess of Windsor were staying in the same hotel.

We had not been long in Antibes before the news came that Hitler's troops had marched into Prague, and we returned hastily to England, in time to hear Chamberlain's wild pledge to Poland to come to her aid if attacked. L.G.'s speech commenting on this pledge was a memorable one. The House was crowded to its utmost capacity and every point went home. It was another instance of L.G.'s vision. How right he was, and how helpless we were to carry out our promise, the position of Poland today is sufficient testimony. He had some support, for it was rumoured that this guarantee had been given without consultation with our military chiefs. But there were men on the benches opposite who jeered at him and one of them taunted him with lack of patriotism. Tempers ran high.

But a few months later and we were in the war ourselves. L.G. and I drove up to the House of Commons on the Sunday morning when the ultimatum expired. We stopped in Richmond Park just before eleven, and turned on the wireless which was in the car. And that was how we heard the declaration of war.

As we reached the House of Commons the sirens went. It was a false alarm—an aeroplane, which turned out to be one of our own, had been seen flying in from the coast. But I think those sirens marked the end of an epoch.

We had lunch in the Members' Room, and Bob Boothby joined us for a short time. The conversation was, of course, on the subject of the European armies, and Bob said that Ironside (our C.-in-C.) had told him that he had barely two recognisable divisions. We returned to Churt very depressed.

I think I am right in saying that at no time had L.G. any intention of taking part in the War Government. His heart was not in the war. He held in the first place, as I have shown, that with wise statesmanship it could have been prevented; and secondly, with his wondrous foresight, he thought that if Europe embarked on another war, she, including Britain, would be ruined. Who shall say that he was wrong?

On October 3rd he delivered a speech which pleaded for another attempt to come to an understanding with Germany before it was too late. The speech elicited a great deal of support and approbation from many thoughtful people of distinction, who were not pacifists: but amongst the warmongers and jingoes it made him very unpopular. And now, in May 1940, he spoke again with his old fire and force, when the 'phoney war' was showing signs of breaking into the war of undreamed-of proportions which it subsequently became. The news of the failure of the Norway expedition was coming in, and Neville Chamberlain was attempting to defend the Government. L.G. was ready, and Neville's somewhat whining references to his friends gave L.G. his chance. He made a savage attack on the Prime Minister. And in his advancing years—and alas for the last time—there was still the same terrifying ring of scorn and anger in his voice. Chamberlain, who four years before had recorded that 'L.G. had ceased to interest', winced and wilted as the crushing blow descended upon him.

L.G. contended that a speech should have *action* as its objective. No rolling phrases and polished sentences were of avail unless they produced works as a result of words. He used to say that he had listened to very few speeches in the House of Commons which had actually changed the decided views of members or the policy of the Government. I can bear witness to this in the impassioned speeches of the Labour members during the years of unemployment—I particularly remember a most moving maiden speech by James

Griffiths delivered in an apathetic House—which fell on deaf ears and unresponding hearts. L.G.'s own speeches in the House during this period on agriculture and unemployment were similarly unsuccessful.

But the speech on the Norway debate came into a different category. It was a supreme example of a speech resulting in action. It is true that opinion against the Prime Minister and his Government was ripe for action, but it was L.G.'s speech which brought it to a head, and crystallised it. Next day Chamberlain resigned office. In six months he was dead.

And now the two men of genius, whose lives had been linked for so long, were destined to separate, as it turned out, for ever. L.G. had, I think, always been aware, perhaps unconsciously, that the other had the advantage of him in age—an advantage which became so apparent, so finally conclusive, when the war at last broke out. It gave Churchill his supreme opportunity, and at the same time it brought home to L.G. the fact that he was out of the running. Churchill had already made an attempt to have L.G. included in the War Government and now was genuinely anxious to include L.G. in his own Cabinet, for the sake of friendship as well as prestige. But L.G. was adamant.

I was amongst those who pleaded with him, on the fall of France in June 1940, to go up to London and talk with Winston, and offer him *some* kind of help in the terrible task which lay before him. It was his patriotic duty, I said, not to withhold his experience and his strength at such a time. I knew the kind of attack that was being made on him for hesitating to help to rally the nation. Ned Grigg (later Lord Altrincham) was insistent that he should take a part, if only a small one, in the Churchill Government.

On June 19th there appeared in *The Times* a vigorous leading article:

Organising Victory

An article which appears on this page presents an argument which, in one form or another, is commanding more and more attention . . . if (the P.M.) could be relieved of some of the . . . burdens which he is bearing. The case is for a better distribution of effort, a better system of planning, a more scientific method of organisation.

The author's suggestion (on long-range planning) . . . is a Defence Committee (three Service Secretaries of State and the Minister of Civil Defence) . . . to be presided over by a Minister of Defence, not the P.M. . . . a reconstituted War Cabinet . . . to adjudicate on major plans. . . .

The Times then suggests a possible 'Planning Committee' of specialists . . . to establish 'Planning Machinery, staffed by professionals . . . The apex of these activities will be the War Cabinet—so constituted as thoroughly to justify that title, supervising and directing them—at its head the P.M. . . .'

It seemed to me that these articles, heralding or representing a large block of opinion in the country, were very like the campaign which brought Asquith down in 1916. There was a special article in the same edition of *The Times*, obviously inspired by Printing House Square:

The War Cabinet must be small and not representative of special interests or political parties. Its members must possess acute analytical brains, like those of Mr. Lloyd George's War Cabinet, with Lord Milner, Sir Edward Carson, and General Smuts. Many proposals as to membership can be put forward. Shall it be imperial in character? From the members of the present team freed from departmental work can the right men be found? It is clear that the Prime Minister and, secondly, the Minister of Defence must be its leading members. Add two more, or at the most three, and the numbers are enough. The Empire had never lacked for quality. Finally, all along the line, here and abroad, we are losing the battle of political warfare, or propaganda, as it is often called. A new outlook and new methods in this vital field would be an early task of this new War Cabinet.

That night I was roused from a deep sleep by the ringing of the telephone by my bedside and the voice of Brendan Bracken speaking from the Cabinet Room at Downing Street and asking to speak to L.G. I said that L.G. was in bed and that I could not disturb him. Bracken went on to say that Churchill wished to offer him a post in his Cabinet, and I gathered that L.G. could have anything he liked to ask for, provided he would lend his name to Churchill's team, and his policies. L.G.'s friends, so said Bracken, all thought he should come in. But I knew by this time that L.G. would not, and there was no point in waking him.

The next day I had a letter from Ned Grigg:

Brendan Bracken was asked at a dinner given him by the Chairman of the 1922 Committee last night what he thought of *The Times* article and why was not L.G. brought in. He said once again that Winston saw no advantage in a War Cabinet of that type, and that L.G. anyhow was a defeatist. That is being put about everywhere, and *it simply must be scotched*. It is the one thing that is hanging up a real popular demand for L.G.'s return, since it is repeated quite sincerely by people who say with a sigh 'If only L.G. were his former self!'

Only L.G. himself can scotch it. It is of vital national and imperial—and human and cosmic and ultra-stellar—importance that he should.

I was dining with Geoffrey Dawson last night and in the course of it a message was brought in from his Lobby man saying 'Much interest in the lobbies about *The Times* article and some talk about L.G. being the only man to get it followed up. But most people seemed afraid of his defeatist attitude.'

There you are again! It must be scotched, handsomely and finally.

E.G.

But I had already done all I could, and I knew that L.G.'s iron will was set against working with Churchill, or taking any part in the war. We had discussed it many times, and he had said to me, 'Winston and I would never work together.

I would be certain to disagree with him, and finally I would have to resign, leaving the position much worse than if I had refused to take office, and leaving us bad friends, which would be a great grief to me. His policies would not be my policies, and I should have to attack him publicly which would be a bad thing for this country. Winston *likes* wars: I don't.'

It was not that L.G. lacked courage. I knew him well enough to be sure that in the event he could show courage of a sublime order, though it was not the fierce, compelling, magnificent physical courage of Churchill that the trumpets applaud, but the mystical, more sensitive quality.

I did not realise till later that he was ill, but I realise now that the beginnings of illness were making their mark on him, and that his vitality was already being sapped. But when Beaverbrook begged him to go to London to talk with Winston he did finally agree to go, and I went up with him, hoping that he would be persuaded. When he came back to the office after lunch, however, he said to my dismay that in spite of entreaties he did not intend to join the Government. Later in the day he sent a message to this effect. The next morning Beaverbrook telephoned me, very cross and almost abusive. He said it was *my* fault that L.G. had refused to take office. When they were all lunching together yesterday, he said, L.G. had practically agreed to come in, and that later, after he had seen me, he had said that he would not. It must therefore be *I* who was dissuading him and who did not want him to take the risks of becoming a Minister. Beaverbrook would listen to nothing that I said, and it was only many years afterwards—long after L.G. had died—that I told him how I had tried to persuade L.G. and failed. I told him that in fact no one was more anxious than myself for him to join the Government for the sake of his own reputation, and because I thought he should make any sacrifice to help his country in her time of need. But throughout his life L.G. made up his own mind on things, great or small.

He may have given an impression of indecision, of being open to argument or persuasion, but my considered conclusion is that at no time was it possible for anyone to influence L.G. The fact was that no one was ever able to persuade him to do something he did not want to do, or, conversely, not to do anything he wanted to do. He had a will of granite, upon which it was not possible to make any impression at all. Influencing others, he was himself impervious to influence.

He would have his own way, and once he had made up his mind, no one could move him. He knew what he wanted, and he would have it: all obstacles were brushed on one side. To reason, to argue, to plead with him, were all in vain. He planned his goal, and he would reach it, whatever the cost. I almost said, whatever the method. In the achievement of an end he was ruthless, unbendable, adamantine. It was, I expect, this quality which led him to expect so much of others, which enabled him to galvanise men into action —even when they would halt and say 'I can no more'. It was part of the equipment of the man born to lead—the man who, feeling the power within him, was resolute in his determination to redress wrong, to strengthen weakness, to put plans into execution. In short it was the symbol of the supreme man of action, the fundamental executive.

And it must be remembered that for close on sixty years he *had* had his own way. He got it because he was *able* to do so. He conquered all along the line, overcoming difficulties which to others seemed unsurmountable, indefatigable in his labours, unshaken in his purpose. He might appear to listen to those who doubted that he was right in his judgment, but I never saw him changed in his fundamental purpose.

On the other hand, if L.G. had been unjust or mistaken about a person, and had become convinced of this, he was prepared to make amends and reparation. Take the case of General Sir Hubert Gough, who had commanded the Fifth Army from 1916 to 1918, and was sacked after the breakthrough of the Germans on 1918. L.G. had for years regarded Gough as largely responsible for the breakthrough and behaved to him accordingly. Later, however, Captain Liddell Hart took up Gough's case with L.G., and managed to prove to him that Gough personally was not to blame—that it was the General Staff, and in his memoirs Liddell Hart says:

It was unfair to blame L.G. for holding back the reserves in 1918. For it was on the advice of the War Office that the general reserve of 120,000 men was kept at home instead of in France. The advice they formulated was governed by the assurance given in a note from Haig, that in face of the German offensive he would be able to hold his 3-line front in France for 18 days with the forces he had.

Gough himself said that 'during the whole eight-day period of the March 1918 battle he had received no guidance from G.H.Q.'

L.G. dined with Liddell Hart to meet Gough at the Athenaeum the night before we left for Morocco, and on his return from Morocco L.G. invited Gough and Liddell Hart to dine at the Reform Club to continue the discussion. There was as a result a reconciliation between the two men, and L.G. in his memoirs endeavoured to put right his previous criticisms of Gough.

I often think that the words which Milton used about the English (no doubt he meant the British!) nation in general could be used of L.G. in particular, with all truth: 'Of a quick, ingenious, and piercing spirit, acute to invent, subtle and sinewy to discourse, not beneath the reach of any point the highest that human capacity can soar to.'

And yet compare this man—the same man—with the L.G. who became distraught in the face of an illness of one he loved, whom such sickness could reduce to despair and bewilderment. At such a time he was capable of infinite tenderness, of an almost selfless devotion, expending such

overwhelming care and attention and solicitude as almost
to embarrass the object of his affections. He wrote to me
once, when I was 'laid up' with a temperature: 'You really
must not get ill. Every time you do I get fonder and fonder
of you, so I beg you for my sake not to contract another illness, otherwise the results may well be fatal to the shattered
remnants of my judgment and discretion.'

For such a nature the frustrations which he encountered
towards the end of his life, when jeers instead of cheers met
his words of advice and warning, were bitter indeed—hard
to endure, almost impossible of acceptance.

So now, as I say, he made up his mind for himself, and
refused all entreaties.

When he was offered the Embassy at Washington at the
end of 1940 he appeared to toy with the idea of accepting it,
and came to London to see Lord Dawson for his advice.
Dawson advised against it, but I am quite sure that L.G.
had no intention from the first of accepting the offer.

The truth was, I think, that he did not feel equal to any
sustained job of work, and realised that if he took on anything onerous he would probably have to lay it down. He
was twelve years older than Churchill—he was, in fact, now
an old man, and he was aware of it. It is worth noting that
Churchill himself, after retiring at the age of eighty, showed
no readiness to resume any official task when, a couple of
years later, the country was in the throes of the Suez crisis
and relying on a sick man for leadership.

So L.G. stayed at Churt, caring for his farm, and intensi-
fying its cultivation; or sitting in the big window which,
contrary to many accounts, had been planned long before
he ever went to Berchtesgarten and saw Hitler's house there.
The architect of the window, Sir Owen Williams, will bear
witness to this.

He sat in this window, silent, for many an hour for many
days after Hitler had attacked Russia, and what was going
on in his mind I could not fathom.

Gwilym and his wife and their sons came down to Churt often for week-ends, and the breach that had existed between us for so long appeared to be healed. At one point after Gwilym had been ill in London he came down to Bron-y-de to convalesce. Smuts came down to see us early in the war to express his anxiety about the conduct of the campaign in North Africa. 'They are sacrificing the flower of the British Army,' he said.

A matter which bothered us all was L.G.'s preoccupation with the 'Haw Haw' broadcasts. As everyone knows, they were anti-British from start to finish, full of lies about events which were detrimental to the British image, forecasting evil and disaster to the British future, magnifying any truth which was hurtful to our pride and our hopes, sneering at anything that was creditable, mocking our soldiers and our statesmen and our history. All of us at Bron-y-de regarded him as a devil, and did our best to avoid being present at the broadcasts, which L.G. never missed. His visitors, including his family, resented the broadcasts very strongly and being obliged to listen to them; but no protests or criticisms were of any use. L.G. insisted that he must hear both sides, and when he went out a member of the staff was detailed to take down the broadcasts and type them out for him. No one else read them, but it seemed as though it was a ritual for L.G. to hear every word that Haw Haw uttered. L.G. could not possibly have been taken in by them. Perhaps it was a good thing to hear what the other side was saying, but it was *not* good for L.G. The fact that Haw Haw was a traitor should have been sufficient for him to be suspect. L.G. had had to deal with Casement, and he had no hesitation in condemning him. One day perhaps a psychiatrist will be able to give an explanation of this extraordinary phase in L.G.'s life.

19

Death of L.G.

Dame Margaret became ill early in January 1941, and I felt
that L.G. ought to go down to Criccieth. But he would not
go, and his family did not persuade him; finally Lord Dawson telephoned and said he should go. I went as far as
Shrewsbury with him by car, and then came back by train.
By that time it was snowing hard and I only hoped that L.G.
would be able to finish his journey. But he could not. He
had one of the best chauffeurs in the country—Rolls-Royce
trained—but the car ran into a snow-drift at Cerrig-y-drui-
dion and could not be pulled out that night. When L.G.
arrived in Criccieth, Dame Margaret had died. He and
Megan came back to Bron-y-de after the funeral.

'You must be prepared for remorse,' Lord Dawson said
to me, and so I was. I let him and Megan comfort each
other, and L.G. let Megan order a memorial garden for her
mother at Brynawelon.

In 1943, on L.G.'s eightieth birthday, we had great celebrations at Bron-y-de. All the family, including the grandchildren, were there and many friends, and the *Daily
Mirror* sent an enormous birthday cake which was greatly
appreciated by the younger members of the party. Lord
Boothby had written a wonderful article on L.G. and his
life, which gave L.G. much pleasure. Bob Boothby had been
a very loyal visitor to Churt during the lean years, and L.G.
had taken his side when Churchill jettisoned him in the early

part of the war. I had known him from the time he entered Parliament in 1923 when going into my room in the House of Commons one day I met a dark, handsome young man who was waiting to pay his respects to L.G., and who ever since has been a true friend and someone whose judgment I would always respect, and whom the British public rightly love.

Lord Dawson wrote congratulating L.G. and saying how glad he was that the nation had paid him so many tributes. 'They show,' he said, 'that the great things you have done are remembered. . . . Your picture on this birthday make one think you will never need a doctor again! . . . I hope the problem we lunched over has had a happy solution . . . I hope Miss Stevenson is well and content.'

Dawson and L.G. had lunched together some time before this and, knowing the situation, he had asked L.G. if he would like him (Dawson) to interview his children with a view to persuading them to take a more friendly attitude to our marriage. L.G. willingly gave his permission. Gwilym was sympathetic to his father and to me. I don't think Richard was consulted—my recollection is that he was ill at that time. Olwen, who had been helpful ever since she knew that the question of our marriage was being discussed, said she would support anything her father wished—but Megan! Dawson said that he could not influence her, that she 'blew up' completely when discussing the matter and threatened all kinds of tragedies. I told L.G. that we ought to put the whole idea of marriage off, if he was going to be made unhappy as a result. He had hopes that she would 'come round' if we postponed the marriage and if we met agreeably on common ground at Bron-y-de. But not until the last moment did she agree to joining the party on his birthday. L.G. thought she had broken faith with him and was very upset.

My birthday was on October 7th, and L.G. offered me a wedding ring as a birthday present. We were married on

October 23rd, 1943, at the Guildford Registrar's office. My sister Muriel and Sylvester were our witnesses. A kind friend had filled the office with flowers and the registrar was most helpful in avoiding the Press. L.G. was looking gay and handsome, and after the ceremony we drove up to Hindhead around the Punch Bowl. Then L.G. told the chauffeur to drive to the farm office and introduced me to the manager as 'Mrs. Lloyd George'. The whole countryside was bathed in sunshine, as was my heart, and a deep contentment possessed me; contentment, but not the thrills of the usual bride. Our real marriage had taken place thirty years before.

We had managed to keep the arrangements for our marriage secret, in order not to be bothered by the Press, but when the news broke we were overwhelmed with messages from friends and well-wishers, known and unknown, including Mr. and Mrs. Churchill and Field Marshal Smuts. We had many lovely presents, from a case of champagne from Lord Camrose to one which especially touched us, from an old Greek, who sent a beautiful rug as a token of gratitude for what L.G. had done for Greece.

*   *   *   *   *

About a year after we were married, in the autumn of 1944, I became alarmed at symptoms of ill-health in L.G. Our local doctor, who was a friend, often dropped in, and I asked him to make an excuse for a more careful examination than usual. He diagnosed cancer and I asked for Lord Dawson's opinion to correct or confirm the verdict. Alas! He could only bear out all that Dr. Smith, our doctor, had told me, and there was nothing that we could do.

L.G. had wanted to take me to Wales as his wife, and the house at Llanystumdwy which had been modernised and beautified by that incomparable architect Clough Williams-

Ellis was ready for our occupation. One lovely evening at
the end of September 1944 we came over the glorious Welsh
hills down to the blue of the Cambrian Sea. Along the
coast to the little village and the old bridge over the
Dwyfor we drove, and so he came home again.

We had intended to be away from Churt for about a fortnight, but I believe that L.G. suspected he might not come
back, so reluctant was he to leave it. Two or three times we
were all ready to go, with the car at the door, and then he
decided to stay. Even on the day we actually went he postponed his departure, going through the rooms again and
again, and coming back to his lovely library with its gorgeous view, for a last, long look. 'I don't want to go!' he
said to my sister as she bade him goodbye.

The house at Llanystumdwy was a welcoming one, and
here again he had in his library a large window which took
in the view of the sea and mountain. He was content to stay
here, becoming gradually, almost imperceptibly, weaker.
Ann Parry, L.G.'s Welsh secretary and my friend, whose
unselfish devotion helped me during every difficult time,
had come with us to Wales, and between us we tended him
during these last months, and I think helped to make them
easier for him.

L.G. took me to walk by the river and to the haunts of
his boyhood. The tree in the garden of his old cottage was
still standing, in whose branches he used to sit to learn his
Euclid. He showed me the spots where he found wild
cherries, and the island in the river where they would play
the war-game of 'Napoleon'. We drove to Cwm Pennant, of
which Dafydd ap Gwilym wrote: 'Oh God, why dids't thou
make Cwm Pennant so beautiful, and the life of an old
shepherd so short?'

In November we were entertained in Caernarvon by the
newly elected mayor, and L.G. made a short speech. But now
he was noticeably failing, and it was pathetic to see him
making a brave effort to be his old self.

s

He said:

Great men sometimes lose the reins and lose their heads. This time let us hope they will retain them and that when victory is assured they will sit down and reckon what the future is going to be for their own countries as well as for other lands.

I think this was his last public utterance.

And then came the offer of the earldom. It was quite obvious that an election would take place before many months were out, and it was equally clear that L.G.'s health would not allow him to fight it. What was certain, however, was that it would break his heart if he were defeated after his fifty-five years of unbroken membership of the House of Commons—a melancholy end, indeed.

When Churchill asked him if he would accept an earldom L.G. realised that it would relieve him of the worry which was looming ahead of having to fight a tough election. He was most anxious to voice his opinions when the war was over on the subject of the Peace Treaty, and he felt certain that he could make a worth-while contribution. Who was to know that L.G.'s life would end before the life of Parliament, that by the time the war was over L.G. would be lying in his grave by the Dwyfor: that in any case there would be no Peace Treaty with our chief enemy?

L.G.'s acceptance of an earldom has been severely criticised in many quarters. At the time I thought he was completely justified in accepting it. I know that it has been suggested that I influenced him in his decision to take it, but indeed I did not do so. My brother-in-law, William George, has described how, when the three of us were discussing whether L.G. should accept or not, and the pros and cons were being examined, I said: 'If you have any doubts about it, why not send a telegram refusing—that would be an end of the matter.' I also said: 'To bear the name of Lloyd George is sufficient honour for me.' Nevertheless I must confess that when L.G. drafted his telegram 'Gratefully accept', and sent

Ann Parry with it to the village post office, my heart beat
a little more quickly.

There seemed to be a good precedent in the Asquith
earldom, the only difference being that Asquith accepted
an earldom when he found he could no longer sit in the
House of Commons, and L.G. did so while he was still un-
defeated. But what Asquith could presumably do with
impunity, and even with honour, Lloyd George apparently
could not do—though quite why this should be so, it is
difficult to see.

The title did at least decide the controversy as to whether
L.G.'s name was 'George' or 'Lloyd-George', for it emerged
that he could not be Earl Lloyd George unless a hyphen
joined the two names! How L.G. hated being addressed as
'George'! It was usually, so he thought, intended as a minor
insult on the part of people who did not like him, so refused
to give him his full name.

Part of L.G.'s doubt as to whether to accept or not was
the fact that his successor was Dick, now in hospital. Father
and son had never got on, and personally I think that the
trouble started when Dick was born. L.G. had passionately
wanted a girl, and here was a boy. There was little sympathy
between them, and when the Boer War came Dick was
tormented and insulted by the boys at school, and began
to resent his father. During the 1914–18 War he did not distinguish himself. At the end of the war he married a rich
girl, the daughter of Sir Robert McAlpine, the millionare
contractor. However, in 1932 there was a divorce and again
he had come to his parents for help. He went to America
for a time, but on his return before the second war he
needed help again, and his father resented this. When L.G.
was in the last stages of his illness the doctor asked him if
he would like to see Dick, who was in hospital at Denbigh.
L.G. said he would rather not. He left nothing in his will to
Dick. He said:

I have made no provision by this my Will for my son Richard Lloyd George because he has already received substantial pecuniary benefits from me.

Dick, of course, was very angry about this. At the first meeting of the executors I proposed that I myself and L.G.'s children (Olwen, Gwilym and Megan) should together donate an income to Dick which would enable him to live.

There was no response to my proposal. But although I have often been very angry with Dick's efforts to make me unhappy I have discovered that, in view of what he must have suffered, anger can be translated into pity—and indeed it is better so.

L.G. had begun to lose interest in the war. He was totally opposed to the policy of unconditional surrender, and when a punitive peace had been finally decided upon he was angered and horrified, and I think he gave up hope. Part of his genius lay in the fact that he was at all times able to see so much farther ahead than any other living statesman. He said, as he had done in 1919, when Foch wanted to pursue the Germans to the Rhine: 'You must have someone to make peace with.' I think he would have avoided the mistake of allowing Russia to become the dominant power in Europe, just as sagacious statesmen did after the Napoleonic wars. And in saying this I am not talking of something that came to my mind after the event. L.G. saw the results far ahead, and feared for the chaos which he foresaw would ensue on 'unconditional surrender'.

But as his strength began to fail him he wisely put aside his preoccupations and cares. By now he had achieved a serenity which was foreign to him in his fighting days. It contented him that he lay in his beloved village, encircled by mountains, river, and sea.

I wrote to my mother on December 29th to prepare her for the news of the earldom:

I hope you will be pleased at the news which is appearing on New Year's Day. I cannot really believe it is true—it seems more like a fairy tale to me. L.G. is really *very* pleased about it. It is softening his resignation from the House of Commons and I think most people will be very glad. Gwilym and Edna are very pleased and so is Olwen.

His weakness increased, but his patience and serenity with it. He seemed even more lovable in his helplessness than he was in his strength. Fortunately he had no pain.

In previous weeks, during the early stages of his illness, he had concentrated on reading Macaulay—the *History of England*, and the *Essays*—from cover to cover. Now his beloved Dickens was once more pressed into service—*Martin Chuzzlewit*, *Nicholas Nickleby* and the *Pickwick Papers*. But at last the process of reading became oh, so slow, and finally it was abandoned altogether.

His children, his grandchildren, his brother, and many friends paid him frequent visits and sat with him in the lovely window with its broad view. Megan came every day, with a show of friendliness to me, and she would bring flowers from her garden nearby. L.G. was pleased that she and I—to all appearances—were friends. His old friend and supporter, E. P. Evans, who had been the President of the Liberal Association for many years, and of whom L.G. had the highest opinion, came and talked to him about past conflicts. 'Who is coming today?' he would ask me in the morning. And he would enjoy the visit, albeit he became quickly tired.

At other times he would sit silent, deep in thought, and dozing from time to time. Not once during the whole of that time did he give any sign that he was conscious of his increasing weakness, or that he was nearing the end.

I remembered then how one day soon after Ramsay Macdonald's sudden death, L.G. said he thought it was an ideal way of passing and that he would himself prefer such a death. 'I would like to be called quite unexpectedly and without warning,' he said, 'just as when one evening at Buckingham Palace someone touched me on the shoulder, and said, "The King wants you".' L.G. did not pass like that, but his end was none the less gentle. It seemed like a quiet translation from this world to the next.

One afternoon, when I thought he was asleep, he opened his eyes and turned to me, and said, 'Play "Who will lead me to the strong City?".' It was one of the Welsh hymns which I had played to him on so many occasions during the years, especially at times of stress and trial. The last verse begins: 'Christ will lead me to the strong city.'

I wrote to my mother on February 11th:

I expect you will have been interested to see that the Earldom has been gazetted and we are now a full-blown Earl and Countess. L.G. is really very pleased about it. But I am not very happy about him, poor darling. He is very poorly. I had another doctor to see him last Saturday, one that Dawson recommended (Dawson himself is ill and could not come) and he confirmed what the others had said, that there is really nothing to be done except to take things quietly. That is all he wants to do, and he only gets up for a short time each day, and does not feel equal to going out now. Fortunately he has no pain at all, and seems very happy and peaceful. There is a good deal of nursing to do but I am equal to that and Ann Parry is a wonderful help.

My mother died on March 13th, a fortnight before L.G., but I could not go to her, being unable to leave my husband, whom I was nursing night and day. My sister telephoned me that my mother was asking for me, and the fact that it was impossible for me to make the journey and be with her at the last, added to the heaviness of my grief.

I wrote to my father on the 14th:

I can't tell you how desperately sorry I am not to be able to come to you, but the Doctor said it would have a very adverse effect upon L.G. if I went away, so that I clearly cannot leave him.

He is not so well to-day, and the Doctor fears that the end cannot be far off. . . .

I wrote to him again on the 21st:

I am afraid L.G. is seriously ill and we are very anxious about him. I have had advice from Lord Dawson and the head doctor at Ruthin Castle. They confirm that nothing can be done. But fortunately L.G. has no pain whatever and is most happy and serene, and he has no idea how ill he is. So that all I can do is to keep him happy and nurse him, and pray that he will have no pain. Everyone is most kind and telegrams have been pouring in, including one from the King and Queen. Gwilym and Edna came down for the weekend and were very happy to see him so contented and peaceful. It is really lovely to see him sitting in the window here, with the glorious view and the sunshine, completely at peace with everything.

And then, on a cloudless and windless March day, we watched beside the bedside for the end. He had become oblivious of us and of this world, and in the evening, after the sun had set, quietly, happily, he answered the last great 'Who goes Home?'[1]

After L.G.'s death, letters of sympathy poured in from all parts of the world, from high and low, rich and poor. It would be idle to try to describe the many tributes which these messages conveyed. There was no discrimination of party or nationality. The message of Ernest Bevin said:

The passing of David Lloyd George has robbed the nation not only of a great political figure but of one who was a great law giver and whose work transformed the outlook and life of the whole nation.

And Mr. L. S. Amery wrote, after speaking of L.G.'s

1. The call that goes through the corridors of the House of Commons when it rises.

'courage and grasp of the necessities of the hour [in 1918] which turned disaster into triumph', went on:

How he will compare in history with Churchill is indeed an interesting speculation. He had not the same knowledge of war in the narrower sense, but a much wider grasp of all the many other factors which come into the picture of war on the modern scale. In other ways it would be difficult to imagine two more wholly dissimilar types of mind and character. I only hope that someone who has known them both will some day draw the comparison.

And Aneurin Bevan wrote:

I wish that I had had more opportunities of talking to L.G. before his death. It was a great misfortune to me on many occasions that I could not call upon his sagacity, experience and quick sympathy.

Through the Foreign Office came a sheaf of tributes from Governments all over the world. General de Gaulle telegraphed Mr. Churchill—one of his rare communications, I imagine:

Nous déplorons avec vous la disparition en la personne de Lloyd George d'un grand homme d'état et de l'un des meilleurs artisans de notre première et commune victoire.

General de Gaulle.

And from Athens came a small bag containing soil from the Acropolis which the Pan-Hellenic Union of Reserve Officers and other ranks of the National Defence Movement of 1916 wished should be placed on L.G.'s grave. This was done in 1946 on the anniversary of L.G.'s death, sprinkled on the grave during the dedication by the Rector of Llanystumdwy.

20

Epilogue

For a long time I was bewildered by the circumstances which presented themselves to me after L.G.'s death. So much had my life been bound up with his, so much occupied had I been, especially since our marriage, with working for and looking after him, cheering him, nursing him, that I had not visualised life without him at all. During the war years he had inevitably seen less and less of his friends, and so had I of mine. Even before the war our circle had diminished considerably now that he was more and more at Churt. I found myself almost completely cut off from the world as I had previously known it.

After L.G.'s death I realised how active and potent jealousy and malice could become when restraint is removed, and when the object of them has 'no arms, no armour'. I considered with much care the idea of living in Wales. The house in Wales was a lovely one, a Tudor farmhouse with a Queen Anne façade added in 1720. It was the house I had always dreamed of, with a lovely view of the bay of Cardigan, and near the sea. But I became more and more aware that I should have to fight, in spite of many good friends, if I stayed there to live. I am not a born fighter, and I decided to come back to Churt to live, amongst friends and with my own family. I have never regretted it. It was at Churt that I had spent more than twenty years with L.G. and every field and orchard and path had been trodden by us together. My brother-in-law wrote to me after I had taken my decision: 'You have left the battlefield after winning the battle.'

I thought that it would be fitting for L.G. to have a memorial in the village where he had been brought up, and it occurred to me that an agricultural centre for young people would be the sort of venture of which he would have approved. I approached the officials at Bangor University and they were willing to support the scheme, and as the idea of county colleges was gaining ground at that time, they—especially Professor Trevor Jenkins, who was a tower of strength—helped me to outline such a college, and Clough William-Ellis drew up plans for building it. Then came the question of finance. I thought it would be a simple matter to launch a memorial fund for the purpose, and I conveyed the plan to members of L.G.'s family, feeling sure of their support. But they were not enthusiastic, and when Mr. Churchill declined to be a signatory to a letter to the Press suggesting a memorial, on the ground that he had discovered that L.G.'s family did not support the idea, I realised the difficulties facing me.

When I was planning the building of an enclosure of the place where L.G. was buried on the bank above the river and surrounding the large stone which he had asked should mark his resting-place—a stone on which he himself had often rested—I wrote to each member of his family asking for their opinions on the plan, and encouraging their suggestions. (A sketch of the plan was sent to each one of them.) Not an answer was received, with the exception of a subscription sent by one of his grand-daughters to the memorial fund, with a message of approval. When the enclosure was finished, a key to the gate was sent to each of L.G.'s children, but they were not acknowledged. There were many distinguished supporters of the idea—Sir Anthony Eden, Bertrand Russell, Sir Archibald and Lady Sinclair, Lord Lindsay of Birker, Mr. James Griffiths, Lord Camrose, Lord

Kemsley, Mr. Richard Crossman, Dame Sybil Thorndike, Mr. William Hughes of Australia, Lord Hankey and, as I have mentioned earlier, General Smuts.

The fund, however, never amounted to a great deal—certainly not enough to build even the beginnings of a college: and as very soon the County Council decided that no such schemes would be permitted for many years, the idea was given up and our committee decided to build a small museum to house the freedoms which had been left to me by L.G., and which he suggested might be available sometimes for the public to view. This has developed into a large collection of articles belonging to L.G., which have been added to over the years by friends who possessed objects of interest. A splendid Rembrandtesque portrait of Uncle Lloyd by Christopher Williams hangs there. A generous Cambridge scholar gave us a whole series of original cartoons for *Punch* by Bernard Partridge. The broken lock from the Llanfrothen churchyard is also there, and the seal with which L.G. signed the Treaty of Versailles.

I have handed over to the Caernarvonshire County Council eleven acres of land adjoining the museum for the purpose of building a county college if this were ever to become possible. So far it has not, but perhaps in a future generation one of L.G.'s descendants will feel moved to taking up the idea and do him honour. I find letters in my files from people who were asked to contribute to the fund saying that they could not do so because members of the family were not consulted. But they were consulted at every point. It is surely not necessary for hatreds to endure so long and so widely. When L.G. lay dying he thought that we were all friends and it made him happy. It seems, however, that nothing can eradicate my original offence against the family. There can be no doubt that Megan thought her behaviour was justified. She had taken a vow many years before that because I had supplanted her mother she would never speak

to me again. I ought to have realised that in all the demon-
strations against me her justification was that she was
keeping faith with her mother. Looking at the case quite
dispassionately, it was I who was to blame, not Megan, in
the first place, and I suppose she was entitled so to regard it.

There were kind people in Churt who were anxious to
make the transition from Wales to Surrey a happy and peaceful one. I was surrounded by welcoming friends, including
the vicar and his wife, in spite of the fact that L.G. had
never, being a nonconformist, attended the village church.
But he had, ever since he came to live there, taken an interest in village welfare, being one of the first trustees of the
new village hall. Admiral James was another of the trustees,
and he and his wife became my firm and loved friends and
helpers. And, of course, a great many of the villagers were
employed by L.G. on his farm. I now see the children, who
were then in their prams, grown up and doing honour to
the new Churt, and I cannot help feeling very proud of this,
though the farm lands and the estate have been broken up
and sold by his children, as he always said they would be.
I had my home and my orchards there, and I did not mind
how much hard work I put in. My sister encouraged me,
and I had expert help also from many people who had helped
L.G. many years before. But the cost was another matter.
My capital was not inexhaustible and the years after the war
were increasingly difficult for the farmer. I had already spent
—and lost—a lot of money trying to make the farm at Llanystumdwy profitable, to no avail. Churt is not a good farming
district—the extra land I needed was expensive both to buy
and to cultivate, and experienced labour was hard to find.
But I pushed ahead with experiments as I knew L.G. would
have done, and decided that a small dairy farm was desirable
and would become an asset to the orchards. In actual fact,
the dairy farm absorbed its own assets and, in addition, required help from the fruit profits! I had twenty-three acres
of rough woodland which, in the enthusiasm of ignorance,

I decided to clear to provide pasture or crops for our herd, and I asked advice from our local agricultural committee. Their opinion was unequivocal; it was a hopeless proposition. The woodland had been cut to the ground by the Government when wood was badly needed during the war and could not be bulldozed. Clearing the ground would incur a large expense for land which, according to the committee, would never yield anything of value. I obstinately felt this was a challenge, but met with the same discouragement from various land-clearance contractors. But one day a valiant young Irishman presented himself and offered to do the job. It was a slow and laborious business, winching out an average of six hundred roots to the acre, and then the land was cultivated. I then approached Sir George Stapledon, of Aberystwith University Research Station, about the first crop, and he gave me the name of the appropriate oats to be sown on such reclaimed land. The result was so amazing that people from various quarters, including a somewhat apologetic party from our agricultural committee, came to inspect this apparently miraculous crop.

But in the end I was beaten and faced with the necessity of giving up my farm while I still had some money left. I have the satisfaction, however, of seeing the orchards and the reclaimed land now being profitably used by young people who are far better farmers than I ever could have been.

My sister and I finally decided to make our home in a farm cottage, with a piece of land which has given us the interest of making a new garden. There was plenty to do in Churt, in the village, and I have enjoyed my part in it.

The writing of this book has been good for my soul, letting a breath of fresh air into the accumulated difficulties of the past and making an assessment of my spiritual faults and failures. In the early part of my career, my life, with so many different interests, seemed to assume the texture and quality of a patchwork, but now, when I am nearing the end, it seems to me like a tapestry into which the Lord, in His Grace, has woven so many mercies and blessings, and I say with the Psalmist: 'Thou hast anointed my head with oil, my cup runneth over.'

Index

287